A Key to the Apocalypse,
Discovered and Demonstarated from the Internal and Inserted Characters of the Visions
By Joseph Mede (1586-1638)
Translated By R. Bransby Cooper, Esq.
This edition edited by Anthony Uyl

Woodstock, Ontario, 2017

A Key to the Apocalypse

A Key to the Apocalypse,

Discovered and Demonstarated from the Internal and Inserted Characters of the Visions

By Joseph Mede (1586-1638)

A Translation of Mede's Clavis Apocalyptica

By R. Bransby Cooper, Esq.

This edition edited by Anthony Uyl

Originally Published by:
London; Printed for J. G. & F. Rivington, St. Paul's Church Yard, and Waterloo Place, Pall Mall. 1833.

Originally Printed by:
London: Gilbert & Rivington, Printers, St. John's Square

For the Use of Those Whom God Has Endued With the Love and Desire of Knowing and Investigating That Wonderful Prophecy

From the Latest Edition, Revised by the Author, the Rev. Joseph Mede

"Blessed is he that readeth, (or interpreteth) and they that hear, (or listen to him that interpreteth) the words of this Prophecy, and keep those things which are written therein, for the time is at hand."--Apocalypse, chap. i. ver. 3.
That is, the time is even now come, when those things have begun to be fulfilled, and they will be fulfilled more and more from day to day.

The Apocalyptical Key;
or,
The synchronism and order of the Apocalyptical Prophecies, according to the things transacted, on no hypothetical interpretation, nor preconjecture about the events; but firmly demonstrated from the very characters of the visions themselves, purposely inserted by the Holy Spirit, and offered to examination according to a self-evident scheme: so that it may prove, as it were, a Thesean clew to those who are involved in this sacred labyrinth, and a Lydian stone to discover the true, and to refute every erroneous interpretation.

The text of A Key to the Apocalypse is all in the Public Domain. The layout, covers, backgrounds and Devoted Publishing logo are Copyright ©2017 Devoted Publishing. This edition is published by Devoted Publishing a division of 2165467 Ontario Inc.

**What kind of philosophies do you have?
Let us know!**

Visit our online store: www.devotedpublishing.com
Contact us at: devotedpub@hotmail.com
Visit us on Facebook: @DevotedPublishing

Published in Woodstock, Ontario, Canada 2017

ISBN: 978-1-77356-133-2

Table of Contents

PREVIOUS REMARKS 5
    Footnotes: 5
PART I 6
    SYNCHRONISM I 6
        Footnotes: 7
    SYNCHRONISM II 7
        APPENDIX 7
    SYNCHRONISM III 8
    SYNCHRONISM IV 8
    SYNCHRONISM V 9
    SYNCHRONISM VI 9
    SYNCHRONISM VII 10
PART II 11
    SYNCHRONISM I 11
    SYNCHRONISM II 13
    SYNCHRONISM III 13
    SYNCHRONISM IV 13
    SYNCHRONISM V 15
    SYNCHRONISM VI 16
    SYNCHRONISM VII 16
THE EPOCH OF THE APOCALYPSE 17
THE CLOSE OF THE SYNCHRONISMS AND OF THE APOCALYPSE 18
A COMMENTARY ON THE REVELATION OF SAINT JOHN, ACCORDING TO THE RULE OF THE APOCALYPTICAL KEY 20
    THE FIRST PART 20
    Of the two Apocalyptical Prophecies 24
        Of the first Prophecy, which is that of the Seals; and in the first place, of the events signified by the six first Seals 24
        Of the First Seal 25
        Of the Second Seal 25
        Of the Third Seal 26
        Another mode of interpreting the symbol of Wheat and Barley 28
        Of the Fourth Seal 28
        Of the Fifth Seal 30
        Of the Sixth Seal 30
    APPENDIX 35
        Footnotes: 36
    THE VISION 38
    A MEMORABLE SENTENCE 42
        The First Trumpet 44

- The Second Trumpet 46
- The Third Trumpet 48
- The Fourth Trumpet 49
- Of the Three Woe Trumpets 50
- THE PROCLAMATION 59
- Footnotes: 60

THE INTERPRETATION 61
- THE MEANING 61
  - Footnote: 63
- THE ICHNOGRAPHY 63
- THE MYSTERY 63
  - Footnotes: 73
- THE MEANING 74
  - Footnotes: 79
- THE MYSTERY 79
  - Footnotes: 104
  - NOTE 105
  - Footnotes: 107

THE FALL OF ANTICHRIST, ... 108
- Footnote: 108
- HYPOTHESIS 108
- AN EXPOSITION 109
  - Footnote: 112

OF THE THOUSAND YEARS 113
- Footnotes: 114
- A REMARKABLE PASSAGE 115
- Footnotes: 116

THE OPINIONS 117
- Footnotes: 119

PREVIOUS REMARKS

1. I CALL a synchronism of the prophecies a concurrence of events predicted therein within the same time; which may be called a contemporary or coetaneous period; for prophecies of contemporary things synchronize.

2. The order of the seals and of the trumpets included under them, is certain and indubitable; namely, that which the number points out from I. to VII. When the rest of the prophecies are compared with one another, and then with the seals by synchronism, the order of the whole Apocalypse will be manifest; and this, with God's assistance, we now proceed to exhibit.

O thou that sittest on the throne, and thou, O Lamb, the root and the offspring [1] of David, who alone vast worthy to receive and open the book, open the eyes of thy servant, direct his hand and his mind, that in these thy mysteries he may discern and disclose something to the glory of thy name, and to the advantage of the Church!

Footnotes:
1. Stirps may imply both.

PART I

SYNCHRONISM I

Of the Woman driven into the Wilderness.
Of the Seven-Headed Beast restored.
Of the Outer Court trodden down by the Gentiles.
Of the Witnesses on Earth prophesying in Sackcloth.

IT is from hence that I begin, and my first synchronism shall be that of the remarkable quaternion of prophecies displayed in equal intervals of time. First, Of the woman living in the wilderness for a time, times, and a half, or (as it is there more fully expressed) for 1260 days. Secondly, Of the seven-headed beast restored, and endued with power for forty-two months. Thirdly, Of the exterior court (or of the Holy City) trodden down by the Gentiles for the same number of months. Fourthly, and lastly, Of the witnesses prophesying in sackcloth for 1260 days.

The truth of this synchronism is almost evident of itself, and seems capable of being confirmed, as it generally is, by the very equality of the periods; for a time, times, and half a time, i. e. three years and a half (as appears from the collation of the 6th verse with the 14th of chapter xii.), make up forty-two months, and forty-two months 1260 days.

But because it does not necessarily follow, (though in visions presented at the same time it is extremely probable) that equal times are also synchronic, since equality does not prevent some things being prior, and some subsequent to others, the character of equality will not be adapted to compel reluctant assent; I will search, therefore, for characters elsewhere, from which I may put an end to the matter by clear and irrefragable demonstration.

Of the Beast and the Woman
The times of the beast and of the woman residing in the wilderness, begin from one and the same point; namely, from the red dragon's being conquered, and cast out on the earth. As therefore they are equal, they must of necessity run together through the whole period, and at length complete their course together. That the times of each commence from the same point or terminus, is evident from the 12th chapter; since as soon as the dragon is cast out by Michael, the woman flies from his face into the wilderness, and the dragon being angry, that he had in vain attempted to overwhelm her, as she was departing thither, went to make war on the remnant of her seed, with those whom she was about to bring forth in the wilderness [2], and standing on the sand of the sea, he delivered to the ten-horned beast ascending from thence, his power, and his throne, and great authority.

Of the Beast and the Prophecy of the Witnesses
The times of the beast and of the prophecy of the witnesses being also equal, finish together at the end of the sixth trumpet. It is manifest that they began together, and were contemporary through the whole intervening space.

Now that the times of the beast, and of the witnesses of God prophesying in sackcloth [3] finish at the end of the sixth trumpet, is clear from v. 14. c. xi., where not only both the ascent of the witnesses into heaven (which is the termination of this mourning prophecy), but the great earthquake (by which the royal city is thrown down, and the kingdom of the beast destroyed), is marked out by the point of time at which the second woe (or sixth trumpet) is past, and the third woe (or seventh trumpet) is immediately about to commence. For in that moment of time, the witnesses, whom the beast risen out of the abyss had killed, as they were just about to finish their testimony (for that is the meaning of ὅταν τελέσωσι), being divinely revived, ascended into heaven. And in the same hour there was a great earthquake, and the tenth part of the city fell, and then it came to pass, at the sound of the seventh trumpet, that the kingdoms of this world became the kingdoms of our Lord and his Christ.

Of the Witnesses and Court (or Holy City) occupied by the Gentiles

It is plain that the times of the witnesses and of the court (or Holy City) occupied by the Gentiles, are contemporary, from the meaning of the text, c. xi. v. 2, 3. as from the wrath of the Gentiles, who are thrust out at the beginning of the seventh trumpet; that is, at the end of the sixth, when the days of the witnesses likewise expire, as has just been shown. For the nations or Gentiles, who at v. 18. are said to be inflamed with anger at the sound of the seventh trumpet, are no other than those, who for the whole forty-two months had trodden down the outer court of the temple; that is, the Holy City, and who are now, on that account, about to be destroyed by the wrath of God.

This synchronism is not wont to be called in question by any one that I know or recollect.

Of the Witnesses, Court, Beast, and Woman

If the treading down of the court and Holy City be contemporary with the prophecy of the witnesses, it will be contemporary likewise with the beast with whom the witnesses contemporize, and therefore with the woman in the wilderness also, with whom the beast contemporizes. So that the woman in the wilderness, the dominion of the beast, the conculcation of the Holy City, and the prophecy of the witnesses, all synchronize with one another.

Footnotes:

2. Query.
3. Sacco et cilicio, in sackcloth and haircloth.

SYNCHRONISM II

Of the Two-Horned Beast (who is also the False Prophet), with the Ten-Horned Beast (who is likewise called the Image of the Beast).

The two-horned beast is the founder, or re-establisher of the seven-headed beast, crowned with a diadem of ten horns, which, in fact, after his deadly wound, he restored to the image of his former state, to the great detriment of the saints, and who became possessed of power for forty-two months. Having done which, he exercises all his power before him, and shows forth, or performs, great wonders in his sight. But at length, this same two-horned beast (which John otherwise calls the false prophet), together with the other beast, in whose sight he wrought miracles, are taken as inseparable companions, and are both cast alive into the lake of fire burning with brimstone. Since, therefore, the ten-horned beast (for so I may be permitted to call the seven-headed beast when reinstated, for the sake of perspicuity), and the two-horned false prophet are not separated from each other either in their origin or destruction; but the one administers the power of the other, ενωπιον αυτου; that is, in his presence; who does not perceive that they are necessarily contemporary through their whole period of time? But that the whole matter may be rightly understood, we ought to be aware that no other state of the seven-headed beast is described in the 13th chapter, than that of his restoration, or last head, in which he became ten-horned, as the whole series of the description evinces. For whatever mischief the beast is said to have perpetrated, whatever worship and adoration was paid to him by the inhabitants of the earth, is all reported as having been done after his re-establishment, or the cure of his wound. Moreover, it is manifest from the interpretation of the angel, c. xvii., that the ten horns belong to the last head or state of the beast, which is the state of his restoration; since at that time, after five heads had fallen, that is, had fulfilled their parts, the sixth was even then performing his in the age of John, and yet "the time of the horns" is said to be "not yet come." Therefore they must necessarily belong to the seventh or last head.

APPENDIX

On the alternate Use of the Names of the Beast and False Prophet; as also of the Beast and Image of the Beast

The title of the synchronism reminds us of both. And first, Iræneus has observed, that, from the most ancient writers on the Apocalypse, the bicorned beast and the false prophet are the same; which, from the comparison of v. 13, 14, 15, 16, of c. xiii. with v. 20 of c. xix., is so clear and manifest, that it requires no farther confirmation. But what the title sets forth in addition, that the ten-horned beast is otherwise accustomed to be denoted by the name of the image of the beast, is less apparent, and would not perhaps be suspected by a reader who was not very attentive: Yet, that it is so, I am persuaded I have not rashly remarked; and therefore, wherever the beast occurs with

A Key to the Apocalypse

the false prophet, (which I find it does three times,) then by the name of the beast, the ten-horned beast is alone to be understood; since, by the false prophet, it is sufficiently clear that the two-horned beast is designated. On the other hand, when you find the beast compared with the image of the beast there, by the beast the false prophet is to be understood; but by his image, the ten-horned beast, or the seven-horned beast restored: for, since the latter acknowledges the false prophet as his restorer, and suffers himself to be wholly guided by his will, as by that of a supreme lord, he is not improperly called his image; not, indeed, the image of one whose similitude he bears, as if the genitive were used passively, (for, in that respect, he is the image of another, perhaps of the seven-headed dragon, or of the state in which he flourished before his wound, in resemblance of whom he blasphemes God anew, and wages war against the Saints,) but an image, of whose restoration that two-horned and dragon-speaking beast was the author, and whom he claimed as his own; the genitive denoting the agent and possessor, as, in the same passage, the mark of the beast is not a mark impressed on the beast itself, but one with which the beast brands his worshippers.

And that what I have said is the right interpretation of the image of the beast, the first proof I would bring is, that it is said, c. xiii. v. 15, that the very image of the beast, which the false prophet had just animated, caused that as many as would not worship the image of the beast should be slain; nay, in other places, (that you may acknowledge the beast,) it is generally subjoined to a word expressive of worship, or as something to which worship is suited. Since, therefore, the Apocalypse describes two beasts only, and not more, this wicked majesty, with an equal power of commanding or compelling, cannot but belong to one or the other of them. Moreover, when the beast is present at the same time as the false prophet, the image of the beast does not occur in the same sentence, as if then, in fact, the appellation of beast supplied its place. Lastly, it is said to be the image of the beast, of which there is a number and a name; but the name and number of no other beast seem to be mentioned than that of the two-horned. Of the same, then, (as of a maker and lord,) he is justly said to be the image. But this image, whether it be or not the ten-horned beast, is of no consequence to our system; for the synchronism of the beasts does not rest on this hypothesis.

SYNCHRONISM III

Of the great Harlot, or Mystic Babylon, with the same Seven-headed and Ten-horned Beast.

1. The time of the beast is the time of the wilderness. (Syn. i. s. 1.) Now, the harlot is seen by John in the wilderness; but this description is not of much force.
2. The ten-horned beast carries the harlot or adulteress, and the harlot sits on the beast: therefore, both exist at one and the same time.
3. The ten horns of the beast (which, in truth, spring from its highest and last head,) and under whose dominion alone the harlot manages the beast, and the beast carries the harlot, (the times of the other heads having been previously completed after it revived as from a deadly wound); these ten horns, I say, "are ten kings which receive their authority as kings for one hour with the beast;" viz. with the reinstated beast, which carries the adulteress, and is now ten-horned; that is, exercising the office of the last head. These, when the time has been fulfilled, during which "they were to deliver up their power to the beast;" that is, when the connexion with the beast is just ready to be dissolved, "will hate the harlot, render her desolate and naked, and at length burn her with fire." So then the beast, which in its ten-horned state (the only state in which it is prophetically contemplated by John) first commenced with the harlot or adulteress, will not survive her, nor will the harlot survive the beast. The harlot and beast, therefore, universally and exactly synchronize, which was the object to be proved.

SYNCHRONISM IV

Of the Hundred and Forty-four Thousand Sealed, who were Virgins, with the Babylonian Harlot and the Beast

1. In the first place, they are called virgins, and are praised on that account, because they had not defiled themselves with meretricious embraces. They coincide, therefore, with the meretricious times of the Babylonian harlot, "with whom the kings and inhabitants of the earth committed fornication."
2. Out of this virgin choir proceed those who denounce the ruin of Babylon, and who deter men from all communion with the beast, his image, and mark. Therefore, the virgin assembly is contemporary with Babylon and the beast.
3. These, lastly, are those that are called the chosen and faithful attendants on the Lamb,

accompanied by whom, he wages war with the kings, or horns, of the Babylonian beast, and who, under his auspices, (as King of kings and Lord of lords,) will at length obtain the victory. For those words, relative to the Lord of lords and King of kings, ought, I think, to be read in a parenthesis, where the angel says, "These shall make war with the Lamb, and the Lamb shall overcome them, (for he is Lord of lords and King of kings,) and they who are with him, are called, and chosen, and faithful;" that is, the Lamb, and those who are with him, called, and elect, and faithful, shall overcome the Babylonish kings.

4. But these observations are not sufficient for the firm establishment of a complete contemporary agreement; for all these things may be consistent with partial contemporation. I therefore proceed, in the following manner, to demonstrate that the assembly of the sealed attendants on the Lamb are universally and exactly contemporary with the beast. That assembly of the sealed ones is an Αντιστοιχον, or opposite state, coeval with the beast, or the whole company of the followers of the beast; that is, the forces of those holy soldiers remaining still in the faith of the Lamb, when the other inhabitants of the world, as deserters and rebels, have received the mark of the beast. This is obvious from the text: whence, as formerly, by ancient custom, slaves and soldiers were wont to be distinguished by the mark, and inscribed by the name of him to whom they had pledged their faith, so these are said to bear "the name of the Lamb and his Father on their foreheads." Since this is the case, it follows that the duration of the one is commensurate with that of the other, and agrees with it altogether, during the same interval of time: for the mode of this sort of opposition requires that the assembly of the sealed followers of the Lamb, as far as it is pointed out by the vision, should be understood in a manner wholly opposite to that of the beast; beyond which opposition, agreeably to the intention of the vision, it has no meaning, and therefore it begins where that begins, and ends where that ends.

5. Moreover, with respect to the close of the contemporary period, that may be proved from the description in c. vii.; because the palm-bearing multitude is the limit both of the tyranny of the beast, and of the company of those who were sealed;--of the beast, because it is there said, "These are they who have come out of great tribulation;" but out of what tribulation, except that of the beast persecuting the saints? Therefore, they left behind the tyranny of the beast. Of the sealed company, because the palm-bearing multitude immediately follows, as is manifest from that transition, "After these things I saw," &c.

SYNCHRONISM V

A Corollary of the General Synchronism of all the circumstances previously enumerated

It follows that the revived, or ten-horned beast is contemporary with the woman in the wilderness, with the conculcation of the Holy City, and with the lamentation of the witnesses, during the same period, Synch. I. The two-horned beast with the ten-horned beast, Synch. II. The harlot with both, Synch. III. The virgin company of those who are sealed with the harlot and the beast, Synch. IV. Therefore all synchronize with each other.

SYNCHRONISM VI

Of the Measure of the Interior Court by the Reed of God, with the Snares of the Seven-headed Dragon, and his Battle with Michael concerning the Birth of the Child

These are the nearest antecedents of contemporary events; the battle of the dragon and the birth of the child, with the habitation of the woman in the wilderness, and the rise of the ten-horned beast. The interior court, (for what is said of the temple of God, of the altar of incense, and of the priests worshipping there according to custom, is a periphrasis of this expression,) to the exterior court, or that of the people, where the nations are represented to have been unjustly and unlawfully housed as in a stable.

To prove this: In the first place, both the delivery of the woman, and the battle of the dragon with Michael, impinge on the same termination, viz. the flight of the woman into the wilderness, which is said to have followed next to the act of both: For the woman, as soon as she had brought forth a son, "fled into the wilderness," there to be nourished for 1260 days. In like manner, when the dragon was cast out, the woman "fled into the wilderness, there to be nourished from the face of the serpent, for a time, and times, and half a time." These two things, therefore, as you see, the title of the synchronism combines into one, as visions of the same time and subject, completely connected, and which it is unnecessary to separate in this investigation. Moreover, that battle in which Michael conquered the dragon, immediately preceded the restoration of the seven-headed or ten-horned beast; for the dragon, as soon as he was cast out into the earth, "standing on the sand of the sea shore, delivers up for the future his office, that is, his authority, his throne, and great power,

A Key to the Apocalypse

to the beast emerging from thence;" and (as the Complutensian edition renders it, together with Irenæus) "one of his heads, as it were, wounded to death, whose wounds being cured, all the world followed the beast, wondering."

And thus far the matter is plain and obvious; but of the antecedence of the interior to the outer court, (which alone remains to the completion of the synchronism,) the mode of proof is a little more difficult, because the subject has long been otherwise understood, and is therefore impeded by prejudices.

The inner court, in consequence of the structure of the temple, precedes the outer court in situation and order, as being nearest to the throne of God, or τῷ Ναῷ, the head of the whole structure. Therefore, if things should be significant of different times, (for it is not a novelty that order of situation should denote order of time, as in the statue which Nebuchadnezzar dreamt he saw,) then it is agreeable to reason that the indicated time of the interior court should be prior to the indicated time of the exterior.

Now that there is an indication of different times relative to the courts, and consequently that the indication of the interior court is more ancient, and prior to the other, I thus farther demonstrate. Because this vision of the measurement of the court of the temple and altar, or of the inner court, is the beginning of a repeated prophecy, which, indeed, (as will soon be more fully shown,) rehearses from the beginning, and as it were above, the times of the prophecy of the seals, whose commencement no one can have doubted, must be sought for from that epoch of the apocalyptical period. "You must prophesy" (says he) "again," (thus he explains the symbol of the eaten book) "before many people, and nations, and tongues, and kings." "Πάλιν," that is, in a renewed order of the times of which he had before prophesied. But he begins from the measurement of the temple and altar of incense, and of those who worshipped there. If, then, the vision concerning the delivery of the woman, and the battle of the dragon, (which is itself a part of this repeated prophecy), ascend to the very commencement of the period or apocalyptical time, even so far, that the Apocalypse has nothing more ancient, or that deduces its origin from a higher source, (and this will appear, both from the nature of the circumstance, the birth of a child, and from synchronisms already confirmed, and to be still farther confirmed,) why should not the beginning of the same prophecy and the first of all the visions, with still greater probability, be presumed to ascend as far? But the months of the outer court cannot reach so high, as they are wholly contemporary with the ten-horned beast: therefore, it is very evident to me, that the times of the inner and measured court not only precede the months of the outer and unmeasured one, but ought to be derived from the origin of the repeated prophecy, as well as the vision of the birth of the child, and of the dragon.

Now, these three events--the habitation of the woman in the wilderness, the ten-horned beast, and the outer court trodden down by the Gentiles, appear to be contemporary from the first synchronism: therefore the times of the inner court measured, and the delivery of the woman, together with the wiles of the dragon, and the battle with Michael, being the nearest antecedents of those contemporary events, must contemporize with one another. Q. E. D.

SYNCHRONISM VII

Of the Seven Phials; with the Beast and Babylon declining to their Fall

The effusion of the phials brings ruin and destruction on the beast, as is manifest from the text. For the conquerors of the beast sing the song of Moses, ἐπινίκιον or the song of victory. c. xv. v. 2, 3. And it appears especially, from the first phial, c. xvi. v. 2, which sends the plague of an ulcer "on the men who had the mark of the beast, and on those who adore his image;" from the fifth, which is poured "on the throne of the beast," and which renders his kingdom dark; and also from the last, on the pouring out of which Babylon is wholly overthrown. Therefore, the effusion of the phials is contemporary with the concluding scenes of the beast and Babylon.

PART II

I have completed the First Part in Seven Synchronisms: The other Part, that of the Seals, follows, in which I will demonstrate the connexion of all the prophecies which have been hitherto recited; and if there are any besides, of those likewise with the seals, in as many other synchronisms: Whence it will plainly appear, (and it may be adduced as a matter very worthy of observation, and, unless I am deceived, of no small consequence in the subsequent interpretation,) that the whole Apocalypse, from the fourth chapter, (for I introduce nothing now about the seven churches,) is divided into two principal prophecies, of which each commences from the same epoch, and, as it were, from one barrier, and ends at the same goal. The first is that of the seals, and in them of the trumpets, for the seventh seal is the seal of the trumpets, which I take every where for granted, from the grammatical sense of the context. For it is not to be supposed that the order of sense is preserved in all the other seals, but is unsuitable to the seventh alone, as what is submitted to view on the opening of a seal, that is, τὸ πρᾶγμα, the subject of the seal. Now, the vision of the seven angels with the seven trumpets follows the unclosing of the seventh seal. The other prophecy (or, if you will, the system of prophetic visions) is that τοῦ βιβλαριδάου, or of the open book, which, commencing from the same beginning of apocalyptical time, retraces the times of the former prophecy, namely, that of the seals, from the 8th verse of the 10th chapter to the end of the book. And this repetition of the prophecy is indicated by that transition in the 11th verse of the same chapter, where the angel says to John, "Thou must prophesy again (πάλιν) before many people, and nations, and tongues, and kings."

Moreover, it will not perhaps be unworthy of the reader's attention, that at the beginning of each of those visions, as well of the first of all the visions, that of the seven churches, as of three entire prophecies, the commencement is proclaimed by "the voice, as it were, of a trumpet talking with St. John;" as if the Holy Spirit meant to distinguish them by this mark from other prophecies, which are parts of these principal ones, in which you will see nothing of a similar nature.

Now, these are the beginnings of the prophecies to which I allude. Of the vision of the seven churches, in these words: "I was in the spirit on the Lord's day, and I heard a great voice behind me, as of a trumpet, saying," &c. Of the prophecy of the seals, in this manner: "And the first voice which I heard was as it were of a trumpet talking with me," &c. Lastly, of the prophecy of the little book: "And the voice which I had heard from heaven" (i. e. as of a trumpet speaking) "spake again unto me, and said," &c.

Thus far is prefatory, and, as I hope, not foreign from the subject of which we are treating. The Synchronisms now follow.

SYNCHRONISM I

THE CARDINAL POINT OF THE SYNCHRONISMS; OR, THE SYNCHRONISM

Of the Seventh Seal, which relates to the first Six Trumpets; with the Ten-horned and Two-horned Beast, and other contemporary matters

And first, the beginning of the beast is contemporary with the beginning of the seventh seal, which is that of the trumpets.

Since the assembly of those who were sealed, as the antithesis or opposite of the reign of the beast, synchronizes rightly and exactly with the beast; and since the same assembly begins with the opening of the seventh seal, or that of the trumpets, it follows clearly that the beast also must begin with the same seventh seal, or that of the trumpets.

Now, it has been already shown by Synch. IV. Part I. that the assembly of the sealed must be altogether and exactly contemporary with the beast. That the same assembly begins with the seventh seal, is plain from the seventh chapter, where the act of sealing immediately follows the sixth seal; since, as soon as the vision of the sixth seal is finished, and when the seventh, which is that of the trumpets, is just about to open, attention is paid to the elect servants of God by the impression of a seal, that they might not be destroyed by the storm of calamities which was brooding over the earthly globe.

Now, the four angels who presided over the four quarters of the world, were just ready to let loose the winds (which they had hitherto restrained), at the sound of the trumpets. Attention must likewise be paid to the sound of the fifth trumpet, c. ix. v. 4. that you may understand, even from that indication, that the sealing belongs to the times of the trumpets. It is beyond all doubt that the conclusion and termination of the sixth seal is the beginning of the seventh, since the series of the seals with respect to each other, cannot and ought not to be interrupted. Therefore, it is necessary that the assembly of the 144,000 who are sealed, which follows the close of the sixth seal, should begin with the seventh, which succeeds not less immediately to the sixth. And so, with wonderful judgment (as I conceive), the Holy Spirit has pointed out to us beforehand, by this act of sealing, the connexion between the beginning of the beast, and the commencement of the seventh seal, since no other reason can be given why the series of the seals, which is not otherwise to be interrupted, should be disturbed by this vision of the sealed ones interposed in chap. vii. Secondly, the end of the beast is contemporary with the close of the sixth trumpet. For since the 1260 days of the witnesses' mourning in sackcloth finish at the end of the sixth trumpet, or the beginning of the seventh, there also must the forty-two months of the beast finish, and by consequence, the tyranny of the beast is comprised within the compass of the six first trumpets. Q. E. Δ.

Now it has just been demonstrated, Part I. Synch. I. s. 3. that the forty-two months of the beast, in the same manner as the 1260 days of the mourning of the witnesses, contemporary with them, must finish at the close of the sixth trumpet, as it is shown from the 11th chapter, when the witnesses, after three days' death, being again restored to life, and carried up into heaven, had completed the days of their sorrowful prophecy, "a great convulsion of the earth having taken place at the same hour or time," the great city suffered destruction, and the beast, the cruel enemy of the witnesses, in consequence of the defeat which he then underwent, breathed his last. That we might know at what period of the seals and trumpets this happened, the Spirit has immediately subjoined, "The second woe (that is, the sixth trumpet) is now past, and the third woe (the seventh trumpet) cometh quickly." Which character I believe to be inserted here as another index of this great synchronism, or principally for this purpose, that it might be another of the hinges on which that great and universal frame of the prophecy of the little book and the seals might turn. Since otherwise, both this notice and the sound of the seventh trumpet, which immediately follows, would have been placed in right and natural order, at the end of the prophecy of the seals, chap. x. But the Holy Spirit, by the mystery of the seventh trumpet in that place presignified, in the manner of a proclamation briefly only, and as much as appeared sufficient at that time, (namely, that it would come to pass while that was sounding, "that the mystery of God should be finished as he had declared by the prophets,") wishes to suspend and postpone the uttering of that sound, and the full disclosure of the mystery for a little while, (and without doubt for some important purpose,) until, having made a transition to the new prophecy of the little book, he might bring the first vision, when it had run its apocalyptic course, to the same conclusion of events. For I would wish the reader very attentively to remark, that in this one vision of the 11th chapter, as the first of the renewed prophecy, the all-wise Spirit runs through the whole period of the sealed prophecy, as a warp through a woof, and connects the same with the seventh trumpet as with a sort of clasp, for the sake of directing the time to the series of the seals. But for what purpose, except that to the first vision thus fixed and compared with the seals, the remaining prophecies of the little book which succeed, being connected also by their own characters, the whole system of the renewed prophecy with the seals might be dexterously accommodated?

Moreover, lest a scruple should occur to any one, that those things which are related in the text, of the consternation of the beast, of the ruin of the city, and of the slaughter of men occasioned by the earthquake, by no means appear as if they ought to be understood of the total abolition of the beast; I say that this is not requisite for that synchronism of which we have been treating; but that they should be taken at least of the concluding time of his power and kingdom, which is determined in forty-two months, and which, the synchronism of the beast and witnesses being acknowledged, must end at the same time with the days of the witnesses. But whatever shall survive of the beast for a little while, will therefore, as may here be collected, be under an appearance dissimilar from the former, so that it cannot be reckoned under the same description; but is likewise not long after to be wholly destroyed and abolished under the seventh trumpet, when "the kingdoms of this world shall become the kingdoms of the Lord, and of his Christ."

And so it will be manifest, that by this cardinal synchronism well established, the rest may be easily deduced from it and connected with the seals.

SYNCHRONISM II

Of the contemporary term of the Interior Court, and the Battle between the Dragon and Michael concerning the Man Child, with the first Six Seals

Because they are the events next antecedent to the contemporary ones which succeed them; for the six first seals are the nearest antecedents of the seventh. The inner court and the battle of Michael with the dragon are the nearest antecedents of the beast, and of the assembly of the 144,000 sealed ones. Now the seventh seal (or what is nearly the same thing), the six first trumpets, are contemporaneous with the assembly of the sealed and the beast, as was shown by the former synchronism.

SYNCHRONISM III

Of the Phials with the Sixth Trumpet

The seven phials of the last wrath of God, since they are so many gradations of the ruin and fall of the beast, must necessarily begin from the commencement of this ruin and fall. But the kingdom of the beast, while the sixth trumpet was yet sounding, had so far begun to be undermined, and had proceeded to such an extent of ruin, that at the end of the same trumpet the power which was given it to exercise dominion, and to overcome the saints for forty-two months, was finished. But the beast could not have fallen to such a state of ruin and fatal calamity before the fifth phial at least was poured out, for then it appears at length that his seat was shaken, and his kingdom darkened. Therefore five, at least, of the phials are poured out before the sound of the sixth trumpet has ceased: I believe even the sixth, but the seventh phial, which is the phial of consummation, will therefore concur with the beginning of the seventh trumpet, which is also the trumpet of consummation.

SYNCHRONISM IV

Of the Thousand Years in which the Dragon or Satan is bound, with the Seventh Trumpet, or the Interval from the Destruction of the Beast

That this account of the binding of Satan may be better understood, it must be premised for a demonstration that it is said in the text, Satan was not only cast into the abyss, but shut up there, and that the angel set a seal upon him, that he might no longer seduce the nations until the 1000 years were completed. For it was the custom of the Hebrews and neighbouring nations, when they wished to have a door firmly secured and barred up, to affix a seal to it.

Thus king Darius sealed with his signet and the signet of his nobles, the stone which was placed over the den of lions into which Daniel was cast. In the story in the Apocrypha, the servants of Daniel shut the doors of the Temple of Bel, and sealed them with the king's seal. In like manner the Jews secured the sepulchre of our Saviour, "sealing the stone and setting a watch;" or made it sure by sealing the stone, where it is to be observed that the Greek words ἀσφαλίζειν and σφαγίζειν mutually explain each other. It is one thing then, and far different to be cast down from heaven, (which many accommodate to this place), and another to be bound, shut up in an abyss, and sealed. The former did not deprive him of his power of wandering about and doing mischief, the latter does not suffer him by any means to come out of his prison. Nay, I dare to affirm that not one of those things which are related in the 20th chapter is to be found in the 12th, nor, on the other hand, is there one word to be found in the 20th of what is related in the 12th. So far from truth is the supposition that the same event is represented on both occasions. Let us, however, examine a little. In the 20th chapter four things are related of the dragon: first, that he was seized by the angel who descended from heaven; secondly, that he was bound; thirdly, that he was cast into the abyss; fourthly, that he was shut up and sealed there.

You will find none of these things in the 12th. On the other hand, of what alone is narrated in the 12th chapter of the casting down the dragon from heaven to earth, not even a trace is to be found in the 20th. Nay, from the very context it is easy to collect that no such transaction then took place. For there it is said, that the angel who came to bind the dragon, came down from heaven. Therefore the dragon was already on earth; for otherwise why should the angel have descended to lay hold of him? Hence, Michael did not descend from heaven, but had an engagement with the Devil in heaven itself. These things being premised, let us proceed to the exposition of the synchronism.

A Key to the Apocalypse

Argument 1.--Under the first six seals the dragon, or Satan, was free and at large, and also under the first six trumpets of the seventh seal. It follows, therefore, that the 1000 years for which Satan is bound, are brought within the seventh trumpet. That Satan or the dragon was not bound while the first six seals were yet running their course, is plain from this circumstance, that in all that interval, as a red dragon with his seven heads and crowns, he was contending with Michael about the offspring of the woman, as was just now demonstrated. But neither did this take place under the first six trumpets of the following seal; for this is the period of the woman in the wilderness, and of the domination of the ten-horned beast, as appears from Synch. I. of this Part. In truth, while the woman was living in the wilderness, it was very unlikely that the dragon could be considered as bound, who, when free and precipitated from heaven, in the first place attempted to overwhelm her with a flood of waters which he cast out of his mouth, as she was preparing to depart; and afterwards, when this attempt did not succeed according to his intention, (the earth having absorbed the flood, and the woman having withdrawn into the wilderness,) inflamed with wrath and fury, he went to make war with the remnant of her seed which keep the commandments of God, and have the testimony of Jesus Christ. Are these proofs of Satan's being bound? But let us see likewise (what is said of him) respecting the beast, and hear how the dragon was bound under his reign: Namely, the dragon gave him his power and his throne, and great authority, and all the world wondered after the beast, and worshipped the dragon which gave power to the beast. But could Satan perform all these acts while he was in prison Certainly in one shut up and sealed it was not possible. But that there may be no room for subterfuge, and that it may clearly appear how far the dragon was still free, and at liberty to perform such deeds, from those into whose custody he is said to be committed, in order to be restrained, behold his other pupil, the false prophet, the inseparable companion of the ten-horned beast, and the minister of the bestial power, of whom you have it written expressly, that he should perform great wonders, and deceive the inhabitants of the earth by the miracles which it was given him to perform. Now, who can readily believe that while these beasts were in possession of authority, the dragon, or Satan, was cast into the abyss, and a seal put upon him, that he might not deceive the nations any more? But from the trumpets themselves, (of the intermediate time at least,) there is not wanting an argument of the devil's being free and unbound. For is not that king of the locusts of the fifth trumpet, who is called the angel of the abyss, to whom the Hebrew name of Abaddon is applied, and the Greek of Apollyon, and whom John points out as him who had long since fallen to the earth, that very dragon himself and Satan whom Michael, before the trumpets had begun to sound, had cast down from heaven to earth? For in the whole Apocalypse, I do not remember to have read of any other besides him who fell to the earth, nor do I know any one else to whom those titles of the angel of the abyss and Abaddon could apply. However that may be, Satan was certainly not bound at that time; the bottomless pit (as it is there called) was not closed upon him and sealed, but open to that degree, that the smoke arose out of it, like the smoke of a great furnace, and the sun and air were darkened by the smoke: And lastly, the liberty of the dragon, or Satan, to deceive the nations, must have continued to the very ruin of the beast, and was therefore entirely coeval with the six first trumpets, which I think it impossible for any one to doubt, who has sufficiently attended to what is said to be done after the effusion of the sixth phial, that when the seventh, which is the last phial, is just about to be poured out, and therefore the last day of the beast was just at hand--"Out of the mouth of the dragon and his vicars, the beast, and the false prophet, three unclean spirits of demons working miracles go forth unto the kings of the earth, and of the whole world, to gather them to the battle of that great day of God Almighty."

So the thousand years of Satan's bondage, in order that he might no longer deceive the nations, cannot be placed under the first six seals, nor under the first six trumpets. They must consequently be referred to the seventh trumpet.

Argument 2.--Afterwards, when the thousand years are finished, and Satan, having been loosed from his prison for a short time, had excited new commotions, the rabble of deceived nations which he had collected having been consumed by fire sent down from heaven, he himself being taken as a deceiver, is said to be cast into a lake of fire and sulphur, where the beast and false prophet were. Observe here, reader, the mark of the time by which it is intimated that this event, whatever it is, of Satan's captivity and condemnation, after his renewed deliverance, succeeds as well in order of relation, as also in time of action, to the vision of the former chapter concerning the beast and false prophet being vanquished, captured, and in like manner cast into a lake of fire burning with sulphur, by him who sat on the white horse. For it would not otherwise be said that Satan was cast into the place where the beast and the false prophet were, unless the beast and the false prophet had been previously sent there.

Nor let any shrewd person say, by way of evasion, that there is no difference between this war of the 20th chapter, after the one thousand years, and that of the former chapter; since not only the character displayed, but all the circumstances likewise, on both sides, are in direct contradiction to it--the parties, kind of battle, and mode of destruction. There by the sword; here by fire; nay, the event of each battle is also dissimilar, as will presently appear by demonstration. In that instance, it was the binding of Satan for a time; but in this, it is his condemnation to eternal fire.

Since the war then in which the beast and the false prophet, when captured, are cast into a lake of fire, is different from the last, to which Satan, who was to be finally cast into the same lake, had excited the nations immediately after his liberation, it must have been waged either within the thousand years, or before they began. But within the thousand years it could not be waged, because so long Satan is said to have been shut up in the abyss, that he might not deceive the nations any longer until the thousand years were completed; c. xx. v. 3. But in the war in which victory was at length obtained over the beast, the false prophet, and their associates, (if ever otherwise,) lie was most free and at perfect liberty to deceive, as is apparent from what we have justly alleged from the 16th chapter, of the preparation for this war; namely, that after the effusion of the sixth phial, when the seventh, by which the beast was utterly destroyed, was just ready to be poured out, "from the mouth of the dragon, and from the mouth of the beast, and the false prophet, three impure spirits, like frogs, being the spirits of demons working miracles, went forth to the kings of the earth and of the whole world, to gather them to the battle of the great day of God Almighty." Since then the period of the thousand years by no means admits of these disturbances and satanic commotions, it follows that this war of the beast preceded them in time. And thus at length the thousand years of Satan's bondage will contemporize with the interval from the destruction of the beast. Q. E. Δ.

Argument 3.--Lastly, since, during the thousand years in which Satan is detained in custody, Christ may be said to have reigned with his followers over that august and magnificent kingdom, therefore, by the same arguments and marks by which the synchronism of the one is established, that of the other will be confirmed. That this august kingdom of Christ then begins with the seventh trumpet, or from the destruction of the beast, it is now our business to show.

SYNCHRONISM V

Of the Thousand Years of the august Kingdom of Christ, and of the Seventh Trumpet, or the Interval from the Destruction of the Beast

That extraordinary and august kingdom of Christ, repeatedly mentioned in the Apocalypse, and of whose approach the chorus of animated beings and elders rejoicing together, are wont to sing hymns and doxologies to God, every where succeeds to the beast and Babylon, subdued and led in triumph. For, first, in the 20th chapter, where this reign of a thousand years is expressly treated of, in the number of those who reign with Christ, are they who have not worshipped the beast, nor his image, nor received his mark upon their foreheads or in their hands. Do not these words sufficiently show that this reign of Christ succeeded the reign of the beast, his image, and his marks? For why should this eulogium be bestowed on the children of the kingdom, that they had not adored the beast, &c. unless the beast had preceded it? For the good desert is certainly antecedent to the remuneration and reward. But this kingdom, (as the series of the narration points out) is bestowed on the saints as a reward of their faith and constancy, their cause having been first heard in solemn judgment; the assembly of which is described in these words, "And I saw thrones, and they sat upon them, and judgment was given unto them;" that is, the power of judging facts, &c. Therefore the time in which, while the beast was reigning, the saints approved their faith and their constancy to God, preceded the judgment. The remuneration follows the decree then established.

2. The same likewise farther appears from the paean of the elders and living creatures, which was sung at the fall of Babylon: "Ἀλληλούϊα, ὅτι ἐβασίλευσε Κύριος ὁ Θεὸς ὁ παντοκράτωρ," v. 7. "Let us rejoice, and exult, and give glory to him; for the marriage of the Lamb is come, and his wife hath made herself ready." For that the kingdom in both cases is the same, I cannot entertain a doubt.

3. But most clearly of all does it appear, from c. xi. v. 15, 16, &c. when, at the sound of the seventh trumpet, the days of the witnesses, and the months of the beast, and the Gentiles being concluded, there was that exclamation in heaven, "The kingdoms of this world are become the kingdoms of our Lord and of his Christ, and he shall reign for ever and ever. And the four and twenty elders who sat on their thrones before God, fell on their faces and worshipped God, saying, We give thanks, Ω Lord God Almighty, who art, and who vast, and who art to come, because Thou hast taken to Thee thy great power, and hast reigned."

This is that consummation of the mystery of God, proclaimed by the prophets, which, at the sounding of the seventh trumpet, the angel had before predicted should come to pass; when neither the months of the beast, nor the days of the witnesses in mourning, nor any part of the period of "a time, and times, and half a time," should remain to be completed, precisely according to the prediction of Daniel, c. vii. v.25, 26. concerning the oecumenical dominion of Christ, or the reign

A Key to the Apocalypse

of the saints, which was to take place after the same times and the same sessions of judgment. Likewise where the same angel who here addresses John, in the same gesture, manner, and (what is chiefly to be remarked) under the same form of swearing, is said to have asseverated that the interval of a time, and times, and half a time, being completed, the dispersion of the holy people, and with it, the last of wonderful events, should be consummated.

Whoever desires a farther confirmation, let him apply the characters of the foregoing synchronism to the present; for they afford, as I have said, mutual corroboration to each other.

SYNCHRONISM VI

Of the New Jerusalem, the Spouse of the Lamb, with the Seventh Trumpet, or the Period from the Destruction of the Beast

The marriage of the Lamb, and the august kingdom of the Lord God Omnipotent, both begin from the fall of Babylon, from whence the seventh trumpet begins. This appears from the hymn of the elders and living creatures, which are quoted in the former synchronism, c. xix. v. 6, 7. "Alleluia! for our Lord God Omnipotent has begun to reign. Let us be glad, and rejoice, and give glory to Him; for the marriage of the Lamb is come, and his wife hath made herself ready." But the "new Jerusalem is the spouse of the Lamb, adorned and prepared for her husband," c. xxi. v. 2. "And I saw," says he, "the Holy City, New Jerusalem, coming down out of heaven from God, as a wife adorned for her husband;" and, v. 9, "Come, and I will show you, the bride, the Lamb's wife." Therefore, it will both begin and be contemporary with the seventh trumpet.

2. New Jerusalem is the beloved city; but that beloved city, as soon as the thousand years are finished, is said to be compassed out by the last forces of Satan, then set at liberty. c. xx. v. 9. "And they compassed the camp of the saints about, and the beloved city." Therefore it must have existed before, while Satan was bound. To these two arguments, either for the sake of confirmation, or of illustration and ornament, two others seem proper to be subjoined.

3. As soon as the seventh phial has been poured out, "a great voice proceeded from the Throne, saying, Γέγονε, It is done, c. xvi. 19. In like manner, c. xxi. v. 5, 6. "He who sat on the Throne" said to John, as he saw the New Jerusalem descending from heaven, "Behold, I make all things new. Γέγονε, It is done. I am A and Ω, the Beginning and the End." Therefore the new Jerusalem, the wife of the Lamb, begins from the final termination of the phials: "It is done," the harlot being now extinct, and so is contemporary with the interval from the destruction of the beast.

4. One of the angels of the phials, c. xvii. showed John the judgment of the harlot, while the phials were pouring out, and which was to be effected by one of them at least; and the same angel of the c. xxi. v. 10. shows the same John the bride of the Lamb, the great and holy city Jerusalem; because it was to become conspicuous when the phials were discharged, that is, when the beast and Babylon were extinct.

SYNCHRONISM VII

Of the Palm-bearing Multitude of Persons innumerable, rejoicing in triumph, out of all nations, and kindreds, and peoples, and tongues; with the Seventh Trumpet, or Period after the Destruction of the Beast

I. The palm-bearing multitude immediately succeeds the company of a hundred and forty-four thousand sealed; but that company which is to be considered as the opposite to the beast, with which it is contemporary, both in meaning and duration, completed its period likewise with the beast. (Synch. IV. Part. I.) Therefore the palm-bearing multitude follows both, and consequently falls in with the seventh trumpet, which is the interval from the downfal of the beast.

The palm-bearing multitude are citizens of the new Jerusalem; for of both it is said, "that they shall not hunger any more, nor thirst any more; that the Lamb shall feed them, and lead them to living fountains of waters; and that God shall wipe away all tears from their eyes."

Now, the new Jerusalem is contemporary with the seventh trumpet, and therefore the palm-bearing multitude is so likewise.

THE EPOCH OF THE APOCALYPSE

The epoch of the Apocalypse, as far as it is a prophecy of the future, whether you are inclined to consider it as commencing from the beginning of Christianity, or from the ruin of the Jewish polity and church, or from the moment of time in which the revelation was made to St. John, or in whatever way it may be understood, (for I will not act as an interpreter, when I recollect my design,) I think no one will be inclined to doubt but that the beginning of the seals, which relates to things to be transacted therein, must be deduced from thence. But from the same epoch must be derived also the beginning of the second prophecy, or of the Little Book, if those words of the context, about the repetition of the prophecy, and what we have besides treated of above in Synch. VI. Part I. and in the Introduction to Part II. have not been sufficiently convincing to any individual, he will be compelled at length to acknowledge, from the necessity of the synchronism, when he shall have attempted to place the several prophecies in order and method according to the explanations which have just been made.

THE CLOSE OF THE SYNCHRONISMS AND OF THE APOCALYPSE

The universal resurrection of the dead, and the last judgment with Gehenna follow the thousand years of the kingdom and the condemnation of Satan, c. xx. from verse 11 to the end.

Paradise follows the description of New Jerusalem, through which runs a river like Eden, winds about here and there, having in the midst

[page 46 is missing]

be extracted, compared, and demonstrated, with the supposition and assistance of any given interpretation.

2. Then, besides, as it is the custom in historical works, that many different transactions which took place together and at the same time, with many other transactions, cannot, notwithstanding, be related together, but separately and in succession; so likewise it is usual, in the case of those prophecies and visions of things performed, (but displayed in the most commodious and wisest order,) that they would be altogether in the wrong who would proceed to interpret the Apocalypse in such a manner, as if the events succeeded each other always in the same order and series as the visions.

3. By successfully examining the meaning of the Apocalyptical visions, the series and connexion in the chief of them among each other, according to the events, being investigated by remarkable characters and marks, and demonstrated by internal arguments, is to be constituted as the basis and foundation of all solid and legitimate interpretation. For the order itself is to be confirmed, not according to the will of the interpreter, (as we see unadvisedly done by many,) on account of some congruity of the interpretation, but every interpretation is to be tried by the characters of the synchronisms, according to the already constructed idea of this chronic order, as by a rule and standard. For without a foundation of this kind, it is scarcely possible that you should extract any thing from the Apocalypse which can solidly give an assurance of its interpretation and application, and which may rely on Divine authority, and not on assumed principles and mere conjectures. But, on the contrary, if this foundation be admitted, since even the bounds of time and order will not permit the application to wander at licence and at will, you will be surprised, out of so many varying and even contending interpretations, how many are almost entirely removed, few doubtful places, upon the whole, being left, and those generally of small consequence, in which the intention yet remains doubtful, at least as to its general application; so that from this book henceforth, as well as from the other books of the New Testament, arguments may be obtained, even on the subject of prophecy, secure of interpretation, and on which reliance may be placed as on the oracles of the Holy Spirit, and not merely on the inventions of the human understanding.

5. Now, Ω Reader, such an Apocalyptical Key, or Compass, (if you prefer calling it so,) according to the measure of intelligence with which a good and beneficent God has favoured me, an unworthy sinner, in the investigation of these mysteries, I demonstrate to the best of my power in the above synchronisms, and propose to your view in the accompanying scheme, as in a brief and easy compendium; in which, (that you may not be ignorant of its use,) if you have once made up your mind about the sense of some principal prophecy, and of the times in which it was fulfilled, you will then have a method pointed out, from which, by the clew of the synchronisms, and the order of the whole, you will be able to investigate, nay, even to demonstrate, the meaning of the other visions; since those other prophecies which are contemporary with that known prophecy of yours, are without doubt to be applied to the same times; but those which precede are only to be interpreted of preceding, those which succeed in like manner, only of subsequent events.

6. And lest you should be inclined to doubt whether there is any one of all the visions in the Apocalypse to be found on which you can safely fix your foot, in the manner I have pointed out, and from thence, as from some station or watch-tower, measure the rest of the Apocalypse, lo! on this very point a discovery has been made by the Holy Spirit, in that illustrious vision of the great harlot; in truth, the only one of all the visions which the angel, contrary to custom, explains to John. But for what purpose? unless that by it an approach may be opened to the rest, which would be otherwise inaccessible?

Joseph Mede

What would you wish for more? Here then, having invoked the Father of Lights, enter; and having entered, apply the key to unlock the remainder. Make a trial; and when you have tried, you will confess that this prophecy is most admirable, and that when the subject is thoroughly investigated, there is none of the Old Testament, not even that of Daniel, (so it becomes the Gospel,) which can be compared with it for certainty, either in the singular contrivance of its manifestation, or in the mode and manner of discovering its interpretation.

Lastly, I will intreat of you, Ω Reader, who may meet with this work, that if you shall perceive any thing perchance to have been revealed to me, while an attentive observer, which may be of service to yourself or others, in the understanding of these mysteries, you would refer it wholly to the mercy of God, bestowed upon me; to whom I likewise shall never cease to return my grateful thanks for the slenderest raylet of His wisdom; but whatever may be erroneous, that I beseech you to impute to myself alone, a man of very little ability, and by no means fitted of myself (of which I am fully conscious) to such an undertaking.

Blessing, and honour, and glory be unto Him that sitteth on the Throne, and to the Lamb, for ever and ever!

A COMMENTARY ON THE REVELATION OF SAINT JOHN, ACCORDING TO THE RULE OF THE APOCALYPTICAL KEY

Apoc. c. vi. 2. "Exivit vincens et ut vinceret."
Apoc. c. i. 7. "Ecce venit cum nubibus et videbit eum omnis oculus, etiam qui eum transfixerunt."

THE FIRST PART

Of the Apocalyptical Commentaries, according to the Rule of the Apocalyptical Key, on the First Prophecy which is contained in the Seals and Trumpets; with an Introduction concerning the Scene of the Apocalypse.

As it is my design to investigate the meaning of the Apocalyptical visions, it is requisite for me to treat, in the first place, of that celestial theatre to which John was called, in order to behold them, exhibited as on a stage, and afterwards of the prophecies in succession, examined by the Apocalyptical Key.

Ω Christ! the Wisdom of God! to whom "the Revelation was given by the Father, to show unto us his servants things which must come to pass," illuminate my mind with Thy bright beams, cleanse me from impurity by Thy blood. Grant me, with Thy assistance, and with the Spirit for my guide, to investigate these abstruse mysteries, and to explain them to others!

I give the name of Apocalyptical theatre to that august session of God and the Church, described in the fourth chapter, and exactly conformable to the type of the ancient encampment of Israel in the desert, which will be fully manifest on comparing the disposition of one with the other. Thus, in the midst of the camp of Israel, was placed the tabernacle. The Levites were stationed nearest the camp; and after the Levites, to the four quarters of the world, the rest of the assembly of Israel, marshalled under four standards, three tribes being disposed under one standard, and receiving its name from the first tribe of its cohort. Each standard exhibited a signal, which, though Moses only mentions in a general manner, and does not always express what figure was inscribed on each standard, yet the Hebrews, from the ancient traditions of their elders, (in this instance not rashly to be despised,) proceed to the description of the whole in the following manner:--

On the east was the standard of Judah, with his associate tribes, under the sign of a Lion.
On the west the standard of Ephraim, under the sign of an Ox.
On the south that of Reuben, under the sign of a Man.
On the north that of Dan, under the sign of an Eagle.

Aben Ezra observes on Numbers ii. רכינוכק רדטא. Our ancestors have said, that there was the figure of a man on the standard of Reuben, on account of the mandrakes which he found, (but this is a foolish observation). On the standard of Judah the figure of a lion, because Jacob compared him to one. On the standard of Ephraim the figure of an ox, with reference to what is said, Deut. c. xxxiii. v. 17. "The firstling of his bullock." And lastly, on the standard of Dan the figure of an eagle. Bar Nachman, and Chuzkuni in his third chapter, have the same observations on this subject.

If any one should be very curious to inquire on what account the figures of these animals were selected for this purpose, besides what may be deduced, not improperly, from the blessing of Judah and Ephraim, the writers on the Talmud seem to intimate a reason of this nature. There are four proud ones, (say they,) or those who bear pre-eminence in the world; the lion among the wild beasts, the ox among cattle, the eagle among birds, and man, upon whom God bestowed super-eminent beauty, that he might rule over all. Whatever the reason may be, this tradition of the Jews may be confirmed by the quadruple face of the cherubim, in Ezekiel, (for do not imagine there were so many heads,) by which was signified, that he who was carried by them was the Lord and King of the four cohorts, or camps of Israel. For as the chariots of princes are emblazoned with the ensigns of their lords, so are the cherubim with the signs of Jehovah, King of the Tetrarchs of Israel.

Joseph Mede

Nor would it be very difficult to collect, from the position of Ezekiel, and the cherubim in that vision, with respect to each other, to which quarter of the world each face of the cherubim was directed: For when Ezekiel, with his countenance turned to the north, saw the cherubim, as it were, coming forth to meet him, undoubtedly that which then appeared before him was the anterior and direct face of the cherubim, namely, that of a man, and consequently the face of the man looked towards the south: Whence it follows, that what is said to have been on the right hand of Ezekiel, the face of the lion, looked towards the east, that of the ox, which was on his left hand, looked towards the west; and lastly, that of the eagle towards the north.

And the same reason induces us to believe that those cherubim which overshadowed the ark of God, in the recess of the temple, were of a similar, that is, of a quadriform face, especially, since it may be proved, that this was the fact with regard to those which were engraven on the walls of the temple; because in the same prophet, c. xli. v. 19, we read of half their sculpture, when two faces, as must have been the case in bas-relief of this kind, being buried in the plane of the wait, the two remaining ones, those of the man and the lion, are represented as having stood forward, in opposite directions, towards the palms embossed on each side. And permit me to ask, why should the cherubim have been sculptured in any other form than that in which they were exhibited? We may add, that some understand of the four animals, as so many ensigns of the cohorts of Israel, a passage of Psalm lxviii. v. 10, which, indeed, Jerome, in that version which has its reputation from its conformity with the Hebrew verity, has thus translated: "Thy animals have dwelt therein;" that is to say, according to what precedes it, "in thy inheritance;" i. e. the camp of thy people, whom thou leddest through the wilderness. In like manner, the Septuagint, and the Vulgate, which is translated from it, have τὰ ζῶά σου, animalia tua; and, in truth, that this passage refers to that time, plainly appears from what is antecedent to this and the preceding verse. "Ω God! when thou wentest out before thy people; when thou wentest through the wilderness; the earth trembled and the heavens dropped at the presence of God," &c. And also what is subjoined of "the gracious rain," the rain of manna, if I am not mistaken, and therefore it may be rendered, "A gracious or liberal rain hast thou shed, Ω God! with which thou hast comforted thy labouring inheritance." Not to say, besides, that the beginning of this psalm is borrowed from that form of prayer which Moses used at the going out of the people of Israel, "Rise, Ω Jehovah! and let thy enemies be scattered!"

We have seen the Israelitish encampment of God: Now let us see how the Apocalyptic Assembly conforms to it in every respect. c. iv. v. 2. "And I was (says John) in the Spirit, and behold a throne was set in heaven; and there was One sitting on the throne. And He that sat thereon was to look at like a jasper and a sardine stone, like the appearance of an emerald; and around the throne were four-and-twenty seats, and upon the seats I saw four-and-twenty elders sitting, clothed in white garments, and they had on their heads golden crowns. And out of the throne proceeded lightnings, and thunderings, and voices; and there were seven lamps of fire burning before the throne, which are the seven spirits of God. And before the throne was a sea of glass, like unto chrystal, and in the midst of the throne, and round about the throne, were four animals, full of eyes before and behind; and the first animal was like a lion, and the second animal like a calf, and the third animal had a face as a man, and the fourth animal was like a flying eagle. And the four animals had each of them six wings round about him, and were full of eyes within, and they rest not day and night, saying, Holy, holy, holy, Lord God Almighty, which was, and which is, and which is to come! And when those animals give glory and honour and thanks to Him who is sitting on the throne, and who liveth for ever and ever, the four-and-twenty elders fall down before Him who sitteth on the throne, and worship Him who liveth for ever and ever, and cast their crowns before the throne, saying, Worthy art thou, Ω Lord, to receive glory, and honour, and power, for thou hast created all things, and through thy will they are, and were created!"

Do not these particulars answer exactly to each other? First, as to the tabernacle: That the throne here placed in the midst, on which God was sitting, was no other than the temple, or tabernacle, (for it must be observed, that the description is applicable to the history of both,) appears both from the seven lamps burning before it, and from the glassy sea, like chrystal, of which the former represent the candlestick with its seven lights, likewise burning before the sacred place; the latter that immense laver in the Temple of Solomon, called the sea; but with this difference, that that of Solomon was brass, but ours of glassy or pellucid substance.

I know not, however, whether we may not be allowed to conjecture that an allusion is here made to that more ancient laver of the Mosaic tabernacle, since that also is reported to have been constructed of looking-glass, of I know not what substance; viz. of the looking-glasses of the women assembling at the door of the tabernacle. But you may see the temple remarkably described under the title of the throne of God. Is. vi. 1. "I saw the Lord sitting upon a throne, lofty and elevated, and its skirts filled the temple." So also Jerem. xvii. 12. "A throne of glory from the beginning is the place of our sanctuary." And Ezekiel, xliii. 7. "The place of my throne, and the place of my footsteps, where I dwell in the midst of the sons of Israel for ever."

A Key to the Apocalypse

And that it was a throne of this kind, which John saw placed in the midst of the elders and living creatures, the Apocalypse has every where taken for granted. For where did he see the altar openly, "and under it the souls of those who were slain for the Word of God," except in the temple? How could the golden altar of incense be before the throne, unless that throne were a temple or a tabernacle? What else will "the four horns of the golden altar" imply, which is in the sight of God? What is meant by the temple, the courts of the temple, and the altar, as well those which were to be measured by the reed of the angel, as those which were to be left out? What the temple of God opened in heaven, and therein the ark of the testimony exposed to view? What the angels coming forth from the temple, and that also in heaven? What is meant by the harpers standing on the brink of the sea, or glassy laver, and singing the song of victory, and that likewise in heaven? What in the fifth verse of the same chapter, of the temple of the tabernacle of testimony opened in heaven? and of the same temple "filled with smoke from the glory of God?" But what places the matter beyond all chance of contradiction is, "And there came forth a great voice out of the temple of heaven from the throne."

Moreover, in this throne or temple, lest any doubt should remain, the place of God's seat, (or, as the Greek interpreters speak of the throne of Solomon,) a ὁ θρόνος τῆς καθέδρας, the throne of his resting-place, was that interior and most holy part of the temple, where the ark of the covenant was enclosed with the mercy-seat. For there God was said to dwell, and sit between the cherubim of glory: For which reason, indeed, both the seven lamps in this place, and the golden altar of incense afterwards, are said to have been "before the throne;" that is, before the inmost recess of the temple; for that is plainly said of both in so many words, 2 Chron. iv. and 1 Kings vi. 20, in the former of which the Septuagint has, "τοὺς λύχνους κατὰ τὸ πρόσωπον τοῦ δαβείρ;" i. e. the lamps before the face of the Dabir [4], (for so the inmost recess is called in Hebrew;) in the other place, "Θυσιαστήριον κέδρινον, κατὰ πρόσωπον τοῦ δαβείρ," "the cedar altar of incense before the face of the Dabir;" nearly in the same sense as in the Apocalypse, "before the throne and before God." So the remaining parts, both of the temple and tabernacle, will consist partly of props, partly of steps, and partly of a footstool to the throne properly so called, of which kind that august throne of Solomon is said to have had parts or appendages. Thus far respecting the throne.

2. Four-and-twenty elders, in the next place, surround the throne, who represent the bishops and prelates of the churches, and answer in place and order to the Levites and priests in the camp of Israel, and their number twenty-four corresponds with the daily courses of the priests and Levites, or, what comes to the same result, with the chiefs of the daily courses. Whence beside that they are next to God, they have likewise their thrones there: Moreover, they wear crowns, which are marks of dignity and power bestowed by God.

3. At a proper distance behind the elders, where lines drawn through the middle of the throne bisect its sides on every part of the circumference, towards the four cardinal points of heaven, four living creatures were seen; the first in the figure of a lion, the second of an ox, (for μόσχος is an ox with the Hellenists,) the third in the likeness of a man, the fourth of a flying eagle, representing doubtless the Christian churches towards the four parts of the world, and answering to the four Israelitish camps, which bore standards of the same animals. For what is called in the Apocalyptic text, a little obscurely, "in the midst of the throne, and round about the throne," may be explained by the figure ἓν διὰ δυοῖν; i. e. one through two; familiar to the Hebrews, as if it had been said, in the midst of the circuit or circumference of the throne; and in this sense, if you were to draw round the throne, as a square, a quadrangular parallel figure at a proper distance from the throne, and the elders surrounding it, in the midst, or at the middle of every one of the sides of the quadrangle, (for ἐν μέσῳ, in the midst, is to be taken distributively,) the four animals exhibited themselves, namely, one in the middle of each side.

Figure of the Throne

Moreover, those animals are described as "full of eyes before and behind," having six wings around them, and those full of eyes within. So many eyes denote a multitude of very well-sighted persons, and full of the knowledge of the mysteries of God, of which kind there are many in the animals, that is, in the churches which the animals represent. The wings denote agility and alacrity in executing the commands of God. Wings with eyes denote zeal combined with knowledge and faith. Lastly, six wings around them, denote that they are ready to fly every way, that is, fully prepared to fulfil the commands of God universally and entirely. In addition we are told, lastly, what was the nature of their duty, as well that of the living creatures, as of the elders around the throne, namely, of this kind, that "as often as those animated beings were about to give glory, and honour, and thanks to Him that sat on the throne;" i. e. as often as the churches formed their holy congregations, so often "the four-and-twenty elders, in right of their office preceding the animated beings, are accustomed to "fall down before God," saying, "Worthy art Thou, Ω Lord, to receive glory, and honour, and power; for Thou hast created all things, and for thy pleasure they are and were created." This interpretation being admitted, the diction of John, which many pretend to be a solecism, as improperly using the futures, δώσουσι, πεσοῦνται, προσκυνήσουσι, instead of the preterites, will easily be defended; since, according to the Hebrews, (whose ideas the apostle every where adopts,) the future is used to denote an act of custom or duty, so that John is by no means to be supposed to relate what was there done in the vision, by the animated beings and elders, but what was to be done as occasion should arise, and what he himself saw clone by them afterwards, in the progress of the visions when an opportunity occurred of celebrating God.

And therefore (that I may at length come to a conclusion) I think I have clearly shown, that the throne in this august session answers to the tabernacle or temple; the elders answer to the Levites; the four animals to the four Israelitish camps; that is, that the whole assemblage is the image of that ancient castrametation in the wilderness. Which subject has indeed been more diffusively treated of by me, because I have observed that the reason of many types in the Apocalypse depends chiefly on the knowledge of this, which I doubt not but every one who has thoroughly investigated the matter, will perceive as well as myself.

The theatre being thus prepared, He who sat on the throne stretches forth a book in his right hand, written upon, both in the inside and the out, and fastened with seven seals, and an angel at the same time coming forth on the scene, proclaims, with a loud voice, that if to any one were given the power of opening it, so that the things which were written therein might be seen and read, he should take it into his hands and apply himself to the task; and in so doing, would perform an office very acceptable to all who were ardent in the study of mysteries.

And the book was in truth most worthy of the effort; in the unsealing of which, any one would exert all the powers of his understanding and industry, inasmuch as the volume was predictive of the counsels of God, in which was interwoven the series and order of events, to be transacted up to the second and glorious advent of Christ.

For, of this nature evidently appears to be the double prophecy of the future, which the volume contained. Which is the reason, unless I am mistaken, why John, when he was preparing to expound the visions, prefixed to the beginning of his history the descriptive outline of his glorious advent, as the boundary of the Apocalyptic course. "Behold (says he) he cometh with clouds, and every eye shall see him, and they also that pierced him, and all the tribes of the earth shall lament because of him." As much as to say, this is the scope, this the boundary of the visions which I shall relate.

But when "no one of those who were in heaven, or in the earth, or under the earth, was able to unseal the book," and the object seemed to be given up for lost, so that John, overcome with grief, burst into tears, lo, "a Lamb in appearance, as if it had been slain," that is, bearing the marks and wounds of one that had undergone death, arose in the midst of the elders and animated beings, and took the book, for the purpose of unsealing and opening it, as he alone had worthily obtained the power of doing it.

At the sight of this a chorus of the animated beings and elders, together with the surrounding angels, and all the creatures in the universe, filled with gratitude, immediately sing a hymn to the Lamb and to the Father. On which subject I desire only to remark at present, that they manifestly refer the power of unsealing the book as obtained by the merit of the passion of the Lamb. "Worthy art thou (they say) to open the book and its seals, for thou wert slain, and hast redeemed us to God by thy blood, out of every tribe, and tongue, and people, and nation." By which, perhaps, light may be thrown on that saying of our Saviour before he had suffered and been glorified: "But of that day and hour (alluding to his second coming, whether it would be sooner or later) knoweth no one, neither the angels in heaven, nor the Son, but the Father only;" because the Apocalypse was not yet given to Christ by the Father, nor the order of events relating to his advent yet made known. I assert nothing rashly; let the reader weigh the matter with himself.

While the Lamb is thus unsealing the book at each of the seals, particular images of future things are exhibited, of which the system runs through the whole Apocalyptical course, and thus constitutes the first universal prophecy. The interpretation of which, by the favour of Him who sitteth on the throne and of the Lamb, we will now attempt.

Of the two Apocalyptical Prophecies

The first prophecy, that of the seals, comprehends the fates of the empire: The other, that of the little book, the fates of the Church, or of the Christian Religion, until at length both shall coalesce in the reign of the Church triumphant, "when the kingdoms of this world have become the kingdoms of the Lord and his Christ." For as Daniel in the Old Testament, according to the succession of empires, both presignified the coming of Christ, and explained in order the fates of the Jewish Church; so is the Apocalypse to be understood as measuring out the Christian system by the proceedings of the Roman empire, which was still remaining after Christ. Nor does the event contradict this supposition. The interpretation of the first prophecy thus proceeds upon this general hypothesis.

Of the first Prophecy, which is that of the Seals; and in the first place, of the events signified by the six first Seals

The scope of the seven seals in general is this, that the periods of time, as it continues to flow, being distinguished by the characters of events, it may be shown, that when the succession of occurrences of every kind relative to the Roman empire has been contemplated, it would come to pass that Christ would vanquish the powers of the world with which he was waging war. In the sixth succession, or sixth seal, the gods of the heathen Roman empire; and in the seventh, when the series of the trumpets shall have arrived at the last trump, whatever, even after that time, might have arisen anew, or yet remain in any part of the world, was to be destroyed and abolished. "For he must reign until he bath put all enemies under his feet:" That is, till he has abolished all hostile principality, and power, and authority.

We will treat of the former period, as the order requires, in the first place.

The six first seals then, in their sixfold character of events, (not much unlike those which our Saviour had prescribed for pointing out the time of the ruin of Jerusalem,) distinguish so many periods of the Roman empire, while it was yet subsisting and flourishing, until, at length, in the sixth, Christ should utterly demolish the power of idols and heathen deities in that part of the globe. Now I call characters the very signal events of the Roman empire, by which occurrences, as in a symbol, the periods may be distinguished, and those in this first period, not brought on from without by the barbarous nations, (of which kind will be those of the empire afterwards falling to decay under the plagues of. the seven trumpets,) but intestine misfortunes, arising within the empire itself: Which destruction, indeed, was introduced by the Holy Spirit for this purpose, that the different times of the Roman commonwealth,--the former of its flourishing, the latter of its declining state,--may be described by different marks.

It is here likewise to be observed, that since the characters of the occurrences, of which I have spoken, scarce ever or rarely pervade the whole period of the seal, and consequently may not be sufficient of themselves to circumscribe these periods within a certain beginning and end; therefore, in the four first seals, the Holy Spirit (where that may be most necessary, as well for the cause above mentioned as on account of the inequality of the periods) has had recourse to the four animated beings for that purpose, each of which might indicate the epoch of the seal according to his point of the compass. How this is done we shall presently see. It is sufficient at present to have given a hint of it. C. vi. "And I saw when the Lamb opened one of the seals, and I heard one of the four animated beings saying, as with a voice of thunder, Come and see. And I saw, and behold a white horse, and he that sat thereon held a bow, and a crown was given unto him, and he went forth conquering, and to conquer. And when he opened the second seal, I heard the second animated being saying, Come and see. And there went out another horse that was red [5], and it was given to him that sat thereon to take peace from the earth, and that they might slay one another; and a great sword was given him. And when he opened the third seal, I heard the third animated being say, Come and see. And I beheld, and lo a black horse, and he that sat thereon had a balance in his hand: And I heard a voice in the midst of the four living creatures, saying, A daily measure [6] of wheat for a penny, and three daily measures of barley for a penny; and hurt not the oil and the wine. And when he had opened the fourth seal, I heard the voice of the fourth animated being saying, Come and see. And I saw, and behold a pale [7] horse, and the name of him that sat thereon was Death, and

Hades followed in his company; and power was given them to kill the fourth part of the earth with sword, and with famine, and with death, and by the wild beasts of the earth."

Of the First Seal

The first occurrence of the Roman empire, and that a most illustrious one, is the commencement of the victory of Christ, by which the Roman gods began to be vanquished, and their worshippers to be transfixed with the arrows of the Gospel, to fail on every side, and to submit their necks to Christ the conqueror. "He went out (says he) conquering, and to conquer;" that is, he hath not yet completely conquered, but laid the foundations of victory, to he hereafter more and more fulfilled.

The index of the first seal is the first animal in the likeness of a lion, in station towards the East, and it shows that the rider, viz. the emperor, is to go forth from that quarter of the compass, from the mounting of whom on his horse for the purpose of riding,--that is, from the beginning of his government,--the period of the first seal was to commence, namely, from the glorious exaltation of our Lord Jesus Christ, under the guidance and auspices of which emperor from the East, this battle is waged, and this victory obtained. The beginning of the following seals is pointed out by the Roman emperors; but where the act of Christ is described, he is accounted as the sole emperor [8].

Now indeed, when this seal had run its course, the oracles of the gods, through the whole Roman world, became mute, and John, the last of the twelve apostles of Christ, having received the wages of his warfare, departed from this life, to receive an undecaying crown in the heavens, together with his brethren and co-apostles, ibr a conduct bravely and happily performed.

That riding on horseback is a symbol of power, and of those who hold the reins of government, may be seen even from the interpretation of the Greek translators, Psalm xlv. v. 5, according to whom, prosper and ride on, is rendered, κατευοδοῦ καὶ βασίλευε, Go forth prosperously and reign. Nor does the Chaldee dissent from this sense, which translates, "as horsemen on the throne of the kingdom. So the woman riding on the beast is explained by the angel to be a city having dominion, and the expression of riding is applied in the same sense in other parts of Scripture.

Of the Second Seal

The second memorable event of the Roman empire, the picture of the second seal, is slaughter and intestine butchery; to which there was scarcely any similar in the whole Roman history. "And it was given," says he, "to him who sat on the horse to take away peace from the earth, and that men should massacre one another;" which last part of the sentence confirms the explanation of the former: For in what sense should the words be taken, "It was given to him that men should kill one another," unless it were given, or came to pass, that while he sat thereon, men should fiercely contend in mutual slaughters and butcheries? The index of this seal is the second animal, in the figure of an ox, situated to the west, and which bids them in the vision look towards himself: He thereby informs us, that this seal begins when Trajan, the Spaniard, had taken the reins of government, an emperor from the west. Dion says, Trajan, a Spaniard, was not an Italian, not belonging to Italy: Before him, no one of any other nation had obtained the Roman empire. But from him thenceforward the dominion continued in a descent from the same family down to Commodus, when the interval of this seal terminates.

Beginning, then, from this emperor, let us seek for that memorable event of mutual slaughter. This took place when Trajan and his successor, Hadrian, held the ensigns of imperial sway, among the Gentiles and Jews who then dwelt together throughout the Roman world. What was done under Trajan, take not in my words, but in the joint expressions of Dion and Orosius. "The Jews," says Orosius, "were inflamed with an incredible agitation at one time, as if maddened by rage, through all parts of the earth: For they waged the most atrocious wars throughout the whole of Lybia, against the inhabitants; which was then so desolated, in consequence of the cultivators being killed, that it would have remained wholly void, every inhabitant being cut off, if Hadrian, the emperor, had not afterwards introduced colonies there, collected from other places."

"Those who dwelt about Cyrene, (it is Dion who speaks,) under a certain leader of the name of Andrew, slew Romans as well as Greeks, fed upon their flesh, and ate their entrails [9]. They then smeared themselves with their blood, and put on their skins. They divided many from head to foot with saws, they cast many to the wild beasts, they compelled many to fight together; so that there perished about two hundred and twenty thousand souls." He proceeds: "Besides, a similar slaughter took place in Egypt and in Cyprus, under the direction of Artemion, where there perished also two hundred and forty thousand. They utterly destroyed Salamis, a city of Cyprus, having slain all the inhabitants. (Oros. Eus.) In Alexandria also, having stirred up a warfare, they were conquered and reduced. At length they were subdued by others, and principally by Lysias, whom Trajan sent against them. In Mesopotamia also, when they had rebelled, war was undertaken against them by the command of the emperor; and by these means, many thousands of them were destroyed with a very great slaughter."

Thus far as to what passed under Trajan. But you will ask if there was any thing under Hadrian to be compared to these facts? Let the reader judge if they were not of a similar kind. I dare to affirm, not much inferior. For we have not yet related any thing of that famous rebellion under Barchoshebar, the pseudo Messiah. Listen to that, then, likewise in the words of Dion. "When Hadrian," says he, "had brought a colony into the city of Jerusalem, and in the same place in which the temple of God had been, had ordered another to be erected to Jupiter Capitolinus, all the Jews, wherever they were, began to mutiny, to inflict many injuries, secretly and openly, on the Romans, and many other nations were joined with them, from the desire of plunder; and by this means, almost the whole world was thrown into commotion." He goes on: "Then at length, Hadrian, after he had sent some of his best generals against them, (as their great number and desperation were well known,) not daring to attack them except singly, at length, after a long time, he overpowered and vanquished them, and there were slain, in these excursions and battles, not less than five hundred and eighty thousand persons. But so great was the multitude of those who died by famine, disease, and fire, that the number could not be ascertained." But was this victory easy and bloodless to the Romans? By no means. For he adds: "So many of the Romans perished in that war, that Hadrian, when he wrote to the Senate, did not use that exordium which the emperors were accustomed to adopt: Si vos liberique vestri valetis, bene est; Ego quidem et exercitus meus valemus.'"

These are his observations concerning the commotion among the Jews, under that son of the Star, as they called him, or if you will, the son of Stellio, whom Eusebius also reports to have slain the Christians with all sorts of torments, who were unwilling to render him assistance against the Roman soldiers. But if any one is desirous of hearing how the Jews themselves estimate the slaughter of their nation, the author of the book Juchasin writes, that Hadrian butchered twice as many Jews in this war as went out of Egypt. Another, in the book which is intituled יובדיבלט, which Drusius quotes in his History of Past Events, has said, that neither Nebuchadnezzar nor Titus had afflicted them so sorely as the emperor Hadrian.

Therefore this destruction seems to have been the most grievous paroxysm of that unheard of tribulation, which our Saviour had predicted should befall the Jews, and, by consequence, not undeservedly selected by the Holy Spirit for marking this second period, beyond all the events of that time, since it exceeded them all, as well in the renown of the nation, as in this illustrious completion of prophecy.

Of the Third Seal

The third animated being is the index of the third seal, in a human form, his station being towards the south, and consequently shows that this seal begins with an emperor proceeding from that cardinal point of the compass; probably with Septimius Severus, the African, an emperor from the south, of whom Eutropius writes in the following manner: "Deriving his origin from Africa, from the province of Tripolis, from the town of Leptis, the only emperor from Africa within all remembrance, before or since."

Many will have famine or dearness of provisions the subject of this seal, deducing their proof rather from the black colour of the horse, and from the mention of grain, a measure [10] of wheat for a penny, to which likewise they think the balance in the hands of the rider refers; as if the allowance of corn was not only to be measured, but weighed, in consequence of very great penury. And, in truth, I should never have called this interpretation in question, (which appears so suitable at first sight,) if the event had corresponded with it. But I find nothing particular in this age, and in this course of the seals concerning famine, and deserving the adoption of such a character: For what is reported from Tertullian, according to Scapula, is, I think, by no means to be considered as of much importance; for if, as he relates, the harvest failed once in Africa, when Hilarion was prefect, it was not on that account general through the Roman world, nor was it in the age of Severus. Hence, it comes to pass, that while I examine the meaning of the symbol a little more closely, I seem to myself to collect, and not altogether from uncertain signs, that it is to be regarded in a different light. For it does not appear, as that interpretation requires, that the balance can be aptly compared with the choenix, since the libra or scale is used in weighing, but choenix is the name of a measure. Besides, when the condition of the animal indicated agrees so well with the signification of the other seals,--that of the lion with victory, that of the ox with slaughter, that of the eagle with the carcases of the following seal,--here there would be no ground for the association. For what agreement is there between man and famine? The colour of black, neither in its nature nor in the use of the ancient prophets, is coupled with famine only, but serves equally to describe sorrow, misery, and terror.

The subject of this seal, therefore, may be not famine, nor the dearness of provisions, but an administration of justice throughout the Roman world, and a severity more illustrious and more remarkable than in any of the former or subsequent periods of the seals. For as relates to the figure, the colour of the horse agrees with the severity of justice. That the scales are the symbol of Justice, is a fact handed down to us, as at this day no one is ignorant that Justice is painted with a balance. But what is subjoined by way of explanation, will appear, if attention is paid to it, to imply the same. "Take not away wheat or barley from any without a just price being paid for it. Observe a similar rule of justice also with regard to the oil and the wine;" as if he wished to caution them against plunderers, and had said, Do not steal. A denary, or penny, was the ordinary wages for a day's work, which is obvious from the Gospel; it was also the daily stipend of the soldiers. The choenix signifies the diurnal allowance, the ἡμεροτροφιδα, the food for the day, but of a very uncertain measure, for it varied according to the custom of nations, places, and men. The military choenix (to omit the minor choenices of shepherds, husbandmen, and vintagers) was four quarts; but in an ancient lexicographer in Greek and Latin, χοῖνιξ is half a bushel, i. e. double the military: And in the Septuagint, Ezek. xlv. 10, 11, χοῖνιξ is a bath, the largest measure of the Hebrews. From so uncertain a measure as the chænix, how is it possible that any thing should be extorted concerning famine and the dearness of provisions? A chcenix, therefore, I take here for any diurnal allowance, and a denary for any price of such allowance. In this manner the mode of interpretation which I have adopted will be established.

Now it is wonderful how much the event favours the interpretation, while Severus and Alexander were in power, those very distinguished riders on the black horse. Of Severus, what you may read at large in Aurelius, I will collect together, retaining the author's words, and I will do the same afterwards from Lamprideus concerning Alexander. "No one was more illustrious in the republic," says Aurelius, "than Severus, the founder of very equitable laws. Implacable to faults, he exalted every active person by rewards. He permitted honours to be sold to no one within his dominions. Nor did he suffer the smallest theft to go unpunished; animadverting more particularly on his own dependants, because, though difficult of proof, he understood that they took place through the fault of his generals, or even of his prefects." Spartianus agrees with Aurelius when he calls him "both implacable to faults and the enemy to thieves, whenever they were found." But these assertions were in no respect inferior to those which Lampridius relates of Alexander, the son of Mammea, on which, therefore, the chief part of the character of the seal appears to be founded. "He enacted," says he, "moderate and innumerable laws on the right of the people and the revenue, nor did he ever sanction any constitution without twenty lawyers. He was a most severe judge against thieves, accusing them as guilty of daily crimes, and condemning them with the greatest acrimony, and calling them the only foes and enemies of the republic, (hut he speaks, if I mistake not, of judges who were thieves,) he commanded them never to appear in the cities, and if they were seen, to be banished by the governors of provinces. "Eucolpius," says he, "relates, (with whom he was on the most familiar terms,) that if ever he saw a judge who was a thief; he had his finger ready to pluck out his eye. Septimius adds, who was no stranger to his mode of life, that Alexander had so much animosity against those judges, who had a bad reputation from their successors, that if he saw them by any accident from the penetration of his mind, he blurted out the fervour of his indignation, his whole countenance glowing with wrath, so that he could not articulate. Nay, he caused it to be proclaimed by a herald, that no one should salute the prince who knew himself to be a thief, but if he should ever be detected, he should become liable to capital punishment. He proceeds: "If any of the soldiers turned out of their way into the property of any one, according to the nature of the place, he was subjected in his presence, either to be beaten with clubs or rods, or to be condemned; or if the dignity of the person secured him from these punishments, he was visited with the severest reproaches, since he addressed him thus: `Will you have that done on your own land which you do on another's?' and he very often exclaimed what he had heard and remembered, either from certain Jews or Christians, What you would not wish to have done to yourself, do not to another:' With which sentence he was so much in love, that he ordered it to be inscribed on his palace and on public buildings."

Behold, Ω Reader, the rider on the black horse, magnificently holding that golden heaven-descended balance of justice on the theatre of the world! Which was so remarkable a circumstance in a Pagan emperor, that it ought not to be deemed wonderful that the Holy Spirit should have made an allusion to it in this place.

Another mode of interpreting the symbol of Wheat and Barley

It is possible that these allusions to wheat and barley may be understood of the remarkable supply of corn which took place in these times. For it may seem that this meaning also is included in those words: So it may have a reference to the abundance of grain, that provisions should be sold at a just price. "A measure of wheat for a penny:" i. e. Sell the daily allowance of wheat according to the daily price of labour, or the wages or rent, that they might not furnish to any one who required assistance, more daily food than was sufficient for his daily supply. So likewise, "three measures of barley for a penny," may seem to relate to an equation of price, according to the quality of the commodity. If an interpretation of this sort should be satisfactory, the event will here also correspond exactly with it. Spartian says of Severus, "Though he found very little grain, he took such care, that when he departed this life, he left a seven years' regular allowance to the Roman people, so that 70,000 bushels a day might be expended. He first bestowed on the people of Rome a gratuitous diurnal allowance of oil, but he left so much of it, that there was sufficient for five years, not only for the uses of the city, but of all Italy, which was in want of oil." As if indeed he had intended to fulfil what is here added, καὶ τὸ ἔλαιον καὶ τὸν οἶνον μὴ ἀδικήσῃς, "And be not unjust as to the oil and wine."

Lamprideus has similar remarks respecting Alexander. "He so assisted," says he, "the provision of the Roman people, that when Heliogabalus had destroyed the grain, he in his turn replaced it out of his own revenue. The oil likewise," said he, "which Severus had given to the people, and which Heliogabalus had diminished, he fully restored, and added oil for the lights of the baths [11] ."

Of the Fourth Seal

The index of the fourth seal is the fourth animal, in the likeness of an eagle, its station to the North; by which is shown, that the beginning of the seal is to be deduced from an emperor sprung from that quarter, namely, from Maximin the Thracian, a nursling of the North. Julius Capitolinus says, "Maximin, of a village of Thrace, near the Barbarians, born also of a Barbarian father and mother." The character of this seal is an assemblage of sword, famine, and pestilence, raging together in such a manner as was never known before. Whence, to him who sat on the horse, the name of Death is said to be given; that is, in the acceptation of the notion of the Hebrews, who use abstracts for concretes, meaning deadly or death-bearing, because he brought in so many deaths with him into the world. For among the Hebrews, to be called by a name, sometimes signifies the same as to be, or exist, but in a certain particular manner, so that to have the name of Death in this place, means nothing else than to be, in an especial manner, deadly, or the cause of death; to which purpose likewise is that which follows, namely, that Hell accompanies him, as an attendant on funerals.

Now let us look to the event. And never, in truth, from the beginning of the seals, have these three plagues raged conjointly in so singular a manner. I will begin with slaughter, and omit what this age underwent from an external enemy, though that was very severe, the Barbarians laying waste almost the whole of the empire under the emperors Gallus and Volusianus, with rapines and slaughters. These things are not taken into the account. We are inquiring into intestine and domestic affairs. Ten emperors and Cesars then, or thereabouts, who were accounted legitimate, within the interval of this seal, i. e. within the space of thirty-three years, or a little more, did the sword, not of enemies, but of their own subjects, take off. Throughout the same interval, under the government of Gallienus alone, those thirty tyrants of whom Polio speaks, (though there might be fewer by one or two,) sprung up in different parts of the Roman world; and almost all these were slain, either by their own people or by one another, or were butchered by legitimate emperors; so that Orosius has said not undeservedly of this plague, that it was signalised, not by the slaughter of the common people, but by the wounds and deaths of princes.

Lastly, those emperors, beginning with Maxi-min and ending with Gallienus, with what savage cruelty were they endued! Maximin, as Julius Capitolinus testifies, was so cruel, "that some denominated him Cyclops, others Busiris, others Sciro, some Phalaris, and many Typho and Gyges. The senate feared him so much, that even their wives and children offered up prayers in the temples, publicly and privately, that he might never see the city of Rome. For they heard that some were lifted up on crosses, some enclosed in animals lately killed, some thrown to wild beasts, sonic beaten with clubs, and all without respect to dignity of situation." He proceeds: "In order to hide his ignoble birth, he killed all who were acquainted with his family, and also sonic friends who had often given him many donations from motives of pity and piety, for there was not a more cruel animal on the face of the earth." Lastly, says he, "Without judgment, without accusation, without an informer, without defence, he slew all of the faction of one Magnus, a consular man, took away all their goods, and could not satisfy himself with the slaughter of more than 4000 persons. Hear also what Trebellius Pollio says of Gallienus, in his Book of the Thirty Tyrants. "Ingenuus being slain, who was called Emperor by the legion in Mæsia, he was bitterly enraged against the soldiers as well as the citizens, nor did he leave any one without some mark of his cruelty. He was so fierce and blood-thirsty, that he left most of the cities void of the male sex." The same writer, in the Life of Gallienus, says: "The Scythians, having invaded Cappadocia, the soldiers had again entertained thoughts of making a new emperor, all of whom Gallienus slew according to his custom." He adds, in conclusion: "He acted with excessive cruelty towards the soldiers; for he slew three or four thousand every day." Pollio likewise relates, in the same Life of Gallienus, the very memorable example of the Byzantine butchery, exhibited by the soldiers, and by Gallienus himself: "Lest any evil," says he, should be wanting in the time of Gallienus, the city of the Byzantines, illustrious for naval battles, and the key of the Pontic sea, was so wholly laid waste by the soldiers of Gallienus, that scarcely any remained alive; for vengeance on whose slaughter, when Gallienus was admitted into Byzantium, he killed all the soldiers, while unarmed, and crowned with the warrior's crown, having broken the engagement which he had made with them."

Thus far you have an account of slaughter: I come now to pestilence, which here, according to the Oriental custom, is called death. So the Chaldee paraphrast for the Hebrew דבר, pestilence, is fond of using מותא, death; and the Hellenists generally translate it θάνατον, and, with a similar meaning, it is usually called mortality by ecclesiastical writers, which expression has now passed over into many of our vernacular tongues. With regard to the pestilence, the fact is so notorious and manifest, that there is no need of heaping together many proofs to establish the credit of the oracle. I shall dispatch it in a word. Tonaras is my author, (nor are others silent on the subject,) that under the emperors Gallus and Volusianus, a pestilence, arising from Ethiopia pervaded all the Roman provinces, and for fifteen successive years incredibly exhausted them. "Nor was there ever a greater plague read of by me," (says a celebrated man in our own days,) "within the same space of time or territory."

Famine still remains of that trio of calamities; which indeed, any one may collect, could not possibly be absent in this age, although none of the ancient writers had informed us of it, from this circumstance, that almost all the empire was so despoiled and trodden down by the Scythians, during these times, with rapines and devastations, that if we trust to Zosimus, no nation under the Roman dominion remained free from them; almost all the towns were destitute of walls; and the greater part of those which were destitute were taken by them. How was it possible that the fields should not be deserted in devastations of this kind, that tillage should not be neglected, and that whatever was laid up for food should not be destroyed? And that so indeed it really happened, appears from the epistle of Dionysius of Alexandria, who was then living, to his brothers, in which he bears testimony to that dire pestilence of which we are treating, as having succeeded war and famine. "After these things," says he, that is, after the persecution which took place under Decius, (for lie means that which preceded the pestilence,) "both war and famine followed, which we sustained together with the heathen." And after the introduction of a few words, he adds: "But when both we and they had breathed a little, that pestilence came on--a thing more terrific to them than any other species of terror, more lamentable than any kind of calamity, and to us indeed an exercise and a trial inferior to none of the rest." Cyprian agrees with him in his apology to Demetrian: "When you say," he observes, "that a great many complain, it is to be imputed to us, that wars more frequently arise, that pestilence and famine rage, and that showers and rains interrupt the continuance of serene weather; we ought not any longer to be silent."

Moreover, there is something added in the text respecting wild beasts; if indeed it be a calamity of a different kind from the former ones, and does not imply that the tyrants, who like wild beasts raged in those times through the Roman world, were to be assigned as the causes of those calamities; it will in this case point out an evil common to the eastern and southern regions; that when famine and pestilence are raging, wild beasts would grow too powerful for man, and would destroy them, as you may see, Lev. c. xxvi. Ezek. c. xiv. v. 15, 21. But the change of the syntax rather favours the former opinion, if you render καὶ ὑπὸ τῶν θηρίων τῆς γῆς, "and that by the beasts of the earth."

The fourth part of the earth, τὸ τέταρτον τῆς γῆς, within which the power of exercising their ravages is said to have been committed to hell and death, (unless any one should think that the common interpretation may be here defended to which the τέταρτον τῆς γῆς is the τετράδιον, that is, the quaternion, or four parts of the earth,) I explain of the most powerful and much the greater part of the Roman world: For since the third part of the earth, (as will be observed in its place,) points out the amplitude of the Roman world, it follows that the fourth part of the earth is the same Roman dominion, less by a fourth part, and therefore that triple or quadruple connexion of calamities pervaded three-fourths of the Roman world [12]; and certainly Orosius seems to add, that the pestilence did not extend itself farther than (to use his own words) the edicts of Decius ran to destroy the churches. I have nothing more to say. And thus far of the fourth seal.

Of the Fifth Seal

The two seals which follow receive no explanation, as to the time of their beginning, from the animated beings, and therefore no riders on horses are any longer here to be seen, upon which that index of the animals depended. The period of each, then, is to be sought from the time when the event of the preceding seal ceased; which indeed is very easy, when the events, as here, are of such a nature that their termination cannot be concealed, in consequence of their manifest perspicuity.

The fifth seal, therefore, will begin with the emperor Aurelian, in the year 268, at which time the longest of the calamities of the former seal, the pestilence of fifteen years' duration, was extinct.

Now, the most signal event of the Roman state, under this seal, and which surpassed all other events of that time, is that persecution of the Christians which begun with Diocletian, was continued by others, and was far the most severe of all.

Former ages saw nothing to compare with it. "It was longer, and more cruel," (these are the words of Orosius,) "than all that went before. For it was incessantly carried on for ten years, with the burnings of churches, the proscription of the innocent, the slaughter of martyrs. Immediately on the beginning of the tenth, within thirty days, about seventeen thousand men are said to have been sacrificed; nor did the fury of the persecutors abate with the progress of time. In Egypt alone, (what a small particle of the Roman empire!) if faith is to be given to St. Ignatius, patriarch of Antioch, according to Scaliger, "a hundred and forty-four thousand men were sacrificed, seven hundred (thousand) were driven into exile;" whence the Diocletian era derived its name among the Egyptians, so that it is called, even at this day, the era of martyrs. What now should you suppose was done throughout the other provinces of the Roman empire? "Almost all the world was stained with the sacred blood of martyrs," says Sulpitius Severus. "The world was never more drained of blood by any wars, nor did the Church" (the words are those of the same author) "ever conquer with a greater triumph, than when it could not be overcome with the slaughters of ten years."

This butchery is represented by the vision of "souls slain for the word of God, and for his testimony which they maintained, lying under the altar," that is, on the ground, at the foot of the altar, like victims recently slaughtered. For martyrdom is a certain species of sacrifice; whence that assertion of the apostle to Timothy, when his own martyrdom was near approaching: "I am now about to be offered, and the time of my departure is at hand." 2 Tim. c. iv. 6. To which also applies that expression of the same apostle to the Philippians: "If I am offered for the sacrifice and service of your faith," &c.

Further, as they are said to have cried with a loud voice to God, requiring vengeance for their blood, this is a periphrasis for a cruelty so extreme, and ripe for judgment, that it might for its barbarity solicit even the long suffering of God to vengeance. "How long," say they, "Ω Lord Holy and true, dost Thou not judge and avenge our blood on those who dwell on the earth?" In the mean time, white garments were given to each of them, that is, they were adopted into the order of the blessed. The parable is taken from the custom of the Jews, in approving and admitting priests. Those whom they had judged worthy, from their genealogy and perfect form of body, they received into the hall of priests, "clothed in white garments," and so adopted them into the sacerdotal order. Maimonides in Mishne, β. viii. c. vi. s. 11. Which is plainly expressed in c. vii. vv. 13, 14, 15, where it is said of those who are clothed in white garments, "that they are before the throne of God, and worship him (as priests) day and night in his temple."

The answer to this cry of blood is, "That they should rest for a short time, until (the number of) their fellow servants and of their brethren who should be killed, even as they should be complete;" that is, that they should endure for a little, until some of their brethren, who, after Christianity had begun to prevail, were, under Licinius, Julian, and the Arians, to be butchered in like manner, should be added to the number; and then, on the sounding of the trumpets, a remarkable vengeance should be taken on the empire for the guilt of so much blood.

Of the Sixth Seal

The sixth seal begins where the fifth ends; that is, from the year of Christ 311, in which that terrible persecution of ten years ceased.

The event of this seal is a wonderful commotion of heaven and earth, by which that marvellous change of the heathen Roman state, by Constantine the Great and his successors, the standard-bearers of the Lamb is represented; that is to say, all the gods of the Gentiles, shaken from their heaven, their pontiffs and their priests degraded from their offices, unhallowed, cast down, and

Joseph Mede

for ever deprived of their revenues; the temples, fanes, and images of demons throughout the whole Roman world ruined, overthrown, burnt, and demolished. In addition to this, emperors, kings, and rulers, who had undertaken to succour their gods in such extreme perils, to proclaim war against the ensign-bearers of Christ, to combat with immense forces, and even when subdued in battle, to renew the war with their utmost strength, were slain with unusual slaughter, routed, and dispersed; until at length, in complete despair, no one could be found who would bring assistance to the Roman religion falling with such a crash. So that within the compass of a few words, I think I see comprised whatever the Holy Spirit meant to describe by those sublime allegories under this seal. And this is the first completion of that victory of Christ, of which the foundation was laid in the first seal; to which the seals which have preceded it have been subservient, by pointing out in what state of the empire it should come to pass, by the presignified distinctions of the time which passed away in the interval. It now remains that we should apply the assigned interpretation to the several parts of the prophetic allegory, and should show the meaning of it.

"And I looked when he opened the sixth seal, and behold there was a great earthquake, and the sun became black as a sackcloth of hair, and the moon became as blood, and the stars of heaven fell upon the earth, as a fig-tree casteth forth its unripe fruit, when it is shaken by a strong wind, and the heaven departed as a book, when it is rolled up; and every mountain and island were moved out of their places; and the kings of the earth, and the great men, and the rich men, and the chief captains, and the mighty men, and every slave, and every free man, hid themselves in the caves and rocks of the mountains; and they said unto the mountains and rocks, Fall on us, and hide us from the face of Him that sitteth on the throne, and from the wrath of the Lamb! for the great day of his wrath is come, and who can stand before him?'"

These are accustomed images of very horrid slaughters, and (if I may so speak) of an entire subversion of the state of things, used by the prophets, after the manner of the east, as their figures and pictures likewise are by our poets. So Jerem. c. iv. v. 23, &c. paints the fall of Judea, as if every thing was about to return again into ancient chaos. "I beheld the earth," says he, "and behold it was without form and void, and the heavens, and there was no light in them. I looked at the mountains, and lo they were moved, and all the hills were disturbed." In like manner Joel, c. ii. v. 10, says of the horrid devastation of the same land by the army of northern locusts: "At his face the earth trembled; the heavens also were moved, the sun and moon were darkened, and the stars withdrew their splendour." But we must treat distinctly of every part. "Behold," says he, "there was a great earthquake;" in the Greek σεισμὸς, that is, a commotion of heaven and earth, as is manifest from what follows; for the Latin word terræmotus is not equal to the force of the Greek. Now, an earthquake of that kind, according to the testimony of the apostle, Heb. c. xii. upon the passage in Haggai, "Yet once more will I shake the heavens and the earth," denotes the removing of those things which are shaken; which may be confirmed by the same prophet, v. 21 and 22 of the same chapter, where he himself interprets this parable exegetically: "I will shake the heavens and the earth, and I will overthrow the throne of kingdoms, and I will destroy the strength of the kingdoms of the heathen," &c. We therefore shall consider this commotion of earth and heaven, in this place as elsewhere in the Apocalypse, as the ruin of states, and as their entire subversion.

Now, the object of this revolution, as of the former events under the seals, is the Roman empire; but not as politically governed by the Cæsars, (for in this form it was not yet dissolved,) but as subject to Satan and his angels the demons, under the name of religion. This demonarchy of the Roman empire, the tempest which lowers in this seal, will eventually overthrow, and dissipate with a mighty crash.

"And the sun and the moon became black as sackcloth of hair, and the moon became as blood;" that is, by the ellipsis of an adjective, red as blood. This is a periphrasis of the eclipse of the luminaries, in which the sun is wont to appear dark, but the moon ruddy. Similar to which is that of Isaiah respecting the vengeance on Babylon: "The sun shall be obscured in his rising, and the moon shall not cause her light to shine." Sept. "shall not give her light." Isa. c. xiii. 10. Matt. c. xxiv. 29. Nor has that of the same prophet, c. xxiv. any other sense, according to the opinion of Aben Ezra, concerning the slaughter with which the Lord, when about to reign in Jerusalem, (exactly as in this seal,) should visit the host of heaven on high, and the kings of the earth on the earth. "The moon," says he, "shall blush, and the sun shall be ashamed," (that is, each, as if it covered its face for shame, shall be clothed with darkness,) "when the Lord of Hosts shall reign in Mount Sion, and in Jerusalem, and before his ancients gloriously." But what have these things to do, you will say, with the Roman demonarchy? Attend, and I will tell you. In the prophets, (as you will find also by and by in the following visions,) every kingdom and body of empire represents the world; that the parts, likewise, the heavens, and the earth, and stars, may correspond with that image. To prove which, (not to mention any other passages,) that single place in Isaiah is sufficient, c. li. v. 15. "I am the Lord thy God, who divided the sea, (namely, the red sea,) and his waves roared; the Lord of Hosts is his name. And I put my words in thy mouth," (that is, I gave thee my law,) "and I covered thee with the shadow of my hand, that I might plant the heavens, and lay the foundation of the earth;" that is, that I might make thee a kingdom, or political world, "and I might say unto Sion, Thou art my people."

The subject treated of is the emancipation by which God delivered the people of Israel out of Egypt, that he might, of that people, found for himself a kingdom or republic in the promised land. From whence it will not be difficult to collect what is meant in the same prophet, c. lxv. and lxvi. by the new heaven and the new earth, namely, a new world of the same kind.

According to this image, then, heaven, agreeably to the prophetic idea, will denote whatever is eminent in the universality of any kingdom or republic; the earth, on the contrary, what is lowest; the stars, those who obtain and fill a place in that exalted station. By which construction, the sun and moon, being the principal lights of heaven, the former will indicate the first and chief majesty and dignity of the kingdom, the latter next in order to it; which indeed is so true, that the Chaldee paraphrast on the prophets substitutes afterwards, for the sun and moon, the kingdom and glory; as Isaiah, c. lx. v. 20. Jerem. c. xv. v. 9.

Let the sun, then, in the Roman kingdom of idols, in right of supremacy, be the dragon himself, or Satan, especially since from him the Holy Spirit, c. xii. denominates the whole Roman empire in the state in which he was treating of it--the seven-headed red dragon, as we shall there see.

The moon, the second luminary of this heaven, you may call the supreme pontificate, annexed to the imperatorial majesty, even from its first origin, and, as it were, a part of it; or, if you will, the emperor, as the pontifex of Satan, with the whole pontifical college, who, with the emperor as their head, formed one body, and they presided over the religious rites of the gods, and over the whole of the republic, and were not liable to render an account to the authority of the senate, or of any one as superior to themselves, and therefore in this kingdom were not undeservedly to be considered as second to the dragon himself. It is not always necessary, I confess, that so accurate an explanation of every thing in allegories of this kind should be required; but when it can be done, let us apply every minute particular. The sun then of which we have been speaking became dark at that time, and suffered an eclipse, and obscuration of his baneful majesty, when the Roman emperors, having abjured him by baptism, with all his angels, pomps, and worship, dedicated themselves to Christ, the sun of righteousness. The sun being thus darkened and deprived of light, how could the moon, which borrows her light from the sun, be secure? And that very thing, or the office of pontifex maximus, Constantine, Constantius, Valentinian, Valens, immediately rejected, as it was fit they should, unwilling from thenceforward to work for the devil. The name, however, at which you may be surprised, they did not on that account despise, but retained for a short time inscribed among their titles. Gratian first refused the title, as well as the pontifical garments, when offered to him, according to custom, by the pontiffs, as unworthy a Christian man; (a good act, which deserves to be recorded.) And this indeed was a change of such importance, that the Holy Spirit will thenceforth consider the Roman Cæsar, thus divested of the pontificate, as a new head of the Roman beast and king, as we shall hear in c. xvii. But still this moon shone with some light, though melancholy and weak, till Theodosius the First, that destroyer of heathenism, took away at length the pontifical college itself, with the whole remaining crowd of priests, all their revenues being confiscated, by one edict, to the treasury. Now then was the time when Satan must seek another pontifex maximus for himself. But I proceed to the remaining circumstances.

"And the stars of heaven fell on the earth, as a fig-tree casts her unripe figs when shaken by a great wind, and the heaven departed as a book when it is rolled up." Or, "the heaven vanished away," &c. That is, the stars of heaven disappeared, as letters vanish from a book rolled up in the manner of the ancients. For there is an ellipsis of the former substantive, on both sides common to the Hebrew language, as Deut. c. xx. v. 19; 2 Kings, c. xviii. v. 31; and elsewhere frequently to be found; so that this passage of the disappearance of the heaven, and that of the fall of the stars, mutually explain each other, and ought not to be separated from one another, as erroneously pointed, but ought to be included within the same comma. Indeed, the whole passage being from the thirty-fourth chapter of Isaiah, v. 4, where, evidently under the same image, though in an inverse order, the Holy Spirit paints the slaughter and ruin of the kingdom of Edom,--like this,--a kingdom of idols.

"The heavens," (says he,) "shall be rolled up like a book, and the whole host of them, (that is, the stars,) shall fall as a leaf from the vine, and as a deciduous fruitling from the fig-tree;" which sentence the Apocalyptical Spirit wished to render still clearer by the double addition of the words, ἀπεχωρίσθη, "it departed," and ὑπὸ μεγάλου ἀνέμου σειομένη, "shaken by a great wind." Moreover, Obadiah, Jeremiah, c. xlix. from v. 7 to 22; Ezekiel, c. xxxv. through the whole chapter, and c. xxv. v. 12, treat of the same Edomitish ruin, with circumstances not more mild than Isaiah, which I notice on this account, lest any one should think that the description of Isaiah is suited only to the great day of universal judgment.

But now, to return to the Apocalypse. The stars were the Roman heaven of deities, both the gods themselves, the chiefs of that kingdom, under Satan their prince, and the nobles, the priests, though of inferior rank; for even the stars differ from other stars in order and sublimity. These, therefore, are those who, in this wonderful commotion of the Roman state, shaken from their seats, "fell on the earth as a fig-tree scatters her unripe fruit, when it is shaken by a high wind."

Nor will this interpretation of the stars as of gods and priests of the gods, excite so much surprise in him who remembers that the gods of the heathen are every where spoken of in sacred Scripture as the host of heaven, and by Daniel, that the priests and elders of the glorious land, or of the people of Israel, whom Antiochus Epiphanes had cast to the earth, are called by that name. "He magnified himself (says he,) against the host of heaven, and cast down to the earth some of the host and of the stars, and trampled upon them." What he impiously did against the people of the true God, the very same the Christian emperors did against the people of the dragon; with this difference, however, that in the former case there was only one chief of the host of heaven, the Lord Jehovah, who made heaven and earth, against whom, though Antiochus might magnify himself, he could not disturb him in heaven; but in the latter case, there were many chiefs or demons in the Roman heaven, whom all the emperors who bore the standard of Christ, did utterly overthrow. Add to this, that the above exposition may be confirmed by the Synchronism of the Dragon cast down with his attendants from heaven. Chap. xii. "The dragon fought and his angels, but they prevailed not, neither was there place found any longer in heaven. And the great dragon was cast out; that old Serpent called the Devil and Satan."--"And his angels (that is, demons worshipped under the name of gods,) were cast out with him." It follows,--"And every mountain and island were moved out of their places." Mountains and islands might perhaps be taken for persons of higher or lower conditions of life, who are enumerated in the very next verse, unless the word Island should be thought less favourable to such an interpretation. It might, therefore, seem more probable,--if, indeed, it has a reference to this subject,--that both point out men of higher condition which are eminent in each; the mountains on the earth, the islands in the sea. But what if we understand by islands here, not lands rising in the midst of waters, but edifices, of whatever kind they are called, which, surrounded by a public or private enclosure, are not used in common with neighbouring buildings? May we not then take both mountains and islands for the temples and shrines of idols, overthrown by this whirlwind, throughout the Roman world? For any one may see how conformable the notion of mountains is to an interpretation of this sort, who is not ignorant that it was customary for idolaters to build altars and shrines to their gods in the more lofty places. Whence, in every part of the Old Testament, the name of high-places is very frequent; nay, in Jeremiah, c. iii. v. 23, the names of hills and mountains for the temples of idols. "Surely, (says he,) the hills and multitude of the mountains were vain." Now islands for temples are not inconsistent with a similar interpretation, since it is very appropriate to temples to resemble islands, and they are not polluted by communion, or even a contact with the walls of other edifices. Supposing, however, it should not be satisfactory, that one and the same thing should be represented under two names, consider the mountains, if you will, as applicable to sacred places in the country and in the fields, and islands as temples of idols in the cities. But in such things as these, minutiæ of any sort do not seem to be required; so that, perhaps, in every instance, the small points of allegorical prophecies are not to be so anxiously suited to the event. It is sufficient if the sum and substance of the matter agree on both sides.

The demolition of shrines and temples was effected under the authority of the same most pious Theodosius, the standard-bearer of the Lamb. For Constantine the Great only shut up the temples of the gods; he did not destroy them, except at Constantinople and the adjoining places. Julian opened them again. But this emperor ordered them to be utterly demolished. The history is well known to every one, nor is there any necessity that I should add to what has been already related by the ecclesiastic writers on this subject. Perhaps, however, it will not be unacceptable to hear Zosimus, a Pagan historian, complaining of, or indignant at, this severe fate of his gods. "The sacristies of the gods, (says he,) were overthrown through all cities and countries, and therefore danger threatened the heads of those who thought them gods, or who looked up to heaven at all, and adored what they saw there." In truth, as the Lord, when he was about to conduct ancient Israel out of Egyptian bondage, is said to have exercised judgment on all the gods of the Egyptians, Exod. c. xii. v. 12, Numb. c. xxxiii. v. 4, so here, when he was about to deliver the Christian people from Roman tyranny, he exercised judgment on the gods of the Romans. But you will inquire when there was such a disturbance, and heaven and earth were blended, had those gods no Atlases who applied their shoulders to support the falling heavens, and oppose the standard-bearers of Christ thus overthrowing all things? Yes, they had; but they experienced a similar fate with their demons. "The kings of the earth," says the Scripture, "and the great men, and the rich men, and the chief captains, and the mighty men, and every bond and every free man," that is, the emperors, Maximinian, Galerius, Maxentius, Maximin, with Martinian Cæsar, Licinius, Julian, (add also, if you please, the tyrants Eugenius and Arbogastes,) with all their companions in infidelity, of whatever order and degree, who endeavoured with force of arms to defend the religion of their forefathers, to support the cause of the gods, then falling into ruin, and to restore it when already fallen and desperate, were reduced at length to such straits, that "they hid themselves in caves and rocks of the mountains, and said to the mountains and to the rocks, Fall on us, and hide us from the face of Him who sitteth on the throne, and from the wrath of the Lamb; for the great day of his wrath is come, and who will be able to stand?"

This is a degrading image of persons flying and hiding themselves, and of those who are weary of life, from the desperate state of their affairs; to which you have a similar description in Luke, c. xxiii. v. 30. of the slaughter of Jerusalem; also in Hosea, c. x. v. 8. of the destruction of Samaria and her idols; but the whole is contained in Isaiah, c. xi. v. 18.

Here, let the reader observe in the first place, that the key to unlock the whole vision, is contained in those words; for the matter treated of here, is of some splendid victory of the Lamb, by which he subdued and overthrew his enemies with a universal slaughter. Moreover, since they, whose destruction is described, fly from the Lamb as an enemy, and wish to hide themselves from his wrath, it may from hence clearly appear, that the slaughter, although it be pointed out by no synchronism, can by no means be applied to Christian kings, but to those who were estranged from Christ; and, therefore, ought not to be explained of slaughters by the Goths, and other barbarous nations upon the empire, after it had become Christian. But lastly, what the kings, nobles, and chief captains, and the rest of the Gentiles in the same situation with themselves, say in addition, that the great day of the wrath of the Lamb is come, and no one would be able to stand, are the words of men acknowledging the power of Christ, whom up to that time they had despised, in comparison with their gods; and believing in truth, that every attempt to resist the Christians would be fruitless. And this, in fact, they all thought; but Galerius, Maximin, and Licinius, even by open confession, however unwillingly, attribute the glory to God.

For Eusebius, with others, is our authority, that Galerius (with whom Christ begun in this judgment), being seized with a most filthy and horrible disease, in which his body, in consequence of worms spreading over it, putrified with an intolerable stench, was struck at last with a consciousness of the crimes which he had committed against the Church, and having confessed his guilt to God, abstained from persecution of the Christians, and by laws, and imperial edicts, hastened the building of their churches, and commanded the accustomed prayers to be offered up for him; and a short time after poured forth a soul guilty of such cruelty towards the Christians as had never been equalled. [13]

Maximin, a most inhuman enemy of the Christians, relying on magic, on the divinations of idols, and the oracles of demons, in all which he trusted; nevertheless, being conquered by Licinius more than once, while he was yet defending the Christian faith with Constantine, his colleague, having cast away the ensigns of empire, fled and lurked for some time in the fields and villages in the habit of a slave; and at length, being shut up in Tarsus of Cilicia, and inflamed with fury, he butchered many priests and prophets of the gods, by whose oracles he had been excited to undertake the war, as fortune-tellers, impostors, and at length, betrayers of his safety; and then, giving glory to the God of the Christians, he is said to have promulgated a decree for their deliverance; but suddenly stricken by God, requiring punishment for so many crimes against the Christians, with a dreadful and mortal disease, and his whole flesh being by degrees eaten away, and consumed, and at length (as a just retribution for the punishment which he had meditated against the Christians), his eyes having started out, in consequence of the heat with which he was totally burnt up, he made his confession to the Lord, and breathed out his soul, acknowledging that he deserved to suffer those things on account of his madness and temerity against Christ [14].

Lastly, Licinius, the deserter of the Christians, whose party he had for some time espoused, with Constantine, and boasting proudly to his soldiers of the multitude of his gods in opposition to that one only God of Constantine, and him a novel and a foreign God (for so he called him), having been conquered in two great battles (in one of which, out of an army of 130,000 men, scarce 30,000 escaped), and being still unwilling to remain at rest, was at length condemned by Constantine, with his followers, by the laws of war, and given up to deserved punishment. But when they who were the authors of the war undertaken against God, were brought together with the tyrant to the place of punishment, as on the former occasion, they had insolently exulted in a hope placed in vain gods, so now they were brought to confess that they understood, in truth, how great and wonderful the God of Constantine was, and to acknowledge Him as the true and only God [15].

APPENDIX

From the ancient monuments of the Egyptians, Persians, and Indians, from the authors Tarphanes, interpreter of Pharaoh; Baramus of Saganessa, king of the Persians (a contemporary of Diocletian); Syrbachamus, interpreter of the king of the Indians; Apomasar, or, according to others, Achmet, F. Scirim, an Arab, collected Ὀνειροκριτικὰ, or interpretations of dreams, as that people were very much devoted, from the earliest antiquity, to pursuits of this nature, as well as of other kinds, so were they, while their empire flourished, eager to translate the writings of all nations into Arabic. This little book, which was formerly in Greek, by what author is uncertain, John Leunclavius published in the last century, translated into Latin by himself, out of the library of Joseph Sambucus. The same afterwards, in the year 1603, Nicolas Rigaltius communicated from the library of the most Christian king, in his Oneirocritics, having supplied what was wanting in the copy of Sambucus. In this book you may see that many prophetic images, which create so much difficulty to our countrymen, were familiar to the Oriental nations, and were certainly not unusual in their divinations. Of the authors from whom the collection is made, the most ancient of all appear to be Tarphan, the Egyptian, as one who not only calls himself the interpreter of Pharaoh, but every where in his interpretations, uses the name of Pharaoh for a king.

It would therefore appear, that he lived at a time when Egypt had still kings of its own, and while the same were called Pharaoh. The Persian, with his king Saganissa, was, as I have said, of the same age as Diocletian. The Indian is of a later age, as lie every where proclaims himself a Christian.

But there is a wonderful agreement of both with the Egyptian.

Since, then, we are not unwilling to learn the meaning of words and phrases in the sacred writings from those nations which were formerly the nearest to the Hebrew people, and most connected with them in manners, and the use of language, why should we undervalue the same advantages here, in the signification of figures and prophetic images? (for, according to the Hebrew masters, the determination of prophecy is that of dreams.)

Let no one, then, impute it to me as a fault, if I annex out of this author those passages which appear to me to make the figures of the seal just explained, more intelligible.

The same, likewise, I shall do hereafter, with the reader's good leave, as occasion may offer, on the trumpets, and the other visions.

Circumstances, which throw light on the First Seal, and partly also on those which follow

Chap. ccxxxiii. Of the opinions of the Indians, Persians, and Egyptians.

A noble spirited horse, which is called Pharas, refers to eminence and dignity, in the interpretation of dreams. Common horses are understood of nobility, and of some inferior rank.

If any one in his dreams has seemed to be carried on a fleet and wanton horse, he shall find in the presence of the people, fame, and the greatest estimation, as well as eminence and honour.

Also, if any one seemed to be riding armed on a noble horse, he will find power, together with good reputation, on account of his arms.

Chap. ccxlix. According to the Interpretations of the Persians and Egyptians.

If any one seemed to have held bows and arrows in his hand, he shall exult with joy over his enemies.

There are more passages relating to the same subject, as chap. clii. from the doctrine of the Indians, concerning the large and long tail of a horse, signifying companions and followers of his power; of the short cut tail, signifying the loss of liberty, as well as sovereignty, if it were a prince who dreamt of riding on such a horse. In the same manner, chap. ccxxxiii. the dismounting from a horse, if voluntary, is explained of a spontaneous decrease of power; if unwillingly, of a successor in dignity, assuming his place.

A Key to the Apocalypse
The following things throw light on the Third Seal

Chap. xv. Of the Doctrine of the Indians.

If any one in his dreams has seen a balance, or a bell, as they call it, a species of balance, justly weighing in a certain place, let him understand it, of the person of a judge. But if he has a quarrel, and the things appeared to be equally balanced, he shall obtain his cause.

If he should seem to observe an equal and a pure balance, let him know, that the judge of that place is just. But if he should see the scales broken, and turned upside down, he may conclude, that the judge of the place where he saw the dream, is unjust.

Besides, weights also have the same interpretation as measures, according to their quantities, but they are applied to the persons of inferior judges.

These relate to the Sixth Seal

Chap. clxvii. From the Writings of the Indians, Persians, and Egyptians.

The sun relates, in interpretation, to the person of the king, and the moon to the person of the prince, who is second to the king: Venus to the person of the empress, or Augusta, and also the other largest stars to the greatest persons about the king. While I am collecting these things, I am almost induced to think, that the famous title of Sapor, king of the Persians, in his letters delivered to the emperor Constantius, (Sapor, king of kings, partner of the stars, brother of the sun and moon, to Constantius Cesar, my brother, greeting,) which Ammianus Marcellinus attributes to Persian pride, was no other than the vernacular style of the nation, arising from images of this kind; which ought to appear less wonderful to any one, since we see even our own heralds, in publishing the arms of emperors and kings, apply to them the names of the sun and moon, and of the other planets. Hither, likewise, may be referred Jacob's interpretation of the dream of Joseph, his son, of the sun and moon, and eleven stars, making obeisance to him, which he immediately, as by no means ignorant of the parables of the east, applies to his own family, interpreting the sun and moon of himself and his wife, as king and queen; the stars, of his sons, as the nobles of the family, Gen. c. xxxvii. v. 10. But let us return to our Achmet, for be proceeds in the same chapter.

If any one has thought he saw the sun in the heaven deprived of light and rays, calamity and disgrace appertain to the person of the king.

If the sun has appeared to be in eclipse, that portends affliction and war to the king.

If any one has thought he saw the sun covered with a cloud, the king will fall into distress and diseases, by way of occultation.

If any one has seen the sun, and moon, and stars, collected together without light; if he is of the number of grandees, he absolutely approaches to ruin, on account of that darkness; if he is king surrounded by all, he shall be sought out in battle, and shall fall into great affliction.

Chap. clxviii. Of the Observations of the Persians and Egyptians.

If any one has imagined he saw the stars possessed of very little light, cast down, scattered and obscured, this vision is to be referred to the calamity of the nobles, opulent men, and to the presidents of the king.

The sixth seal being finished, we should proceed forthwith in order to the seventh, (big as it is with its sevenfold plague,) as what coheres with the sixth in an immediate connexion. But the Holy Spirit, by a sure suggestion, has led to the delay of our progress for a little while, until it has placed before our eyes the state of an assembly contemporizing with it, which was to be safe under its plagues, and was also to survive them.

Let us then hold the torch of interpretation, in the first place, to that vision, as far as we are able, and then we will continue the order of the seals which we have begun.

Footnotes:

4. Before the Oracle. English translation.
5. A bright bay.
6. This is the meaning of χοῖνιξ.
7. Dun.
8. Here I must hesitate in agreeing with our learned author. After declaring, as he had just before done, that the seals related to the events connected with the Roman empire, he surely departs from his interpretation when he represents the object of the first seal as descriptive of Christ. Does not this destroy the consistency of the explanation? May it not refer to Vespasian or Titus? the former of whom was proclaimed emperor of Judea, and under whose auspices, Jerusalem was taken and destroyed, and the Jewish nation subdued. Tacitus, in recounting the general persuasion that

had gone forth that the East should prevail, considers the prediction verified in Vespasian and Titus. The first illustrious rider was doubtless the conqueror of the Jews.--R. B. C. This was the opinion of our author at a later period, (V. p. 918.) and it has been the general exposition of subsequent commentators.

9. Query.

10. Choenix, the measure by which masters measured their servants' victuals for a day.

11. Query, if this care were not intended by Providence for the supply of the Christians?--R. B. C.

12. The author means, I believe, that if a third of the earth is the Roman world, a fourth of the earth would be less than its full extent; i. e. supposing the earth to be 12, a third would be 4, and a fourth 3, that is, less than 4.

13. Eus. de victâ Constantini, Lib. 1. c. xxx.

14. Item de vitâ Const., Lib. I. c. li. liii.

15. De vitâ Const., Lib. II. c. iv. v. 18.

THE VISION

Of the Company of the Servants of God, or of the elect and faithful Church to be preserved under the ruins of the Seventh Seal, or of the Trumpets, exhibited under the type of the one hundred and forty-four thousand sealed out of all the tribes of Israel, at the beginning of the Seventh Seal.

The vision of those who are sealed is introduced twice: First, in this place, in the beginning of the trumpets, in the first prophecy; again, as the contrast to the beast, when possessed of power, in the second prophecy, c. xiv.; and that with a double view;--here, for the purpose of preserving them under the ruins resulting from the trumpets; there, for the purpose of extolling them on account of their faith maintained to God and the Lamb, when the other inhabitants of the world, deserters and revolters, had received the mark of the beast. From which it clearly appears, that the prophecy of the beast contemporizes with the events of the trumpets; but to what extent, is to be decided by some other means, namely, not beyond the end of the sixth trumpet, in which the months of the beast conclude with the days of the mourning witnesses. c. xi. v. 14. It is our present design to hold the torch of interpretation to the first vision of the sealed ones, which regards their preservation. Hereafter, when we arrive so far, we shall treat of their commendation.

"After these things," says he, (that is, when the vision of the sixth seal is ended, and the seventh, which is that of the trumpets, is about to begin,) "I saw four angels standing upon the four corners of the earth, restraining the four winds of the earth, that they might not blow on the earth, nor on the sea, nor on any tree."

The sense is, He saw angels who presided over the winds, that is, over the storms of war and calamities, which, from whatever part of the world they were about to issue forth, were to be restrained as long as it pleased God; but at his nod, whenever he gave the signal, were to be let loose on the whole world. Not indeed the same with the angels of the trumpets, but those who were at their sounding, to let loose those winds, now from one and now from another part of the world, to ravage and destroy the Roman state. For the parable of the winds in the prophets implies warlike movements, and hostile attacks and invasions; as Jer. c. xlix. v. 36. "I will bring upon Elam the four winds from the four quarters of heaven, and I will scatter them towards all those winds; and there shall not be a nation to which the outcasts of Elam shall not come." Also, c. li. v. 1, 2. "Behold I, saith the Lord, will raise up upon Babel, &c. a destroying wind; and I will send out upon Babel winnowers, and they shall winnow her, and shall make empty her land." And likewise, c. xviii. v. 17. "As an eastern wind will I scatter them, (that is, the Jews,) before the enemy," namely, the king of Babylon. Hither likewise, it seems, may that passage of Daniel be referred, c. vii. 2, 3. "Behold the four winds of heaven strove on the great sea, and four great beasts ascended out of the sea;" that is, from the conflict of nations on every side, rushing among each other with war and the sword, and contending for dominion and empire, four great kingdoms arose.

"And I saw," says he, "another angel ascending from the rising sun, having the seal of the living God, (perhaps therefore Christ the Lord,) and he cried with a loud voice to the four angels, to whom it was given to hurt the earth and the sea, (namely, by letting loose the winds which they had restrained,) saying, Hurt not the earth, nor the sea, nor the trees, till I have sealed the servants of our God in their foreheads;'" that is, do not let loose the winds, nor give them the power of going forth, and raging over the world. He names the earth, sea, and trees, agreeably to the image of winds, as those objects to which the winds are wont to do damage; to the earth, by the ruin of buildings; to the sea, by shipwrecks; to trees, by manifold injury and laceration.

"Hold!" says he, "till we have sealed the servants of our God in their foreheads;" that is, until we have distinguished them by a mark impressed, as the elect assembly of God, on which those destroying winds, which were to consign to ruin the remaining society of men, should have no power; but over which, marked with his seal, Divine Providence would continually watch, lest in this ruin of the Roman state, which the trumpets would effect, this holy progeny should be extinguished. For the event was to be ordered, that they should not go without punishment who injured them, as having transgressed the limits of the right granted them by God; and farther, that the injury, if any should befall them, should be immediately recompensed by God. There is an allusion to the passage in Ezekiel, c. ix. where those who are sighing and exclaiming for the abominations of Jerusalem, are sealed by an angel for this purpose, that they might not sustain equal destruction with the impious and reprobate, from those who were to smite them. And, in truth, the event which relates to this declaration, (if any one will consider the state of the times of which we are speaking) will appear like a miracle;--that it could have been possible, when the Roman empire was desolated and destroyed, by so great a havock of cities and their inhabitants, so that its ancient population being nearly extinct, it was inhabited by a barbarous people, and by nations who were aliens to Christ; yet that the Church, in the very same place, in the midst of these evils, and while, as it were, the world was falling into ruin over its head, should still endure; nay, even that the beast in the same time, (as we shall hear in its place,) while idolatrous worship was defiling the whole of Christianity, should nevertheless nourish in its bosom an undefiled assembly such as this, and that in the name of a reverence for God. Of such importance was it to have been protected by the seal of God.

"And I heard," says he, "the number of those which were sealed--a hundred and forty-and-four thousand were sealed of all the tribes of Israel;" that is, twelve times twelve thousand, being twelve thousand of each of the tribes.

For as in the beginning, we saw the theatre of the visions, or the Apocalyptical Assembly, described according to the image and state of the ancient synagogue, and great part of this book of types has a reference to the same; so that, as false Christians in the epistles to the churches may on that account be spoken of as false Jews, so likewise here, the universal church of the Gentiles, secured by the seal of God, is figured under the type of Israel, the twelve apostles of the former aptly corresponding with the same number of the patriarchs in the latter.

Nor is it thus done undeservedly; as for other causes, so chiefly because the church, which, from the time of the rejection of the Jews, was collected out of the nations, succeeded in the place of Israel, and became (if I may so speak) the substitute of Israel, and was to be accounted in that state by God, until his ancient people, having at length obtained mercy, "the fulness of the Gentiles should have come in;" that is, the "innumerable multitude out of all nations, tribes, peoples, and tongues," which at last, when the signature of this Israel was finished, John testifies that he saw singing praises to God and to the Lamb. This indeed is that doctrine (I speak of substitution), which the Apostle Paul means to teach in Romans, c. xi. when he inculcates that the fall of the Jews should bring salvation to the Gentiles, and their rejection should be the reconciliation of the world. Not that by other means the Gentiles were not called in their own time, since the whole chorus of the prophets exclaims that the Gentiles should be gathered together to the glory of Israel, and should be converted to the Lord, (which the Jews themselves, either in ancient times or at the present day, did or do distrust,) but that, not by this calling, which was made by anticipation or surrogation, and as an incitement to emulation, if the Jews had not renounced Christ. An intelligent person will understand what I mean. "It was necessary," says the apostle, Acts c. xiii. "that the Word of God should first have been spoken to you; but since ye put it from you, and consider yourselves unworthy of eternal life, lo! we turn to the Gentiles."

That testimony of Amos, quoted by James in the Council of the Apostles, Acts, c. xv. (not to notice this likewise), seems to have been intended of the anticipated conversion of the Gentiles, i. e. of that which would precede the restoration of the Jews; and on that account, was then, perhaps, preferred to the other prophecies, which might have been otherwise understood of the adoption of the Gentiles among the people of God. For he intimates, not only that the name of the Lord should be called on the nations, (i. e. that the Gentiles should become his people,) but also, that this should take place partly at a time when the tabernacle of David should yet lie in ruins; that is, that the kingdom of Israel should not yet be restored by Christ. "After this," says he, "I will return, and will build again the tabernacle of David, which is fallen down, and I will build again the ruins thereof, and I will set it up, that the residue of men might seek after the Lord, and all the nations upon whom my name is called;" that is, that the rest of mankind, together with those nations upon whom, even before that period, my name would be called, should at length seek after and worship the true God. For instead of what is now read in the Hebrew text, "that they should inherit the remainder of Idumea," it seems to have been formerly written, that "the residue of men should seek after the Lord." Nay, from the Hebrew reading which now obtains, the same inference may he collected of the anticipated adoption of the Gentiles into the people of God, namely, in this sense,--that the Jews being brought back, when the tabernacle of David, which had fallen down, should at last be restored, the remains of Edom as well as the Gentiles, upon whom the name of God was long previously called, should be admitted by hereditary right. Therefore, some of the Gentiles would become the people of God before the restoration of the tabernacle of David. But of this enough.

With respect to the number of the sealed, the number twelve is a mark of the apostolical family, which denotes the apostolical progeny, by multiplying thousands of each tribe as well as all together; a progeny, we may suppose, though increased to many thousands, yet by no means degenerate, but representing their parents in faith and sanctity. For, doubtless, as "to have the number of the beast" (of which we shall hereafter hear), signifies being of the people or followers of the beast,--so, to bear the number of the apostles, signifies being the legitimate offspring of the apostles. The analogy of the New Jerusalem shows this to be the truest interpretation of the multiplication by twelve, in the structure of which, and in the dimensions of its gates, of the area of its foundation, of the circuit, length, breadth, and height of its walls, the same number twelve, or the multiplication by twelve is adopted. And that we might have no farther hesitation to what that twelve-fold multiplication refers, lo! it is expressly said, of the twelve foundations of the wall, that they were inscribed with the names of the twelve apostles of the Lamb. c. xxi. v. 14. "Of the tribe of Judah, of the tribes of Reuben, Gad, Aser, Naphtali, Manasses, Simeon, Levi, Issachar, Zabulon, Joseph, and Benjamin, of each of these tribes were sealed twelve thousand." The tribes are in no other part of Scripture enumerated in this order, although in other places they are reckoned in various modes. For besides that Dan does not appear with them at all, nor is the name of Ephraim spoken of in the rest, there is a departure here from the rule of all the enumerations which are made elsewhere, and neither the order of nativity, nor dignity of family is preserved; but the last are blended with the intermediate, and the younger sons of servants are preferred more than once to the elder children of wives, so that it can by no means be doubted but that some remarkable mystery of a typical kind lies concealed under such a novel and unusual order. This, with God's favour on our undertaking, we think that we have discovered, and it is in this manner:--

First, Dan is rejected from this type, and Ephraim is passed over, in silence, as the standard bearers and leaders of the Israelitish apostasy (Jud. c. xvii. and xviii.), and the same as were the patrons of the public idols in Dan and Bethel, in the time of the kingdom. They were therefore, altogether unfit to represent the followers of a purer religion.

But that, nevertheless, the number of twelve might be complete, Levi is substituted in the room of Dan, and the name of Joseph with the omission of that of Ephraim. The number being thus constituted, the sons of wives and servants, independent of the accustomed dignity of the family, are intermingled, and the children of servants are adopted as those of their mistresses. "For in Christ there is neither bond nor free," but all are of equal estimation. Since, then, the sons of Leah, both natural and adoptive, are double the number of Rachel, for there are eight of the former, and only four of the latter, therefore such an order is observed in reckoning them, that the four sons of Leah might be compared in a double mode, alternately with the two of Rachel: But on both sides, those tribes are preferred as more excellent than the rest, which some transaction, either of their own, or of their offspring, related in the Holy Scriptures, respecting the true worship of God, and zeal towards Him, had rendered worthy of commendation.

The family of Leah are at the head of the first troop in virtue of the prerogative of Christ, the Prince of the company, as sprung from that stock. In the following manner:

First Quaternion of the Sons of Leah. { 1. Judah Second Quaternion of the Sons of Leah. { 7. Simeon 2. Reuben 8. Levi 3. Gad 9. Issachar 4. Aser 10. Zabulon First Couple of the Sons of Rachel. { 5. Naphtali Second Couple of the Sons of Rachel. { 11. Joseph 6. Manasseh 12. Benjamin

The Reason of the Order of the Sons of Leah

Judah, Reuben, Gad, Aser, constitute, as you see, the first quaternion of the sons of Leah, as superior to the rest in respect to Him of whom the type points out the nobility.

Among those, the first place, as justly due, is bestowed on Judah, on account of Christ, the King of the faithful, descended from that tribe. The second on Reuben, whom that illustrious protestation concerning building the altar of remembrance on the banks of Jordan, ennobled, and which he deserved, that he might not yield the prerogative of his nativity (for he was the first-born) to any other than to the royal tribe of Judah. The third place is allotted to Gad, as the associate of Reuben in that celebrated protestation of retaining the true worship of God, and illustrious besides for Elias the prophet, and him the king, the destroyer of Baalism.

Aser, in fine, assumes the fourth and last place in this quaternion, illustrious for the widow of Sarepta, who reverenced Elijah, (Sarepta lying in the lot of Aser,) and noted also for Anna the prophetess, of the tribe of Aser, who bore testimony to Christ, when she was remaining in the temple according to the law, but by no means to be compared with the three preceding, because each was a female.

Simeon, Levi, Issachar, and Zabulon are deferred to the last quaternion, either because they were embellished with no names, or with fewer than the former; or if they had any, by such as were obliterated afterwards by some kind of wickedness. For Levi blotted out the remembrance of the zeal by which he approved himself in the wilderness, (to pass over the sedition of Korah,) by his fellowship with Israelitish apostates and idolaters, even from the beginning. For Jonathan the Levite, the grandson of Moses, gave up his services in introducing the worship of images to Micah the Ephraimite and the Danish robbers. Judg. c. xvii. v. 10, and c. xviii. v. 30. It is possible also, that the substitution of Levi in the place of Dan might have degraded him into the fourth quaternion. Moreover, since the brethren of this quaternion have no quality in which some excel others, they preserve the order of their nativity unaltered, and every one is enumerated in that order in which he was born.

The Reason of the Order of the Sons of Rachel

Observe that among the posterity of Rachel, two of them paired together, Naphtali and Manasseh, head the family: Joseph and Benjamin bring up the rear. Naphtali and Manasseh are preferred, because he was illustrious, as well in Barak, the conqueror of Sisera the Canaanite, as in Hiram, a Naphtalite on his father's side, the artificer of the instruments and furniture of the temple of God; (1 Kings, c. vii. v. 14. 2 Chron. c. ii. v. 14.) and in a name yet greater, of whom hereafter; the latter was noted for Gideon, the subverter of Baal, and Elisha the prophet.

But the glory of Christ's inhabitation exalts Naphtali, though the son of a maid-servant, above Manasseh, as when Christ was about to enter on his office, he fixed his residence and seat of his preaching in the noblest city of the tribe of Naphtali, and the metropolis of all Galilee, Capernaum, whence, as from an episcopal city, he went forth many times over all Galilee with his apostles, into all the synagogues and villages, teaching the gospel of the kingdom, and shining forth with miracles of healing. For, Reader, I wish to remark, from the Evangelical History, (because it escapes many,) that our Saviour dwelt in Galilee during the whole time that he abode on earth; but that he was seen in Judea, the principal seat both of the nation and of his own tribe, only at the time of the festivals. And this is what Isaiah of old had predicted, Isa. c. ix. Matt. c. iv. v. 14.; that "the wonderful Counsellor, the mighty God, the everlasting Father, (Sept. the Father of the age to come,) the Prince of Peace,"--in one word, the Messiah, should be a Galilean; and, as if in compensation and consolation of the captivity, which Galilee, first of all the regions in the Holy Land, had then recently undergone from the Assyrian, (2 Kings, c. xv. v. 29.) that the tract in question should be peculiarly enlightened by his presence; apparently, indeed, that public way, called "the Way of the Sea," which, coming out of Syria to Jordan, passes through the middle of Capernaum, and from thence, proceeding near the Sea of Galilee, leads into Egypt. Let us hear what he says, (vide Hebrew.) "As in former times he rendered vile the land of Zabulon and the land of Naphtali, (viz. as I have observed by Tiglathpileser,) so at the last he will render it glorious." For "the way of the sea (trodden by the Assyrian) to the passage of Jordan, (where Capernaum was situated,) Galilee of the Gentiles,--the people which walked in darkness, (namely, of afflictions,) have seen a great light; to those who dwelt in the region of the shadow of death, on them has the light shined," &c. Would you know whence and under whose influence Galilee will be so blessed, and within that maritime way where the passage of the Jordan was? he immediately subjoins, "For unto us a Child is born, unto us a Son is given, and the government shall be upon his shoulder, and his name shall be called Wonderful, the Counsellor, the Mighty God, the Father of Eternity, the Prince of Peace."

But those words (with which our transcribers, almost treading in the footsteps of the Jews, who never understood this prophecy, begin the chapter with a great disturbance of the sense,) I annex with Jerome and the Royal Bibles to the last sentence of the preceding chapter; and I render them, "For there is no obscurity in Him who is the cause of their trouble," that is, in the calamitous and afflicted state of things into which the Israelitish republic at that time is reported to have fallen, according to the threatening of the law, and which is as it were submitted to our sight; men were driven to indignation and despair because they saw the enemy by which they were oppressed enjoy perpetual success, and that no misfortune befel him. It is of great importance to the Christian faith, that this oracle concerning the Galilean Messiah should be clearly understood, and the fidelity of Matthew, who alleges it, should be asserted; on which account I. was desirous of throwing some light upon it on this occasion, hoping that the Reader would not consider it as unacceptable. I return to the Apocalypse, and I will add one thing more before I dismiss Naphtali; that, as among the sons of Leah, the first place was allotted to Judah, on account of the generation of Christ, so among those of Rachel Naphtali was noticed on account of his dwelling, that the prerogative of Christ might be supereminent on both sides, in whose name, as that of Lord and Emperor, the assembly (as we shall hear in its proper place) is enrolled.

Joseph and Benjamin remain, transferred to be the last pair of Rachel's children, and of whom the sirname of Ephraim degraded to this place, since it is Ephraim, in truth, who is concealed under the name of Joseph, having been unworthy, on his own account, (because he was the leader of the Israelitish idolatry introduced by Micah, and also because of that enormous apostasy of which Jeroboam and Ahab were the founders,) to have his name repeated in the catalogue. Benjamin likewise, beside being the youngest born, the hatred of Saul the Benjamite, against David, and the curses of Shimei against him who was the head of the family and the type of Christ, deprived of a higher station.

A Key to the Apocalypse

A MEMORABLE SENTENCE

Formed from the signification of the names by which the tribes were called, by which both the order of the tribes sealed, the disposition of the assembly itself, its contest and reward by God are declared.

Judah. . . . confitetur Deo } The blessed Assembly confesses to God by looking to the Son. { Cultus purus et rite Christianus. Pure and truly Christian worship Reuben. . . . .intuendo Filium Gad. . . . cætus Aser. . . . benedictus Naphtalim. . . . luctantur cum } They contend with those who forget their obedience. { Lucta. Contest. Manasseh. . . . obliviscentibus Simeon. . . . obedientiam Levi. . . . Adhæsio (scil. Christo) } Their adherence to Christ adds to them the reward of an eternal habitation with the Son of his right hand. { Præmium. Reward. Isachar. . . . mercedem Zabulon. . . . habituculi (scil. æterni) Joseph. . . . adjicit Benjamin. . . . Filio dextrræ

The blessed assembly, the assembly of those who are sealed, confess or celebrate God, by looking to his Son, that is, to Christ the only Mediator. They contend with those who are forgetful of their obedience, that is, with the antichristians. Adhesion to Christ will add to the Son of His right hand, (that is, to him whom God highly values) the reward of a habitation or eternal mansion. Or otherwise, the Son of His right hand (that is, Christ) will add to those who adhere to God, the reward of a habitation, or mansion of eternal life.

To this more contracted and afflicted state of the Church, under the type of those who are sealed out of the people of Israel, succeeds that most ample, and by far most prosperous state of the same, under the image of an innumerable multitude of palm-bearers, out of every nation, and people, and tribe, and language. "After these I beheld, and lo! a great multitude, which no man could number, out of every nation, and of all tribes, and people, and tongues, standing before the Throne, and before the Lamb, clothed in white robes, and with palms in their hands; and they cried with a loud voice, saying, Salvation to our God that sitteth on the throne, and to the Lamb."

But since this vision pertains to the seventh trumpet, and cannot be conveniently and clearly explained elsewhere, on account of so many things which require to be previously known, we will therefore postpone the exposition of it. At present it may be sufficient that the reader should remember what has been just now generally said, that both the visions in conjunction pervade the whole interval of the seventh seal, or of the trumpets; but separately, that the assembly of the sealed synchronizes with the first six trumpets, and the multitude of the palm-bearers with the seventh.

And thus having completed the interpretation of the interposed vision, or visions, let us resume the discontinued series of the seals.

The Meaning of the Seventh Seal, that is, of the Seven Trumpets.

They were the six first seals, in which the state of the empire, yet standing and flourishing, was described, until the power of idolatry fell by intestine misfortunes. The seventh succeeds, the subject matter of which is seven trumpets, under which the fates of the declining and falling empire, proceeding to ruin by a sevenfold order of plagues, while the trumpets are sounding the alarm, are displayed under images suited to such an event. God, in truth, executing punishment by that destruction for the blood of so many martyrs, shed under Roman auspices. For He, whose will it is that even brute animals should not be spared, if they have slain man, made in His image, would He not require the blood of His servants of the empire which had been a martyricide for so many revolving years?

Neither could the late piety of the Christian emperors, then possessed of the power of the state, avail to intercede with the justice of God, any more than the piety of Josiah, for the kingdom of Judah, guilty of the blood spilt by Manasseh, that it might escape the ruin decreed by God. This revenge, the souls of the martyrs, groaning under that dreadful butchery of the fifth seal, invoked earnestly with their prayers: This God promised, as soon as the Roman tyrant, by the addition of those who still remained to be slaughtered, had filled up the measure of iniquity, c. vi. v. 11]. This time had now arrived.

Wherefore an angel, the priest of heaven, at the altar of incense, offers up those prayers (as was the custom with the prayers of the people made in the temple), by fumigation to the throne of God; and recalls them to His memory.

In the mean time, "there was silence in heaven for the space of half an hour," according to the rites of the temple in performing a sacrifice of this nature. For it is evident, that in sacrifices, in every part of the world, silence was a part of religion. They said, "Attend in silence." That was observed by the people of God, when they offered incense. For, while the sacrifices were offering (which was the first part of their liturgy), the temple resounded with hymns, trumpets, and other musical instruments, 2 Chron. c. xxix. v. 25-28. But at the time of incense every thing was silent, and the people prayed in silence to themselves, Luke, c. i. v. 10. To this, then, there is an allusion, when it is said, that while the angel was about to offer sacrifices at the golden altar, "there was silence in heaven for the space of half an hour;" that is, during the whole time of incense. Which being at length finished, "an angel filled a censer with fire from the altar, and cast it on the earth." And he acted thus to signify by this rite, to what subject those prayers referred, which rising to God, had been imbued with grateful odour; namely, to implore vengeance on the inhabitance of the earth, who had injured the saints, and had even shed their blood.

But the prayers immediately obtained an answer; for "there were," says he, (that is, from the Throne, or inmost recess of the temple,) "voices, and thunderings, and lightnings, and an earthquake." In which words is described the oracle בת לוק--Bath Kol, that is, the daughter of the voice, or of thunder, by which God formerly gave responses to his ancient people, and by the same assented here to the prayers of the saints. Now in the Hebrew language it is to be understood, that voices and thunderings have the same signification. For thunderings are called תולוק, that is, voices. Καί, then, is either to be taken explanatorily, for that is; or as I should prefer by the figure ἓν διὰ δυοῖν, voices and thunderings are voices of thunder, or attended with thunder. God, indeed, for the most part, uttered His decrees with thunder, as he also delivered the law, Ex. c. xix. v. 16. Nay, it was the only oracle which remained to the Jews after the Babylonian captivity; of which there is an example in our evangelist, c. xii. 28. When the Lord had said, "Father, glorify thy name, there came," says he, "a voice from heaven, I have both glorified it and will glorify it again.'" It follows. "And the people which stood by and heard it, said it thundered. Others said, An angel spake to him;" that is, some said it was Divine thunder, or thunder joined with the Divine voice, namely, the daughter of thunder; but others, that an angel spoke. And hence it is that, in the Apocalypse, not only in this place, but elsewhere generally, thunder is connected with Oracles and Divine voices, as c. iv. v. 5, c. vi. v. 1, c. x. v. 3. Vide the sacred Aristarchus of the most illustrious Daniel Heinsius, p. 277 and 455.

The sacrifice being thus ended, and God having assented to the prayers of his saints with the voice of thunder, "the seven angels who had the seven trumpets, prepared themselves to sound." That the works of Divine providence and government are carried on by the administration of angels, is confessed by all theologians. The angels, therefore, preserve their place in those visions, in the transactions to which they are pre-appointed by God, and what is performed by the common agency of angels and men, is said to be performed by the authority of angels, as principals and leaders. So that they appear to me to wander wholly from the mark, who, under the name of angels, imagine that some mystery lies concealed. The angel trumpeters then, who are here mentioned, are those who were appointed to direct the plagues of the trumpets, while men were employed in the performance, by whom it pleased God to execute his decrees. The four first of these trumpets are the cause of the less extensive and minor plagues, inasmuch as they were those during which, while they hung over the greatest part of the Western, or Latin world, the Roman bishop was to be healed, and from that time to become at least the head of that world. For rightly applying the images of which, here likewise let the reader observe, that the Roman community is secretly assimilated by the Holy Spirit with the other empires of the world, to a mundane system, whose parts are the earth, sea, rivers, heaven, and stars; in such a way that the system of every empire may have its earth likewise, which is like the ground itself, a low substance, and the basis on which the mass of the whole political structure rests. Also a sea, which by flowing round its earth, may wear altogether the similitude of a sea; (and this is the amplitude or extent of dominion.) Political rivers likewise, which, in the manner of other rivers, derive their origin from the sea, and return to it again; of which kind are provincial magistrates, and other administrators of government, together with the provinces themselves, the channels of those rivers. The sun lastly, and other stars in the heaven, of supreme power, referring to the sun, moon, and stars, in the mundane system. This analogy being observed, the interpretation, as it is completely fortified by similar figures of the ancient prophets, so it will be easy to be understood, and very apposite in every part to the event recorded.

But what is so often repeated of the third part, as the third part of the trees of the earth, the third part of the sea, of the rivers, of the heaven, I understand of the bounds of the Roman empire, embracing in its circuit the third part of the world, as it was known in the time of John. Which appears capable of being proved from this circumstance, that afterwards, in chap. xii. "the seven-headed ten-horned dragon," (that is, the heathen Roman empire), is said to have drawn "a third part of the stars of heaven with his tail, and cast them to the earth;" that is, to have subjected a third part of the princes and dynasties of the world to his dominion. These things being premised, let us come to the interpretation of particulars.

C. viii. v. 7. "And the first angel sounded, and there came hail and fire mingled with blood, and it was cast upon the earth, and a third part of the trees was burnt up, and every green herb was burnt up."--"And the second angel sounded, and as it were, a great mountain burning with fire, was cast into the sea, and a third part of the sea became blood. And a third part of the creatures in the sea, which had life, died, and a third part of the ships was destroyed."--"And the third angel sounded, and there fell from heaven a great star burning like a torch, and it fell upon the third part of the rivers, and upon the fountains of waters. And the name of the star was Wormwood, and a third part of the waters became as wormwood, and many men died of he waters because they were embittered."--"And the fourth angel sounded, and the third part of the sun was stricken, and the third part of the moon, and the third part of the stars; so that the third part of them was darkened, and the day shone not as to a third part of it, and the night likewise."

The First Trumpet

The first trumpet of the seventh seal begins from the final disturbance and overthrow of the Roman idolarchy at the close of the sixth seal; and as it was to bring the first plague on the empire, now beginning to fall, it lays waste the third part of the earth, with a horrible storm of hail mingled with fire and blood; that is, it depopulates the territory and people of the Roman world, (viz. the basis and ground of its universal polity) with a terrible and bloody irruption of the northern nations, and overthrows and destroys the nobles and plebeians. You may see the image of hail, referring in the same manner to a hostile invasion in Isaiah, c. xxviii. v. 2. "Behold a strong and mighty one from the Lord, (he alludes to Salmanasser,) as a tempest of hail, and a whirlwind of destruction, as a flood of many waters, overflowing, he shall cast down mightily on the earth. The crown of pride, the drunken of Ephraim, shall be trodden under his feet." Also Isaiah, c. xxx. v. 30, of the slaughter to come on the Assyrians: "And the Lord shall cause his glorious voice to be heard, and shall show the descent of his arm in the indignation of his anger, and in the flame of a consuming fire, in dispersion and tempest, and hailstones; for at the voice of the Lord shall the Assyrian be beaten down," &c. Here it is to be observed, that hail is usually accompanied with thunder, especially in the warmer regions. Therefore fire is joined with the mention of hail, both here, in St. John, and in Isaiah, and in the eighteenth Psalm, ver. 13, 14. Nay, in the Scripture history likewise, Exod. c. ix. v. 23. But John mixes blood with it likewise, that he may point out by this index, that the whole image relates to slaughter.--Let the reader likewise consult Isaiah, c. xxxii. v. 19, with regard to the image of hail, and the Chaldee paraphrast upon it. Moreover, the same paraphrast teaches us that trees, in prophetic parables, signify the great and rich, who for oaks of Basan (Isaiah xi. 13.) substitutes the princes of provinces; for cedars, (Isaiah xiv. 8.) rich men; for fir-trees, sometimes princes, (Isaiah xxxvii. 24.) sometimes kings, (Isaiah xiv. 8.) Who likewise paraphrases that passage of Zechariah xi. 2. "Howl, fir-tree; for the cedar is fallen! because the mighty are spoiled. Howl, ye oaks of Basan, for the fenced forest is fallen! Howl, ye kings, for your princes are debased; ye who were rich in wealth are spoiled. Howl, satraps of provinces, for the region of your strength is laid waste." Whence, by analogy, it is easily collected, that herbs are to be taken for the common people, when, as in this place, they are connected with trees.

Now, in order to collect something respecting the event from history, I would deduce the beginning of this trumpet (until something more certain shall be established) from the death of Theodosius the First; that is, from the year of Christ 395; because then the Christian religion seems to have plainly triumphed over the gods of the Gentiles; and at the same time, as combined in a certain common term with the end of the former, and with the beginning of the present seal, the irruptions of the Barbarians having in a small degree been attempted before, but been repressed in the ensuing years, when the empire was again at peace, began at length to take place in a horrible manner, and to hang over the whole Roman world, continually and cruelly wasting and depopulating it with fire and sword.

For in this very year, Alaric first, with an immense army of Goths and other barbarians, broke into Macedonia, from Thrace, sparing neither towns nor inhabitants. From thence, proceeding through Thessaly, and having occupied the straits of Thermopylae, he descended into Greece, that is, into Attica, and overthrew every city except Thebes and Athens. He made an irruption into Peloponnesus, and laid waste Corinth, Argos, and Sparta. From thence he invaded Epirus, where he proceeded to commit the same depopulations and devastations. In the following year, quitting Epirus, he made an incursion into Achaia, and basted to despoil it shamefully, together with Epirus and the neighbouring provinces, by burnings and depopulations. When he had thus, for five years, harassed the east with his cruel ravages, he turned his attention to the invasion of the west, passed into Dalmatia and Pannonia, and laid waste those regions far and wide.

Hear Jerome, who was then alive, deploring the very distressed state of this period, while the tempest was still assailing it. Epist. III. "Between Constantinople and the Julian Alps, Roman blood is every day shed. Scythia, Thrace, Macedonia, Dardania, Dacia, Thessaly, Achaia, Epirus, Dalmatia, and all Pannonia, the Goths, the Sarmatians, the Quadi, the Alans, Huns, Vandals, and Marcomani, invade and seize. How many matrons, how many virgins of God, and free-born and noble persons, are become the sport of these brute beasts! Bishops are taken captive, priests slain, and the functions of divers clergymen suspended! Churches are subverted, horses are stabled at the altars of Christ, the relics of martyrs are dug up. The whole Roman world falls to pieces. What courage do you suppose at this moment is possessed by the Corinthians, Athenians, Lacedemonians, Arcadians, and all Greece, over whom the barbarians rule?"

In the following year, A.Δ. 401, the same Alaric, with Goths, Alans, and Huns following his footsteps, when he was preparing to carry the war into Italy, broke through Noricum, and entered Venetia through the forest of Trent, reduced those cities in a short time under his power, and besieged the emperor Honorius at Hasta; so that almost all men in Italy were beginning to think of changing their habitations. But here at length, Stilico, the general of Honorius, having prepared a great army, checked his fury, and forced him to trace back his steps into Pannonia, from whence he had come, after he had been more than once conquered and worn out by disadvantageous battles. From whence, a short time after, having entered into a league, and being honoured by Honorius with a military prefecture, he withdrew into Illyrium, a province of the east.

While Alaric was quiet for a short time, that the west might not from thenceforth enjoy an hour of rest, immediately after, in the year 404, another memorable irruption of the barbarians was prepared against Italy, Radagaisus, a Scythian, being their leader, who with an army of Goths, Sarmatians, and Germans, to the amount of two hundred thousand, having overthrown the garrisons in the Alps, passed into the territory of Venetia, Emilia, and Etruria, and laid siege to Florence, where being conquered by Stilico with an immense slaughter, he was taken and beheaded. This enemy, however terrible, having been removed in a short space of time, and with little loss, soon after, in the year 406, the third, that most grievous and very destructive irruption of the Vandals and Alans into the west, took place, accompanied by the Marcomanni, Heruli, Suevi, Alemanni, Burgundiones, and a rabble of other barbarians, by which Gallia first, and from thence Hispania, and lastly Africa, were taken possession of, and afflicted with calamities of every kind, which destructions Jerome partly expressed and partly implied in his second epistle. "Innumerable and very fierce nations," says he, "have occupied all the Gallias: Whatever is between the Alps and the Pyrenees, what is included by the ocean and the Rhone, the Quadian, the Vandal, the Sarmatian, the Alans, the Gipedes, the Heruli, Saxon, Burgundian, Allman, and Pannonian enemies have laid waste. Magunciacum [16] has been taken and overthrown, and in the church many thousand of men have been butchered. The Vangiones [17] have been exterminated in a long siege. The city of the Rheni [18], though very strong, the Ambiani, the Atrebates [19], Morini [20], Tornace [21], the Nemeta [22], and Argentorati [23], have been translated into Germany. Aquitania, the country of the Nine People, the provinces of Lyons and Narbonne, except a few cities, have been wholly depopulated. I cannot make mention of Tolosa [24] without tears, which the merits of the holy bishop Exuperius, up to this period, contributed to preserve from ruin. The provinces of Spain are even now trembling, as just ready to perish. Rome redeems its life by gold. And this was that terrible cloud of hail mingled with fire and blood; an image, indeed, of so obvious an application, that I cannot help referring to Nicephorus of Gregora, in book ii. c. vii. never thinking of the Apocalypse, but treating of the Scythians; and yet what fell from him is so suitable to this subject. As,' says he, terrors from heaven are often excited in men by God, as lightnings, fires, and frequent rains, &c. so these northern and hyperborean terrors are reserved by God, that they may be let forth for punishment, when and by whom it may seem right to Providence.'"

But let me add likewise the corollary from Achmet, for the farther confirmation of the Reader.

Corollary taken out of Achmet, of the signification of Hail, Fire, and Trees, in the interpretation of Dreams

Chap. cxci. Of the Explanations of the Indians, Persians, and Egyptians.

"Snow, hail, and cold portend troubles, anxieties, and torments."

"If any one thought he saw hail fallen on any spot, let him expect a sudden hostile attack."

"If he thought he saw hail that injured the stalks of wheat or barley, in that place, as far as the stalks are broken, will warlike slaughters ensue."

To the same purpose is Chap. clxix. Of the Divination of the Indians; Chap. clx. Of the Explication of the Persians and the Egyptians.

"Fire signifies death, war, battles, punishment, and affliction, if any thing or person had been seen to burn."

Also in Chap. cli. The Persians, Indians, and Egyptians interpret Trees by Men, principally Magistrates, Noblemen, and very illustrious men.

"If any one has seen trees watered and flourishing, a very eminent man and the people will be fostered."

"If a king has seemed to himself to have planted trees, he will appoint new magistrates." Also, "If trees by length of time become injured and rotten, the nobles of the king will die a natural

A Key to the Apocalypse
death."

"If he has thought he saw shrubs which grew up into trees, this refers to the promotion of his great men."

"If he has thought he saw the leaves of trees collected into his house, wealth shall be gained from the great in the manner of leaves," &c.

The Second Trumpet

The second trumpet which ushers in ruin on the Roman world by a heavier plague, it being already laid waste as to its land, assails the sea; the third part of which, and what belongs to it, it renders entirely bloody, by the fall of a great mountain threatening it of old, but now set on fire, together with a great slaughter of animals or fishes living in it, and of the vessels navigating therein.

That is, the destruction of Rome, the great city, captured again and again, spoiled and burning with hostile flames, broke forth with the ruin of the amplitude of the Roman dominion or jurisdiction; the barbarians, on account of the weakness of the capital, thus affected, now seizing on its provinces, and dividing them into new kingdoms, with an irreparable slaughter of the legions at that time remaining for its defence, with a loss of all aids of retaining and supporting its power, even by negotiation.

The sea of the political world is, as I have observed, that amplitude of dominion which embraces all the inhabitants in the communion of the same political laws. By this image the dominion of Babylon is expressed, Jer. c. li. v. 36. where the Lord threatens that "He will dry up her sea, and make her springs dry;" which ver. 44 explains by the retention of the same metaphor, "The nations shall no longer flow together to her." The amplitude of the Assyrian kingdom likewise, is thus described, Ezek. c. xxxi. v. 4. "The waters have made her to increase;" (that is, the Assyrian cedar,) "the abyss or the sea has exalted her." Perhaps the dominion of Pharaoh is the sea. Isa. c. xix. v. 5. It is said of the destruction of his kingdom, "The waters of his sea should fail;" that is, his empire should be taken away. Therefore those great empires are seen by Daniel "ascending out of the sea;" that is, arising out of the circumference of dominion.

But as "the third part of the sea," that is, of the Roman sea, is said to have become bloody, it is to be understood that blood is used in the first place for slaughter, and then for death, even without blood. Death is to be taken generally for destruction, even of a substance without life. Vide Ezek. c. xiv. v. 19. and c. iii. v. 18. 20. and c. xviii. v. 13. Amos, c. ii. v. 2. Rom. c. vii. v. 9. Whence blood, or to become bloody, is the image which has suffered destruction, as if it were like an animal slain or butchered, dropping with gore. When, therefore, it is said here that the sea is made bloody by the overthrow of a great mountain, it denotes nothing else than that it should suffer some kind of death, or violent extinction by that event. What is said in the vials, where there is the same image, is a little more clear,--"it became as the blood of a dead man." The meaning is, that the Roman dominion, or extent of power, suffered ruin, was mangled, dismembered, and destroyed.

The like symbol of a mountain, signifying a city, is to be found of ancient Babylon, in Jer. c. li. v. 25, "Behold I am against thee, Ω destroying (or corrupting) mountain, saith the Lord, which destroyeth (or corrupteth) all the earth, and I will stretch out my hand,--and will make thee a burnt mountain, (or a mountain of combustion,)" where the Septuagint has ὄρος ἐμπυριόμενον a burning mountain, in the same sense in which John uses it here, ὄρος πυρὶ καιόμενον a mountain burning with fire. Of the same Isaiah says, c. xiii. v. 2, "Lift ye up a banner on the high mountain." The Targum has it, "On the city which dwelleth confidently." Again, c. cxxxvii. v. 24, to Sennacherib, king of Assyria, "Thou hast reproached the Lord, and hast said, With the multitude of my chariots have I ascended to the height of the mountains:" The Targum, "Have I ascended into their fortified cities." But whether rightly, I doubt.

Moreover, that a mountain should here be said to be cast into the sea, is a proper figure, because, by no other means could a mountain hurt the sea, than by being cast into it. And this you will remember, likewise, takes place in the following trumpet of the falling star.

With relation to history, Rome was first captured in the year 410 by the same Alaric, king of the Goths, who in the former trumpet had exhibited, as it were, a prelude of its fate. But now, after the death of Stilico, exciting new disturbances, and setting on foot a new and fatal expedition against Italy, by which he reduced Honorius to such straits, that the barbarian himself gave to Rome a new emperor of the name of Attalus, with whom he besieged Honorius Augustus at Ravenna, who was already meditating from the desperate state of his affairs, to fly into the east, and to abandon the west. But the enemy, induced by his submission, and Attalus having abdicated the empire, restored Honorius to his power.

The dismemberment of the Roman empire followed immediately the destruction of Rome. I call Sigonius as a witness, who says, "The miserable devastation of Italy, continual wars with Gaul and Spain, and at length, new regal governments of barbarians in both provinces, followed the

Joseph Mede

destruction of Rome."

For, in the first place, Honorius, in order to recover the possession of Rome with the empire, having made a league with Alaric, was compelled to grant settlements to the Goths, and a kingdom in the Gallias. Two years after, in the year 412, the Huns pouring into Pannonia, which the Goths had left, lie being destitute of sufficient force to make resistance, under such difficulties, entered into a treaty with them, giving and accepting hostages.

Then in the year 413, Constantius, the general of the same Honorius, that he might not accidentally fall into any warlike difficulty, willingly received the Burgundians into amity, and assigned them seats on the Rhone, who in the preceding years had thrown themselves into Gaul with the Vandals.

Lastly, in the year 415, the same Honorius, (as Procopius relates,) when the Goths, a little while after, had passed into the neighbouring part of Spain, granted to the Vandals likewise, with their king Gunderic, who had lately been expelled from Gaul by the Franks, the habitation they had occupied, under the engagement of waging war with the Goths.

He who desires to know more may consult the beforenamed Sigonius on the western empire, books x. and xi. from whence we have quoted these particulars.

And thus, from henceforth, the extent of the Roman dominion was daily more and more mangled and dismembered, until Rome being again taken and sacked in the year 455 by Genseric, the Vandal, in the year immediately following, or in rather less time, the whole body of the empire appeared to be divided into ten kingdoms in all; which, together with the names of the people, and kings, and the provinces over which they reigned, the following little table will exhibit, together with some illustrations from history, to throw greater light upon the subject.

And in this manner, at length, those ten kingdoms, into which the Holy Spirit had predeclared, both by Daniel and St. John, that the Roman empire should be divided in the latter days, seem to be made out, and are not altogether to be estimated by the bare names of so many regions, or tracts of the earth, as is commonly done, but by kingdoms, into which the extent and dominion of the empire was to be forcibly torn asunder.

In the mean time, however, we do not think that the circumscription of this denary is to be so rigidly interpreted, as to exclude more kingdoms at any one time, or dynasties of some kind or other; but that the empire was to be rent into ten kingdoms, at least, or into ten principal kingdoms. Which, from the original declaration which we have now represented, down even to the present age, under so many fates and changes of republics and kingdoms, I believe to have been always true; though it might be sufficient to confirm the truth of the oracle, if it had only been divided in the beginning into so many kingdoms, though afterwards, perhaps, the number had diminished.

Now that this circumscription of the decad of kingdoms is to be understood in the manner which I have stated, and not otherwise, the similar prophecy respecting the division of the Alexandrian monarchy may teach us. In which, though over and above those four principal kingdoms of Macedonia, Asia, Syria, and Egypt, a fifth was added, namely, that of Thrace, by its founder Lysimachus, yet the Holy Spirit defined that multiplicity by a quaternion, suggesting there would be so many at least, or so many principal kingdoms. For the Thracian kingdom, though it began at the same time with the rest, and lasted forty years, yet had no successor, but expired with the first king, Lysimachus, and therefore is not to be referred to the number.

In like manner we are to judge of this tenfold Roman division. Therefore, let no one be surprised, if, beside the kingdom enumerated in the Gallias, he should possibly find that of the Aurelian Alani, and also the dynasty of the Armoric States, remaining even from the reign of Honorius to these times. The latter, indeed, he will find to have been of very moderate extent, and the former to have lasted for a very short space of time, (or not more than ten years.) Neither, then, is to be reckoned in the same place and order as the rest, though otherwise something of the same nature may be discovered.

A Type of the Dismemberment of the Empire or Dominion of Rome, about the year of Christ 456, and subsequent to that period

Kingdoms of Provinces under their Dominion. Names of Kings regnant about the year 456. Observations. 1. Britons In Britain Vortimer. 2. Saxons Hengist. 3. Franks In Belgic Gaul first, afterwards in Celtic Childeric. The kingdom of the Burgundians was subjugated and extinguished about 536; but to make up correctly the No. 10, the dominion of the Ostrogoths was divided at that time into two kingdoms; Pannonia having been subject to them, being occupied by the Longobards, and Italy alone left to the King of the Ostrogoths. 4. Burgundians In Gaul, about the Seine and Lyons. Gunderic. 5. Visigoths In Aquitaine and part of Spain Theodosius II. 6. Suevi & Alani In that part of Spain comprised in Gallicia and Lusitania Ricianus. 7. Vandals In Africa; but a little before in Spain Genseric. 8. Allemanni Germans In the tract of Germany, called Rhitea Sumanus. The kingdom of the Allemanni coalesced with that of the Heruli, as long as they had possessions in

Italy, about sixteen years. 9. Ostrogoths In Pannonia, having defeated the Huns, and before the expiration of this age the same people extended their kingdom into Italy. Theodemirus. The Longobards, or Lombards, succeeded the Ostrogoths likewise in Italy, from the time of Narsis. After he had destroyed the kingdom of the Ostrogoths, being called forth in 567, they gave up their seats in Pannonia to the Huns and Avari. 10. Greeks In the remainder of the dominion of the empire. Sinc the ancient empire of Rome being dissolved, that of the Greeks is to be enumberated among the kingdoms into which it was broken to pieces Marianus.

The Third Trumpet

The third trumpet wholly overthrew and extinguished that burning star, the Roman Hesper, or Cæsar of the West, which fell headlong from the time when Genseric, king of the Vandals, pillaged the captured city of Rome; though, for a little time, to contend with death under those merely nominal Cæsars,--Avitus, Majorianus, Severus, Anthemius, Olybrius, Glycerius, and Nepos, who perished by mutual treacheries and murders, at length, in the year 476, drawing its last breath under the fatal name of Augustulus, was entirely hurled from the heaven of his power by Odoacer, king of the Heruli, who had fallen upon him, with a very bitter calamity to the fountains and rivers, that is, to the cities and provincial magistrates.

By the Hesperian Cæsar I understand him, who, from the confirmed division of the empire into eastern and western, even from the death of Theodosius the First, yet remained emperor of ancient Rome, and of the West, but for a very short period, as, after the year 91, he began secretly to fall from his heaven at the sound of this trumpet. For though the Roman bishop, more than 320 years after the Hesperian Cæsar had fallen in Augustulus, substituted the king of the Franks, (and afterwards of the Germans) in the same name and title, he did nothing else but contrive, that by this drawn-curtain of a revived Cæsar, or the sixth head of the beast, he himself might not be so clearly perceived by the less perspicacious, to be the last head, that is, Anti-Christ.

The Papal Cæsar, however, does not appertain to the heads of the Roman beast, but to the horns or kingdoms, into which the empire of the sixth head, just ready to give place to the last head, were to be divided. For, after so long a space as 325 years [25], there could not be a succession, as in continuation of the western Cæsars.

But it is time now to throw light on the text of John, that the reasonableness of the interpretation may appear. "And there fell from heaven, (says he,) a great star, burning as a lamp." He seems to describe a hairy star, or comet, among whose species is enumerated by Pliny the Lampadias, or blazing star, especially so called. And indeed, the Cæsar of the West might not unaptly be designated by a star of this kind, on account of his brief duration. Of whom it is said, c. xviii. "And when he cometh, he must continue a short space." But the star was great, in order more aptly to figure the supreme majesty, whose splendour the sun, in other places, represents in prophetic parables. And it is very well known that there have been comets, which seemed to equal even the sun in magnitude, of which kind, perhaps, he will not be in an error, who affirms this star to have been one. But that you may not entertain a doubt of the application, Isaiah applies a similar image of a falling star, c. xiv. v. 12, to the fall of the king of Babylon. "How (says he) hest thou fallen from heaven, Ω Lucifer, son of the morning! How art thou cut down to the ground which didst weaken the nations [26] !" In other places likewise, as in that passage of Isaiah, c. xxxiv. v. 4, just now quoted, stars falling from heaven are understood of the ruin of princes and nobles. A star, therefore, of a singular and unusual magnitude, designates a prince above the common lot of princes, that is, great and illustrious. It follows: "And the name of the star is called Wormwood." It is the prophetic plan, that the quality or fate of the thing or person of which it treats should be pointed out by the imposition of a certain proper name, since there are other instances in the Hebrew language where ρῆμα, רבד, is the same as τὸ πρᾶγμα, that is, the word signifies the thing, as Luke c. i. v. 37, "There is not any word impossible with God [27] ," to be called signifies the same as to be or exist, as Isaiah c. lvi. v. 7, "My house shall be called the house of prayer," for which Luke has, c. xix. v. 4, "My house is, (that is, shall be accounted,) the house of prayer." And Gen. c. xxi. v. 12, "In Isaac shall thy seed be called," that is, "shall be." See likewise the Septuagint Isa. c. xiv. v. 20. Ruth, c. iv. v. 11.

But examples of the figure which I have noticed are every where to be met with. For thus says Isaiah, c. vii. v. 14, "His name shall be called Emmanuel [28] ;" that is, He shall be θεάνθρωπος, God-man; and c. ix. v. 6, "His name shall be called Wonderful, the Counsellor, the Mighty God, the Father of the world to come, the Prince of Peace;" that is, he shall be all these. Also Jerem. c. xxiii. v. 6, "And this is the name by which he shall be called, The Lord our Righteousness;" and Zech. c. vi. v. 12, "Behold a man whose name is the Branch." It follows, "For he shall grow up out of his place," &c. add Rev. c. xix. v. 13, "His name is called the Word of God." Akin to these examples are what we find in Jer. c. xx. v. 3, 4, "The Lord doth not call thy name Pashur, but Magor

Missabib, (i. e. fear on every side). "For thus saith the Lord, Behold, I will make thee a terror to thyself and all thy friends;" and Ezek. c. xxiii. v. 4, "Their names (i. e. the names of Samaria and Jerusalem) are Aholah and Aholibah." Add Isa. c. viii. Hosea, c. i. 6, 7. By a similar figure in every respect, is this fallen star called Wormwood; that is, according to the Hebrew notion, (by which abstracts are used for concretes,) Absinthites, or the prince of bitterness and troubles. Of this kind in truth, if ever there was one, was that Hesperian Cæsar, exercised with perpetual troubles from his first rise to his end; during whose possession of power the Roman empire was ready to fall; nay, in whose appointment was given an occasion of falling, because in the division of empire thus introduced, a way was opened for the barbarians, and the Roman commonwealth was exposed to the most dreadful calamities. Might not he be properly called Wormwood, on account of a fate so bitter to himself and others? According to that saying of Naomi, "Call me not Naomi, call me Marah; for the Almighty has afflicted me with bitterness," Ruth c. i. v. 20.

But before I quit this subject, something must be said of the state of the city and the Roman commonwealth, that the way may be prepared for the interpretation of the following trumpet.

The Cæsar of the West, then, being thus overthrown and extinct, in the mean time Odoacer, king of the Heruli, held Rome for sixteen years under the name of king, who, after two years restored, and from that time preserved, the consulate to Rome and the West, which in his anger he had at first taken away. Theodoric, king of the Ostrogoths, succeeded him, and that, as Paul the Deacon relates, by Zeno, the emperor of the East, delivering Italy to him in a formal manner, and confirming it by the imposition of the second veil on his head. He, after Odoacer was conquered and slain, besides Dalmatia and Rhetia, which were provinces of Odoacer, added Sicily also to his kingdom, rebuilt the walls, and some of the edifices of the city of Rome, having collected a large sum of money for that purpose; so that nothing seemed to be wanted to its attainment of its former state, except the infamy of a city plundered and burned. He regulated the kingdom most wisely; he changed no Roman institution, but retained the senate and consuls, the patricians, prefects of the prætorium, prefect of the city, questor, commissary of the sacred largesses, offices of the privates, and of the military, masters of the foot and horse, and the other magistrates, who were then in the empire, and entrusted the offices only to Romans. Which regulations were for some time continued by his successors also, Athalaric, Theodostratus, and Vitiges, Ostrogoth kings of Italy.--Vide Sigonius on the Western Empire, Lib. xv. Anno, 479, Lib. xvi. Annis, 493, 494, 500.

The Fourth Trumpet

The fourth trumpet having advanced a little farther, proceeded to take away entirely the light of Roman majesty in the city -of Rome, with which it had hitherto shone under the Ostrogoth kings, after the consulate of Rome had failed;- namely, from the year 452, in that Ostrogothic war, waged first by Belisarius, and then by Narses, general of Justinian, for the purpose of recovering Italy: And then the city itself, having been repeatedly taken by Totila, burnt, and a third of it demolished, deprived, moreover, of all its inhabitants, (a memorable sport of fortune!) being recovered at length by Narses, after so many deaths and so much slaughter, was thrown down -a short time after by a whirlwind and thunderbolts. Once the queen of cities, but now at length deprived of the consular power, of the authority of the senate, and of the other magistrates, with which, as stars, she had hitherto irradiated the globe, she fell from such splendour of glory into I know not what ignoble Duchy of Ravenna, over which she had formerly ruled, and was afterwards compelled (what obscurity!) to be subject to the Exarchy, and to pay tribute.

And this was that percussion of "the third part of the sun, and of the moon, and of the stars," by which it came to pass that "a third part of the day did not shine, and likewise a third part of the night." Where the diurnal light, which is that of the sun, is called by the name of day, and the nocturnal light of the moon and stars, by that of night. Like that in Jerem. c. xxxi. v. 35, "Who giveth the sun for the light of the day, and the ordinances of the moon and the stars for a light by night."

The sun shone at Rome as long as the consular dignity and the kingdom was possessed of authority over other cities and provinces. The moon and the stars shone there, as long as the ancient power of the senate, and of the other magistrates, remained. But these being all taken away, (which was done by this trumpet,) what was there but darkness, and a universal failure of light, both diurnal and nocturnal? namely, what belonged to that city, to which a third part of the light of heaven was attributed.

The image of the sun, moon, and stars, in this sense, is very frequent with the prophets. As Isaiah, c. xiii. v. 10, also c. lx. v. 20, where, instead of "Thy sun shall no more set, and thy moon shall not be diminished," the Targum has, "Thy kingdom (it is addressed to Jerusalem) shall no more cease, and thy glory shall not be withdrawn." Also, Jerem. c. xv. v. 9, where of Jerusalem he says, "Her sun is set, while it is yet day," the Targum translates it, "Their glory has departed during

A Key to the Apocalypse

their lives." And Ezek. c. xxxii. v. 7, the same paraphrast turns that passage concerning Pharaoh-- "And when I shall extinguish thee, I will cover the heaven, and make the stars thereof dark"-- "Tribulation shall cover thee, when I shall extinguish the splendour of the glory of thy kingdom." The reader may transfer hither also the observations I have made above from Achmet, in order to throw light on the sixth seal. It is wonderful how they agree.

Of the Three Woe Trumpets

There still remain three trumpets, the greatest and most grievous of all, and therefore discriminated from the former by the appellation of Woes. For after the conclusion of the fourth trumpet, "I saw and heard," says he, "an angel flying in the midst of heaven, and saying with a loud voice, Woe, woe, woe, to the inhabitants of the earth, by reason of the other voices of the trumpets of the three angels, which are yet to sound." Also, c. ix. v. 12, and c. xi. v. 14.

Doubtless, since the Christian inhabitants of the Roman world, whilst the other trumpets were sounding, had contaminated themselves with the worship of new idols, the trumpets which remained were made more important for the purpose of punishing the double sin. For, it is apparent, that this sin, likewise, of the Roman world, together with the former one, of the slaughter of the martyrs, was reckoned in the account of the crime to be avenged, because this enunciation is subjoined to the second woe; namely, "The rest of the men which were not killed by these plagues, repented not of the works of their hands, that they should not worship demons, and idols of gold and silver, and brass and stone, and wood, which neither can see, nor hear, nor walk," c. ix. v. 20.

The First Woe Trumpet, or Trumpet the Fifth.

The first woe trumpet is long since passed. It sent forth those horrid troops of locusts, issuing from the smoke of the Tartarean abyss, now opened by the work of Satan, to devastate the globe; that is, the Saracens, or Arabs, (a nation as populous and numerous as locusts,) were excited to the destruction of so many nations, by the astonishing false prophecy of Mohammed.

For the smoke ascending from the infernal pit is Mohammedism, which the Mohammedan knaves call Islamism. This covered the whole earth with a new obscurity, long since illuminated by the empire and discipline of Christ, the Sun of Righteousness, after the darkness of the Gentiles had been dispersed. And the type of locusts is the more exact, because the Egyptian locusts likewise, came from the same Arabia, bordering on Egypt to the east. For thus says Exodus, c. x. vv. 13, 14, "The Lord brought an east wind on the land, and it brought the locusts; and the locusts went up upon all the land Of Egypt, and settled in all the coasts of Egypt." The Arabs, besides, on account of the remarkable multitude of the nation, are compared to locusts. Judges, c. vii. v. 12, "The Midianites and Amalekites, and all the sons of Kedem, or of the east, lay in the valley as locusts[29] in multitude. Their camels were without number, as the sand by the sea shore for multitude." Where it is to be observed, that the Arabs are peculiarly denominated the sons of the east, as Arabia itself is קדם Kedem, or the east; namely, with respect to Egypt, where the Israelites had learned to speak thus. You may see, Gen. c. x. v. 30, and c. xxv. v. 6. 1 Kings, c. iv. v. 30. Isa. c. xi. v. 14. Jer. c. xlix. v. 28, and perhaps Matt. c. ii. v. 1. Plainly for the same reason as Asia Minor is at this day called Natolia, [30] and Arabia Felix is called by the rest of the Arabians, Ayaman, or south, whence the queen of the south, Matt. c. xii. v. 42. But this by the way.

A similar image of locusts is to be seen in Joel, in the two first chapters, speaking of the Assyrians and Babylonians, who were about to lay waste Judea, from whence he who hath compared the description of both, will not deny that the type was borrowed.

Achmet shows from the use of the east, that the interpretation is to be referred to hostile forces; whose words I have thought proper to insert in this place. It is thus he writes in chap. ccc. from the sciences of the Indians, Persians, and Egyptians: "The locust, no doubt, is generally to be referred to a multitude of enemies: For so it is recorded in the sacred writings, that locusts by Divine command go forth like an army to the devastation of countries." This allusion to sacred writings, applies to those of the Indians alone, as well as every thing in this book, which seems to imply a knowledge of the Christian religion, as will be apparent to the reader. He proceeds,--"If any king or person endued with power has dreamed that he saw locusts going forth towards a particular region, he may expect in that place, a multitude of enemies with great power; and as much injury as the locusts have done, so much damage will they occasion."

Having now then established the image, we will look to the remainder of the description.

"And to them was given power," says ver. 3, "even as the scorpions of the earth have power;" "for they had tails like scorpions, and in them stings with which they hurt; and their torment was as the torment of a scorpion when it striketh a man." That is, they had not only the power proper to locusts of eating up and depopulating the countries through which they passed, but, what was a kind of prodigy, they had tails like scorpions, with the stroke of which, likewise, they diffused poison.

Wonderful A locust scorpion. But the nature of the evil which it implies, the symbol of a serpentine species seems to point out; for the scorpion is of the serpent kind. In that resemblance, in which the devil first deceived mankind, and turned him away from God, the Holy Spirit loves still to introduce him when he is about to deceive men. Whence that expression--"The old serpent, which deceiveth the world," c. xii. v. 9, and c. xx. v. 2. The tail, therefore, of a scorpion, with the sting, denotes the propagation of that diabolical false prophecy of Mohammed, with its whole apparatus, on which the Arabian locusts relying, not less than on warlike force, inflicted hurt, alas! wherever they went. Nay, this train of foulest errors, the Saracens first, from the creation of man, drew after them; and, I believe, no nation before them, relying on a similar imposture, in religion, and under the pretext of destroying the worship of idols, ever contended for the empire of the world.

But it was said to them, "that they should not hurt the grass of the earth, nor any green thing, nor any tree, but only those men who had not the seal of God upon their foreheads."

As to the signification of the particle εἰ μὴ but only, the sense is either exceptive, "that they should not hurt any herb, (for this is the meaning of chortos with the Hellenists,) nor any thing green, nor any tree, unless those herbs, trees, and green things only, which were not inscribed by the seal of God;" so that men and herbs, and green things, mutually explain one another. Or it may be explained not exceptively, but in opposition, according to the use of the particle εἰ μὴ in sacred Hellenism, for ἀλλὰ, Matt. c. xii. v. 4, Rom. xiv. v. 14, and elsewhere; namely, that it might be said to them, that they were not to feed altogether after the manner of common locusts, on herbs or trees, nor on any thing green, but above those things to which they were accustomed, they were to harass men alone; of the number of those whom the seal of the angel, at the beginning of the trumpet, had not exempted from those plagues. In whichever mode it be taken, we might trouble ourselves in vain about the signification and difference of green grass and trees, since those things belong only to the propriety of the figure in which a mystery is not to be sought for. For thus it is said of the Egyptian locusts, Exod. c. x. v. 15, "They covered the face of the whole earth, so that the land was darkened; and they consumed every herb of the land, and all the fruit of the trees, and there remained not any green thing in any tree or herb of the field through all the land of Egypt." But our locusts afflicted the very men, and from hence it is apparent that they were not of the genus of insects, that is, not natural, but symbolical locusts. On which occasion, it will be worth while, once for all, to lay down this rule:--Whenever any thing is attributed to the prophetic type, which is not agreeable to the nature of the same, that will lead us to the understanding of the thing signified by the type, and teach us that the interpretation is to be made according to the condition of the thing so signified; and this, you will observe, is to be done four times, at least, in this vision; as when there is given to locusts not only the power of attacking men, but also a human face, feminine hair, golden crowns, and iron breast-plates; by all which it is intimated that men and not insects are designated; and they, indeed, by no means hooded as some suppose [31], but in all respects such as go forth in arms, for the destruction of others. Of which locusts it is said, "And to them it was given, that they should not kill men, but that they should torment them for five months;" that is, in this respect the Arabian locusts differ from the Euphratean horsemen, of whom mention is made in the following trumpet. It was given to the Saracens to torment for a long time, and in a cruel manner, the nations of the Roman name; but it was by no means given to them to despoil of life that Roman triental, if I may so call it, on any side. For since, while the former trumpets were sounding, out of the ruins of its political state, a new pontifical kingdom of ancient Rome had grown up, with a progress equal, as it were, to the ruin of the other, the Saracens could not destroy this, nor the kingdom of Constantinople, the new Rome. On the other hand, the Turks, after the capture of the royal city, entirely took away the Constantinopolitan dominion, as we shall hear in the following trumpet. Of the five months to which the torment of the locusts is limited, we shall speak with more propriety when we come to the repetition of the same.

"In those days men shall seek death, and shall not find it. And they shall desire to die,. and death shall flee from them." That is, such shall be the calamity of those times, that men shall be weary of their lives. For you are not to imagine that this was done by mere persuasion, or tricks of delusion. The business was effected by arms, and that by the institution of Mohammed himself; the apparatus of which, indeed, and it is sufficiently terrible, together with the amplitude of the dominion to be acquired, and the dress of the nation waging war, is depicted in a lively image. The warlike apparatus is thus described: "And the figures of the locusts were like horses (i. e. cavalry) prepared for battle;" "their teeth were like those of lions," i. e. strong to devour. Joel, c. i. v. 6. Dan. c. vii. v. 7. 23. "And they had breast-plates like breast-plates of iron, and the sound of their wings was as the sound of chariots with many horses rushing to battle." The whole description is taken from Joel, from whence, as I observed, is borrowed the very image of locusts. Vide c. ii. v. 4. c. i. v. 6. c. ii. v. 5.

The crowns, like crowns of gold, placed on their heads, indicate the success and extent of dominion to be acquired nor indeed undeservedly. No nation ever reigned so extensively, nor in so short a space of time were so many kingdoms, so many regions, brought under the yoke of domination. Incredible is it to be told, yet it is most true, that in the short space of eighty, or not many more years, they subjugated and acquired to the diabolical kingdom of Mohammed, Palestine, Syria, both the Armenias, almost the whole of Asia Minor, Persia, India, Egypt, Numidia, all Barbary, as far as the river Niger, Lusitania, and Hispania. Nor did their good fortune or ambition stop here, till they had added great part of Italy, even to the gates of Rome, besides Sicily, Candia, Cyprus, and the other islands of the Mediterranean Sea.

Good God! what a vast tract of land! How many crowns are here! Whence it is worthy of observation, that no mention is here made, as under the other trumpets, of the trient, or third part; since the plague fell not less beyond the bounds of the Roman empire, than within it; stretching even to the extremest parts of India.

The dress of this warlike nation remains to be considered. "And their faces," says he, "were as the faces of men." They were locusts with a human countenance; that is, truly men, (lest any one should suppose that insects were spoken of,) "having hair as the hair of women;" that is, they were Arabs by nation, who, according to Pliny, wear their hair uncut, and in the manner of women, having turbans on their heads. Pliny, lib. vi. c. 28. Whose custom it is at the present day, as travellers affirm, when they are going into battle, to braid their hair into horns and curls. Camerar. operum subciss. Tom. i. c. 93. Whence it appears manifest that a passage quoted from Herodotus in Thalia, as implying the tonsure of the Arabs, is not to be understood as of the shaving of the head, but either of that of the beard, in some mode used by the Arabs, in imitation of Bacchus, (of which Pliny also mentions something, when he says, "the beard was wont to be shaved by them, except upon the upper lip,") or of the roundness of the ends of their hair, beyond the entire tonsure of the head both of which modes perhaps, because it was the mark of the worshippers of Bacchus, a Heathen deity near them, God forbad to his people. Levit. c. xix. v. 27. c. xxi. v. 5. However it might be, I doubt not but Pliny had seen Arabians at Rome.

It follows, with regard to the duration of the plague, that it is to be actually terminated in five months, according to the type of locusts, who last for so many months namely, from the rising of the pleiades, (called by the ancients the end of spring, being about one month from the vernal equinox,) when, from the eggs left in the earth, during winter, they come forth to the light, until the beginning of autumn, when, having deposited other eggs in the earth for the stock of the next year, they immediately die. See Pliny, lib. xi. c. 29.

God, however, intended to suit this notation of time, not only to the type, but also to the antitype, since he delivered up Italy, the chief state of the earth, and of the sin which drew down the foremost plague, to be infested by the Saracenic locusts, from the year 830 to the year 980, that is, 150 years, or five months of years.

In other parts of the world indeed, but in a certain order, and for different periods of time, the plague remained longer; chiefly in the oriental regions of Syria, Egypt, and of Asia Minor, which being conterminous to the head of that empire, which was first at Damascus, and afterwards at Bagdad, fell, as it were, into the anterior parts of the Saracenic body for many ages.

Here I would observe, that though, in whatever lands they occupied, they wounded the inhabitants with the envenomed stroke of that scorpion-tail of which I have spoken, yet the Italians seem to have felt the stroke in some different, unknown, and singular manner. The whole swarm being assimilated to a body, and the anterior parts assigned, as they ought to be, to the east, what will those African troops be, stretched out at so loose a distance from the head towards the west, but the tail? And from thence arose all the calamity of Italy, which they repeatedly struck by an oblique stroke (see the nature of scorpions) through the Mediterranean sea, as well as its. islands of Sardinia and Sicily. As if the Holy Spirit expressly pointed hither when it said, with the reiterated mention of months, "And they had tails like scorpions, and stings, and they had power in their tails to hurt men five months." For so reads the Cornplutensian Codex, according to the testimony of Syrus, Primasius, Andreas, and Aretas. Though an interpretation of this kind be not unsuitable to the designation of the time, yet I do not change my opinion that there is another signification of that serpentine train, and much more widely diffusing itself, as I have said above. If any one will suffer himself to be persuaded of a secondary sense, (which I am not accustomed easily to admit,) he is at liberty to adopt it with my consent.

Now, this is one way by which the five months of the type of locusts may be adapted to the event. There is also another, provided those months are doubled in consequence of those five months being twice mentioned, as if indeed the Holy Spirit meant to apply the number Five according to the analogy and propriety of the type; but to double it that it might answer by another period, to a more illustrious antitype. For why otherwise should he repeat the notation of those months nearly in the same words? Is there not a mystery under this repetition? I do not remember a similar circumstance elsewhere, in the continued description of the same type. If this, then, should be satisfactory, three hundred years, as many as twice five months of years amount to, will comprehend that noted period of the Saracenic kingdom, which, from the beginning of the Caliphate of the Abasides, (who first fixed the seat of empire at Bagdad,) extends to the capture of the same city by Togrulbec, king of the Turks, (who is called by us Tangrophilix); that is, from the year of Christ 750 to the year 1055. This, indeed, is a longer space by about five years; but when the calculation is made by months, no more notice is to be taken of some days, than, when the computation is by days, it is customary to take of hours. It may be added, that this interval will begin commodiously from the removal of the yoke of the exarchate from the city of Rome, with which the calamity of the preceding trumpet ended. It happened at the same time, perhaps even in the same year. If you should still inquire why the Holy Spirit did not comprehend the whole duration of the Saracenic plague within these numbers, since, before this principality of the Abasides, namely, from the year 630, the Saracens had extended their empire by continued successes; so that it had thus then arisen to its acme? It may be answered, that the number of five months has more to do with the type of locusts than with the antitype of Saracens, and therefore it was sufficient, if what properly suits the former was exhibited in some more remarkable kind of period, though it should not measure the whole. I assert nothing, however, on this point, but leave it to others to whom more has been given by God, to search into it farther. (N.B.) This difficulty, notwithstanding, is by no means prejudicial to the interpretation respecting the Saracens; for whichever interpretation you follow, the same difficulty will pursue you.

There yet remains to treat of the king, and his name. "And they had," says he, "a king over them, the angel of the abyss." His name in Hebrew is Abaddon, and in Greek he has the name of Apollyon, that is, the Destroyer.

The Holy Spirit seems to insinuate, as he calls their king the angel of the abyss, that these locusts were not a Christian, but an infidel nation, which had not given their name to Christ. For the children of infidelity, or Pagans, are said by St. Paul to be subject to the prince who had the power "of the air," who is no other than the angel of the abyss; on the contrary, those who become Christians are said "to be delivered from the power of Satan, and to be converted to God."

Whatever the reason may be, the matter is worthy discussion, why he should call this prince of the abyss by a name evidently new and unheard of, and not as he commonly is, the Devil, Satan, the Serpent, or Dragon: or if he had given him one from the notion of destroying, why not rather Asmodeus, from the name Ἰσοδυναμοῦντι, by which the Jews used to call him, but Abaddon never? Is it not because, when the Mohammedans boasted that they worshipped and adored no other God than the one and only God, the Creator of all things, or the Maker of the Universe, who is denominated Abuda by the Chaldeans and Syrians, and is distinguished also by the Arabians themselves by the epithet 'ידבא Abdi, that is, Eternal; the Holy Spirit designed to oppose them with a word of a contrary sense, but of similar sound? By which, in truth, he intimated, that they were so far from venerating (whatever they might assert) Abuda, or Abdi, the Eternal Maker of the World, that in the estimation of God himself, whom they will have to be of one Person, and not to be approached through Christ, they had, in the place of king or deity, not Him, but the evil angel Abaddon, that is, not the Maker, but the Destroyer of the world.

Thus, when the followers of Jeroboam thought that they worshipped the God of Israel in their calves, the Scripture says that they sacrificed to demons. 2 Chron. c. xi. v. 15. Or shall we say that there is here an allusion to the common name of the kings of that portion of Arabia whence Mohammed, in the first place, had issued forth with the locusts; who from an ancient king, Oboda, referred by them into the number of their gods, and from whose sepulchre the name of Oboda remained in a region of the Nabatheans, they were thence called Obodæ, by a name of power, as the kings of Egypt, Pharaohs and Ptolemies, those of the Romans Cæsars, of the Parthians Arsacæ, and the neighbouring kings of the Arabs of Petræa, Aretæ? For Stephen of Byzantium, out of the fourth book of Uranius, a writer on Arabian affairs, says, "Obodas is a country of the Nabatheans, where Obodas the king, whom they made a god, was buried. Now, from this circumstance, Strabo and Josephus induce me to believe that the kings of that country were from thenceforward called by the common name Obodas, the latter of whom commemorates two of this name, the one warlike, and too well known to the Jews by the slaughter of their king Alexander Jamnenus; whom, in fact, Obodas the Arab compelled to fly from Jerusalem, his whole army being slain in the region of Galaad, about ninety years before Christ, whom the Jews, not undeservedly, by a slight alteration, might have called Abaddon, that is, the Destroyer.

The other king was dull and heavy, the contemporary of Herod the Great, whose procurator Syllæus (who administered his affairs according to his pleasure) demanded Salome, the sister of Herod, in marriage; but being deprived of his wish, and rendered the enemy of Herod, brought him into no small dispute with Augustus by his calumnies. Of this Obodas, Strabo makes mention more than once in the expedition of Ælius Gallus into Arabia, and that with the same mark of dulness, and says he was connected by affinity with the neighbouring king Aretas, (and this, as I said, was the common name of the kings bordering on Petræa.) From the same author it is to be collected,

A Key to the Apocalypse

that the more southern kingdom of Obodas reached to the Red Sea, which tract of land, I believe, the Ismaelites and Saracens inhabited; for certainly it appears that the Nabatheans, whose country, by the testimony of Uranius, embraced the region of Obodas, were Ismaelites, having obtained that name from Nabaioth, the first-born son of Ismael. Josephus adds, that Obodas having departed this life, Aretas, by the favour of Augustus, annexed his kingdom to his own. If any one being much struck with such a coincidence and congruity, shall think that the Holy Spirit applied this name Abaddon designedly, that by a certain paranomasia of the royal name he might point out that nation whose custom it was to designate their kings, and even their gods, by a similar appellation, I should think him deserving pardon, especially since both words seem to come from the same root, common to the Hebrews and Arabians, although, as is also the case in other instances, with a contrary signification, and since in the ancient prophets, examples of allusions, not altogether dissimilar, sometimes occur. Thus as Isaiah had called Christ in רצנ, that is, a branch, St. Matthew transfers to Jesus the name of Nazarene, c. ii. ver. ult. You may see likewise Jerem. c. i. v. 11, 12. Schaked, an almond; Schoked, I watch; Amos, c. viii. v. 2. Kajits, a basket of summer fruits, because it comes from Ketz, which means the end, &c. And that the Jews of the latter age were not averse to agnomina of such a kind, may be proved from this, that just before our Saviour's Advent, because Acheron, the river of the infernal regions, did not differ in sound from Accaron, a city of Palestine, (for so was Ekron anciently pronounced,) from Beelzebub, its god, they made a name of Satan, prince of that place, that is, of the infernal regions. For hence, as I conjecture, Beelzebub is called in the Gospel the Prince of the Demons.

The Second Woe Trumpet, or Trumpet the Sixth.

Another woe productive of plagues (which, lamentable to be reflected on, still broods over us), calls forth the tetrarchs of the Turks with a most numerous body of cavalry, from Euphrates, (where they had long rested) to invade the Roman world.

"Loose," says the voice from the four horns of the altar of incense, "the four angels who are bound upon the great river Euphrates." The angels are used for the nations over which they were thought to preside, by a metonymy not unusual in this book. It appears to be so from the circumstance that those who are loosed, immediately, according to the direction of the Oracle, are Equestrian armies, sent forth to slay men. It commands the angels who had been bound, to be loosed, as those who, during the continuance of the former plague, when they burst forth on the Roman regions, had been restrained to the Euphrates for so many ages, that they might not proceed at will. In the beginning, indeed, they advanced a little farther, even to Nice, in Bithynia; but Solyman being conquered in the expedition from Jerusalem by the Argonautic Christians, they were at length confined to the Euphrates. Moreover, the four angels signify so many sultanies, or kingdoms, into which the Turks were divided, when, after crossing the Euphrates, they poured themselves on the neighbouring tracts of Asia and Syria. These, Christopher Richer, from Scilex, a Greek author, thus enumerates:--The Asian, the Aleppian, the Damascene, and the Antiochian. The first of which, the Asian, or that of Asia Minor, owed its original to Cutlumusus, (called, if I am not mistaken, by Elmachinus, by another name, that of Sedijduddaula,) a neighbour of that Tangrophilix who first took Bagdad. He, on the same authority, when Cesarea in Cappadocia was taken and destroyed by the Romans, about the year of Christ, 1080, gave birth to the kingdom in the parts of Asia conterminous to the Euphrates; the bounds of which, his successor, Solyman, enlarged to Nice in Bithynia; but being, conquered by our forces in that well-known expedition from Jerusalem, he was compelled to give up the whole region which he had acquired, and to retreat to the Euphrates. And the seat of this tetrarchy, though elsewhere in the beginning, was still, as to its principal part, in the same Cappadocia of Iconium.

The second tetrarchy was the Aleppian, from its metropolis Aleppo, which is washed by a branch of the Euphrates, and therefore derived from one of the sultans. Its first king (on the authority of Elmachinus) Sjarfuddamlas, who was possessed of Aleppo in the year 1079; to whom succeeded Roduwan Salghucides, in 1095.

The third tetrarchy, with its metropolis Damascus, had for its founder, on the same authority, Tagjuddaulas Nisus, the grandson of Togrulbec, or Tangrophilix, who subjugated Damascus in the same year 1079. His successor was Ducathes, or Decacus, the brother of Rochewan, the sultan of Aleppo, in the year 1095. To whom, says Scilix, the whole region of Decapolis was subject. This bordered on the Euphrates. With these Scilix numbers the fourth, the Antiochian, contained within narrow bounds. For, says he, the caliph of Egypt, of the Saracenic race, possessed Laodicea, even to the regions of Syria. But as that kingdom of Antioch was not only a little too remote from the Euphrates, but lasted only fourteen years, Antioch being taken by our people under their leader, Bohemond, it will be better, perhaps, having expunged that, to add the Bagdadian, or Persian empire, from the other bank of the Euphrates, (for Scilix only took account of the Turks who had passed the Euphrates,) in order to complete the quaternion, that so the whole Turkish empire, both

Joseph Mede

beyond and on this side of that river, should he understood as divided into those four sultanies, which with the series for some time of kings and sultans, may be contemplated by the reader more distinctly in the following

DIAGRAM

Of the Turkish Empire, near the Euphrates, divided into Four Parts, from the year 1080, and thenceforward, taken out of Elmachinus, an Arab, and Scilix, a Greek Author.

Beyond On this side the Euphrates. Bagdad Togrulbec Olbarsalanus Cæarea in Cappadocia, and Iconium in Asia Minor Aleppo Damascus Ghelaluddaulas, Barkyaruccus Muhamedus Mahmudus began hisreign 1117, &c. Sedijduddaulas

Cognomine Cutlumusus Solimannus Tanismanius Masutus Calisastlanus, &c. Sjarfuddulus Roduwanus Tagjuddaulas,

Fil. Bulgarus began his reign 1117 Tagjuddaulas Decacus Abalacus, who was alive in 1115 * * * * * * * * * * Sanguinus Noradinus, &c.

And that was the state of the Turkish affairs when they had first passed the Euphrates; and having given a specimen of their irruption into the Roman dominions, were restrained by the appointed chains to the Euphrates. However, that quaternion of sultanies did not remain entire to the time of relaxation, but underwent several vicissitudes. Notwithstanding, the Holy Spirit estimates the nation from the state of its first irruption, in which, when they had passed the Euphrates, they were bound for an appointed time.

"And the four angels were loosed which were prepared for an hour, and a day, and a month, and a year, that they might kill a third part of men."

This loosing of the Turks happened a little before the year 1300, the caliphate of Bagdad (with which the first woe wholly expired) being now extinguished by the Tartars in the year 1258, and the remnant of the Turks, who had been possessed of the realms from the other bank of the river, even to Persis, being ejected by the same people, as from a sling, in the year 1289, on the Roman countries on this side the Euphrates. For, things being thus prepared, it happened likewise, at the same time, that the Latins, who had now, for almost two hundred years, imposed curbs and fetters on the first irruption of the Turks, were expelled from Syria and Palestine, about the year 1291. In the mean time the Turks, though as yet divided into various satrapies, began to make incursions into almost the whole of Asia Minor, to divide it among themselves, to be possessed by hereditary right, and at length, uniting under the empire of Othman alone, to advance astonishingly, and wholly without restraint, to pass over into Europe; nor could they longer be resisted by any force, until they had destroyed the whole Constantinopolitan empire with miserable devastations. But the Oracle (unless I am deceived) points out the time of this Constantinopolitan destruction, namely, that it should be after a day, a month, and a year; that is, 396 years after the Turks, by the gift of the Saracenic empire to them, had began to be prepared by God; that is, from the time of Bagdad being captured by them.

This was the beginning of the Turkish irruption, by which the Saracenic empire began to be demolished, and the dominion of the Romans to be afflicted; in such a manner, however, that the force of the mischief was to be restrained to the time prescribed for the relaxation. The interval of time certainly agrees exactly; for Elmachinus, the Arabian historian whom I have so often quoted,--than whom, no one marks the successive periods of time more accurately,--relates that Togrulbec Saglucides, the prince of the Turks, (who is called by our writers Tangrolipix, of the Zelzucian family,) having taken the rout of Bagdad, was invested by the caliph Cajim Biamrilla with the imperial garment, and was inaugurated into the kingdom in the year of the Hegira 449, that is, of Christ 1057. "Then," says he, "was the empire confirmed to him."

From this time, then, the stronghold of the Saracenic empire being given to them with the whole Trans-Euphratean dominion, the Turks were prepared, that after a prophetic day, and a month, and a year, they should kill a third part of men; that is, in the year of Christ 1453, they should utterly destroy the remnant of the Roman empire in the East, by the capture of the royal city of Constantinople. For the interval from 1057 to the year 1453, when Constantinople was taken, is precisely 396 years, of which a day forms one, a month thirty, and a year three hundred and sixty-five. Such is here the accuracy of the calculation, that any one may easily be led to suspect the hour likewise, (which, according to the mode of reckoning the other parts of time, would produce fifteen days, would equally correspond with the event, if the month of the inauguration of Togrulbey was handed down to us as well as the year. In the mean time, till that be established, the hour may here be taken for a seasonable time, and the conjunction καὶ may be explained exegetically, as if they were prepared against a seasonable time, namely, for a day, a month, and a year, that they might kill a third part of men.

How many years should thence run on to the destruction of the Turkish dominion, is no where explained; only it is said that it should be about the end of the times of the beast; that is, that the second woe should then be on the point of concluding, when the third woe should threaten the abolition of the kingdom of the beast, c. xi. v. 14, 15.

But, before I quit this subject, I will, not unwillingly, confess, that if the exact correspondence of the prophecy with the event did not, as it were, force conviction upon me, another interpretation of the following kind would have been by no means unpleasing,--that those angels were prepared and appointed for every occasion, whether it were for an hour, or a day, or a month, or even for a year, for performing the work of which there was need. But whether it is likely that so accurate an answer as to time, as the event here exhibits, could have happened by chance, let others judge. It will be for him to form an opinion with whom there is a doubt.

The next point is of the quality and number of the forces. "And the number, (says he,) of the army of horsemen was two myriads of myriads," i. e. two hundred thousand, or two hundred million. He names the horsemen, and not any other kind of force, in the whole description of the plague, as if this enemy from the Euphrates was wholly composed of cavalry. Is it because, in the Turkish army, the cavalry so far exceeds the infantry, that the latter, in comparison with the former, is of no consequence? Yes, (and that, I believe, was principally regarded by the Holy Spirit,) because this is the character of the nation Magog, long ago, consecrated by Ezekiel, from which the Turks were descended. For thus, in that most celebrated prophecy of Gog, which was a common name of the kings of Magog [32], as Pharaoh of the Egyptians, he describes that nation from its equestrian army, c. xxxviii. v. 4. "And I will bring thee forth and all thy army, horse and horsemen, all clothed with breast-plates." Again, v. 15. "And thou shalt come from thy place, from the sides of the North, thou, and many people with thee, all riding on horses," &c. Moreover, Gog himself is called the chief Prince of Mesech, and Tubal; that is, he, who, coming forth from his bounds, ruled in both the Armenias, on this, and on the farther side of the Euphrates. Here, in the name of the hither Armenia, I comprehend the Cappadocians, anciently denominated Meschini, or Moschi, where both the chief town Mazacha, afterwards called Cesarea, and the Moschic mountains in the same tract, are no obscure marks of the inhabitants being sprung from Mesech.

The farther, or greater Armenia, is what is called at this day Turcomania, from the inhabitation of the Turks; in which was formerly the city Thelbalana, the Tibaunian and Balbitenian people, the river Teleboas, and other vestiges of the name of Tubal. The war, however, which Ezekiel relates, is not to be understood of that undertaken in this irruption of the Turks, which John describes, (this he seems only to allude to,) but of another, the last after the return of the Jews; and, if it be lawful to conjecture, when the power which now occupies the country shall have first in some degree receded from it.

But on the type of cavalry, there is something else I would add with the leave of the reader, provided no one will think me too much given to the play of names and etymologies. Even solid and well-cooked food is apt to be more palatable with sauce. Let not the reader, then, be disgusted, if I subjoin something of this kind. The Turks, in truth, before they were set loose, had become, by long inhabitation, Persians, and were every where called by that name in the Byzantine historians. Nicetas, certainly, who embraces in his history the greatest part of the time when they were restrained to the Euphrates, almost always calls them Persians,--very rarely, Turks. But the Persians, you will observe, are horsemen, even from the very sound, since סרפ Paras, by which name Persia is called in the sacred books, (and Parthia is the same, only with another pronunciation,) signifies in the three Oriental languages, the Hebrew, the Chaldee, and the Arabian, a horse or horseman. For this reason, then, the Turco Persians are called the Euphratean horsemen, that is, the inhabitants on the Euphrates, are called by the national name of horsemen. Nor does there appear to be wanting (if any one should object to the irrelevancy of this) an example in Daniel, c. viii., where the Macedonians, who at that time were called Egeades, (that is, goats,) are designated under the type of goats, and their king under the figure of a he-goat. "Behold," says he, "a male of the goats, came from the west," &c. He means Alexander the Great, the king of the Egeades. They are the Macedonians. For so that nation was called, when the first seat of the kingdom was established, from Caranus the founder, two hundred years, more or less, before the time of Daniel. Justin the epitomizer, of Thogus, relates the cause of the name, whose words I shall not think it troublesome to subjoin. "Caranus," says he, "with a great multitude of the Greeks, being commanded by the answer of the oracle to seek for habitations in Macedonia, when he came into Æmathia, occupied the city Edessa, having followed a herd of goats, flying from the rain, the inhabitants not being aware of it, in consequence of the heavy cloud and rain, and recalling the oracle to mind, by which he had been ordered to seek for empire under the guidance of goats, he made it the seat of his kingdom, and afterwards made it a religious observance, wherever his troops moved, to have the same goats before his standards, esteeming them who had been the authors and founders of his kingdom, as the leaders of his undertakings. He called the city Edessa, in memory of the benefit received, Ægeas, and the people Ægeades." Vide cetera.

There is such an agreement here, that one might be tempted to suspect the type of a ram in the same vision, applied to the king of the Persians, alludes to the signification of the name Elam, one of the two by which that nation is called. For ליא in the Hebrew, (whence the name ליא Aries, ram,) and סלא and סלע in the Chaldee, signify the same; namely, strong or robust. Perhaps, therefore, סליע Elam had the same sound as ליא ram to these, and thence the king of Elam is described under this type by Daniel. However it be, when the thing itself is otherwise confirmed, this agreement of names with the type cannot help being matter of pious delight to those who are studious of these matters, whether it be believed to have happened from accident or otherwise. And this by the way.

Now I return again to the Euphratean horse, "whose number," says he, "was two myriads of myriads." Others read myriads of myriads, expunging the two, as c. v. v. 11. It signifies an immense multitude, as Psalm lxviii. "The chariots of God are two myriads,'"--twenty thousand. For a myriad אובר or רְבָבָה is one of those words of number, which in Hebrew are words to be indefinitely taken, as among the Latins six hundred, and does not denote the number ten thousand, but some great number, especially when thus doubled, as may be seen in Daniel, c. vii. v. 10. But how great and how immense the forces of the Turks were in their expeditions, and usually are at this day, must be unknown to no one.

"And I heard," he adds, "their number." Since it might be asked whence John was acquainted with the number, as what was not possible to be represented to him in a vision, he says, "I heard." The like is to be understood likewise in other visions, as often as any thing is related which could not be exhibited to sight; namely, that the apostle was informed by a voice.

The next subject is the armour. "And thus I saw the horses in appearance, and those who sat on them, having breast-plates of fire, and hyacinth, and sulphur, and the heads of the horses were as the heads of lions, and out of their mouths proceeded fire, and smoke, and sulphur. By these three were killed the third part of men."

No where in any part of the prophets, or elsewhere in the sacred writings, occurs an image of this kind, "of fire and hyacinthine smoke and sulphur." Where I understand it literally of that new (and previous to this trumpet) unheard of arms, which those Euphratean enemies made use of, immediately after they had been set loose. I understand it of cannon, vomiting fire, smoke, and sulphur. For gunpowder is ignivomous, with hyacinthine smoke, and sulphureous matter, which those who use in war, obtrude themselves on the senses of their enemies, as covered with breast-plates of fire, hyacinth, and sulphur, from a medium involved in fire, smoke, and the smell of sulphur; on which account the horses' heads are seen to be of a fierce and terrible appearance, like those of lions. Hence John says, that he saw the horses and horsemen, not really, but in appearance, such as he describes. In appearance, I say, ἐν ὁράσει not in reality, having breast-plates of fire, hyacinth, and sulphur; in appearance, having heads like lions; lastly, in appearance, not in reality, out of the mouths of the horses proceed fire, and smoke, and sulphur; since it is wont to appear so to those who behold it on the opposite side. This is the force of the expression ἐν ὁράσει, in semblance, which is used twice in this sense in the fourth chapter, v. 3, "He was in appearance like a jasper stone"--and "a rainbow in appearance, like an emerald." No where else, except once only, does that word appear in the New Testament. By this triple plague of fire-arms, namely, "of fire, smoke, and sulphur," he adds, "were the third part of men killed;" that is, those who were of that trient, or third part, which we called the Roman world. For it is not necessary here, or elsewhere, where a third is mentioned, to understand the whole of that third, but to take it partitively. Examples of which kind of ellipse of the partitive words occur elsewhere in the Scriptures, as well as in this book; as Jud. c. xii. v. 7, "Jephthah was buried in the cities of Gilead;" that is, in one of the cities. And Apo. c. xviii. v. 16, "The ten horns hate the harlot;" that is, some of them. So, τὸ τρίτον, "the third part of men were killed," implies those of that third part.

Who does not know that this was abundantly fulfilled in the destruction of Constantinople? Was not that most illustrious city, the chief of the third part of men, besieged with those fire-breathing machines, and given up to slaughter? Listen to Chalcocondylas! "Mechmet," says he, "in the expedition against Byzantium, ordered the largest cannon to be made, of a size which at that time we had never known to have existed. He dispersed them every where through the camp, that they might throw their balls against the Greeks. One of which was of such magnitude, that it was drawn by seventy yoke of oxen and two thousand men. To this, two others of the largest size were attached, on either side, each of which sent forth a stone, whose weight was equal to half a talent. After these, came that wonderful mortar which threw a ball whose weight amounted to three talents, and threw down great part of the wall. Whose thundering explosion is reported to have been so great that the neighbouring region was shaken to the distance of forty stadia; that is, five miles. This piece of artillery sometimes sent forth seven balls; one by night, which was a signal for the coming day, and indicated to what point in that day the balls would be directed." He who desires to know more, and how, even in the maritime siege, cannon were made use of, and how the walls, after being for forty days stoutly battered by cannon, fell at length; and how Longus, duke of Genoa, with his people, assailed by cannon balls, deserted the place, and opened a way into the city for the Turks, let him resort to Chalcocondylas himself. From the same author, moreover, he will learn that the Peloponnesian Isthmus, having been attacked by Amurath, the father of Mechmet, with the same arms, and the inhabitants compelled to obey his commands, were entirely subjugated by Mechmet himself, Corinth having been attacked likewise with a force of fire-arms, immediately after the capture of Constantinople.

To this account of their arms, is added something about the nature of the horses and their riders. That "their power was not in their mouths" only, (of which we have hitherto treated,) but "in their tails; for they have tails like serpents, having heads with which they hurt." That is, the same as was said above, concerning the Saracens, holds true likewise of the Turks; that they effected mischief, not only by hostile force, but likewise by the train of the Mohammedan imposture, wherever they proceeded. These, therefore, not less than the Saracenic locusts, (whose religion they adopted,) are serpents in their tail. That one kind of serpentine tail may be attributed to the latter, and another to the former, arises from the natural shape of each, and the difference between locusts and horses, by which the pointed tail of scorpions is most suitable to the former, and tails with serpents' heads best adapted to the latter. But "the rest of the men who were not killed by these plagues, yet repented not of the works of their hands, that they should not worship demons, and idols of gold, and silver, and brass, and stone, and wood, which can neither see, nor hear, nor walk," &c.

Now who these are, it will not be difficult to collect; since in the whole Roman world, or on this side the Euphrates, there are none which worship images, with shame and sorrow be it spoken! besides Christians. Does it not necessarily follow, then, that it is they who worship demons also? since the worship of both is ascribed to the same persons in this place. But what in fine you will say, are demons? Not, in truth, what they themselves hold to be impure spirits, and often call them so, (for what Christian would knowingly and willingly worship them?) but what were understood under this name by the theologians of the Gentiles--deities, consecrated under the names either of angels or dead men. "Every demon," says Plato, "is a being between God and mortals." Again, "God holds not communication with man, but through a demon in every conference:" In Symposis, intercourse carried on between the gods and men. The other Platonic philosophers, and most of the various sects, except the Epicureans, held the same. I will quote the words of Apulcius only, in which the opinion of Plato, and the rest, is fully and perspicuously contained: "Demons," says he, "are middle powers, through whom both our desires and merits pass to the gods. They are carriers between mortals and the heavenly inhabitants, from hence of prayers, from thence of gifts; who bear to and fro from hence petitions, and from thence supplies; or, indeed, they are interpreters and ushers on either side. For it would not," says he, "be suitable to the majesty of the celestial gods, to attend to these things."

They had, in truth, two sorts of gods; the celestial, who, perpetually residing in heaven, and the stars, did not humble themselves to these earthly things, and were not to be defiled with their contagion. (These were properly and especially called gods.) The others were demons, who, as mediating powers, and ministers of the celestial or highest gods, had the management of human affairs. The former, (if I rightly conceive,) the Holy Scripture calls the host of heaven; the latter, (especially those who were made of dead men,) it calls Baalim, from Baal, a king of the Babylonians or Assyrians; or in the Chaldaic pronunciation, Bel, who was the first who was consecrated a demon after death by his people; from whence it came to pass afterwards, that powers of this kind were called Baalim or Baals, as Baal Peor, Baalberith, Baalzebub, Baal Moloch, Jer. c. xix., as from the first emperor Julius Cæsar, the rest of the Roman emperors were called Cæsars. Now how this theology of demons agrees with the worship of saints and angels among false Christians, the fact itself declares; only with this difference, that they had many supreme or celestial gods: we have only one, the Father of all. But we ought likewise to have only one Mediator, our Lord Jesus Christ, if false prophets had not introduced more in the nature of demons. Plainly, according to what St. Paul prophesied, 1 Tim. c. iv. vv. 1, 2, 3, "that it should come to pass, in the latter times through the hypocrisy of liars," inventing lying miracles, and through the feigned sanctity of monks abstaining by a vow from marriage and meats, that "the doctrine of demons," that is, the theology of heathen deities, should be brought back again into the world. The interpretation will agree with the words, if we take the genitive demons passively, that is, a doctrine concerning demons, as Heb. c. vi. v. 22, Διδαχὴ βαπτισμῶν, διδαχὴ ἐπιθεσέως χειρῶν, &c. The doctrine of baptisms, of laying on of hands, &c. For, in truth, the expression, "through the hypocrisy of liars," and the words that follow, in order that the construction of the syntax may be preserved, is to be explained by the government of the two substantives, the preposition εν through, denoting the instrument and cause (which is familiar in the Hebrew.) But I have treated more diffusively of this passage in a particular tract, and I have no intention to repeat it here.

Joseph Mede

THE PROCLAMATION

Of the Third Woe Trumpet, or Trumpet the Seventh

The vision of the sixth trumpet being finished, (for there is only one vision under one trumpet, as under the seals and phials,) the next place in order was due to the sounding of the seventh. This, however, is deferred, and the Holy Spirit, in the prophecy of the little book, to which he is now about to pass, in order that nothing might be wanting to the completion of the prophecy of the seals, now just finishing, supplies the place of that trumpet's sound which is deferred, by an oath, under which the effect of that trumpet is generally indicated. That it should surely come to pass, when that angel shall have sounded, that the Roman beast, in the latest times of the last head, having been accused, "the mystery of God should be finished, as he hath declared to his servants the prophets." For so it was predicted long ago to Daniel, that the fourth beast being slain, the, King of the Saints should come to rule over the whole world, (c. vii.) and at the same time, the glorious promise of the restitution of Israel should be completed, (c. xii.) For that this is the kingdom which he calls the fulfilment of the mystery of God, the acclamation subjoined to the sound of that trumpet will not suffer us to doubt. "The kingdoms of this world are become the kingdoms of our Lord and of his Christ, and he shall reign for ever and ever." So that it is wonderful that any persons should be found who understand it in a different sense. The time, of which the angel here swears, that nothing should extend beyond it, can be no other than either the time of the fourth monarchy universally, (or to come more closely to the point, though it is the same thing,) of the last kingdom, that is, the Roman; the last period "of time, and times, and half a time." Since the same which is said by John to come to pass "when time shall be no more; is pointed out by Daniel to come. to pass when the period of the last times shall be finished.

And this consummation of the mystery of God, is the subject matter of the seventh trumpet; to which seven thunders are added as accompaniments, for they are not the very subject which the trumpet exhibits as contemporary with it.

While the angel is making his proclamation about the mystery of the trumpet, seven thunders utter their voices. "He cried," says he, "with a loud voice, as when a lion roareth, and when he cried, seven thunders uttered their voices." That is, when he had begun his proclamation, seven thunders began to speak. And they cannot but contemporize with the seventh trumpet, since what follows the sixth trumpet necessarily falls within the seventh [33] . But what is the voice of thunder? Is it not Bath Kol? If so, the seven thunders will be as many oracles by which the period of the seventh trumpet will be distinguished as by certain dates, but on a subject wholly unknown, and not to be understood until its own times. And this the prohibition given from heaven to St. John, when he was about to write down the words of the seven thunders, seems to intimate: "Seal up those things which the seven thunders have spoken, and write them not." In vain, therefore, will it be for us to inquire, what God wished to have concealed and reserved to its own times. And in this manner sufficient use is made of the seventh trumpet in its place and order, though the explanation of its sound, by which the whole mystery would be fully disclosed, is referred to another time; on the design of which reference, and the whole art of the contrivance, it will not be superfluous or unprofitable to dwell afresh and a little more diffusively, though notice was taken of it in the Apocalyptical Key, since the reason of it escapes most of the interpreters. The diligent contemplation of the system of the Apocalyptical visions, constructed on the characters of the synchronisms, first enlightened me on this subject, and will also, Ω Reader, if I am not deceived, enlighten you.

The fact then is, (for I would unfold it with as much perspicuity and brevity of expression as possible,) both prophecies, as well that of the seals, as of the Biblaridion, are concluded by the same issue of events, by that in truth, which the seventh trumpet exhibits. To indicate which, the Holy Spirit having slightly, but as much as was necessary, there presignified the mystery of the seventh trumpet in its own place, in the series of trumpets, deferred the fuller explanation of its sound, until he had made a transition to the new prophecy of the little book, (ch. x. from v. 8 to the end.) and carried forward the first vision of it, having completed in like manner its Apocalyptical course to the same issue of things, (c. xi. v. 14.) and then that mystery of the seventh trumpet, the common catastrophe of both prophecies, and the former (that of the seals) only promulgated in a general manner, is here at length, on the uttering of the sound, fully unfolded; and that, indeed, in a most commodious manner, since otherwise, and without the previous knowledge of both prophecies, what depended upon each could not have been understood. And hence it is, that the business of this transition was not brought about by any angel of the trumpets, but by that great and illustrious angel who held in his hand the Biblaridion, the symbol of the second prophecy, which was soon to be devoured by St. John.

It belonged to him who revealed the second prophecy, that the manifestation of the trumpets' sound, which contained the catastrophe of both prophecies, should be so far defined. Nay, if that angel, as may seem capable of being collected from his more august clothing and whole apparatus, was Christ the Lord [34]; to no one more properly belonged this right of suspending the last sound for the sake of another prophecy, than to Him who was the author of both.--Hitherto, indeed, he had appeared in the form of a lamb, but now he seems to have taken to him the person of an angel [35], since he was about to reveal to John the same mystery of consummation, which he had formerly revealed to Daniel under the same appearance of an angel [36], and with the same formality and words of an oath. You may compare Dan. c. xii. v. 6, 7, with ver. 5 of the xth chapter.

Footnotes:

16. Mentz, or Mayence.
17. People about Worms, in the Palatinate.
18. Rheims.
19. Artois.
20. Bretons.
21. Inhabitants of Tournay.
22. Near Spire.
23. Argentina Strasburgh.
24. Tholouse.
25. From Augustulus to Charlemagne.
26. The king of Babylon is likened to the morning star, as ruler in the East. This may be considered as the evening star, the emblem of the Emperor of the West.---R. B. C.
27. That is, there is no word spoken by God in prophecy, but what shall surely come to pass.
28. The Sept. has καλέσεις, you shall call.
29. In our version grasshoppers.
30. Anatolia from Ἀνατολή.
31. Mede means to say, they were not monks.--R. R. C.
32. Gog, among the Turks, is at this day called Gioc or Kioc, whence Kioccan; Ciogelp, which is Gugelp.
33. May there not be an interval?--R. B. C.
34. I doubt it, for reasons to be afterwards assigned.--R. B. C.
35. Query?
36. Query?

Joseph Mede

THE INTERPRETATION

Of the Little Book, or, of the other System of Apocalyptical Visions, according to the Rule of the Apocalyptical Key

The course of the seals being finished, in which the affairs of the empire were described, we come now to the other prophecy, much more noble in its kind, as containing the Fates of the Church, or of Religion. John is introduced to it by the delivery and eating up of the open book, being endued as it were with a degree of the prophetic faculty. "And the voice (says he) which I had heard from heaven, spake again unto me saying," (viz. that voice, as of a trumpet, talking with him, ch. iv.) "and said, Go, take the little book which is open in the hand of the angel, standing upon the sea, and upon the earth; and I went to the angel, saying unto him, Give me the little book. And he said unto me, Take and eat it up," &c. Moreover, as the prophecy now to be revealed, as the knowledge of Divine things and secrets, especially those to come, usually is, was to be sweet and pleasant in its foretaste; but, on account of the calamitous state of the Church, or perhaps, of the obscurity of those allegories and types with which it was covered, it would, like aloes taken into the stomach, greatly wound the mind of him who should unfold and penetrate into its sense. Therefore it is said, that the book to be eaten by the apostle would indeed be sweet in the mouth,--that is, in first appearance and first flavour, delightful to the mind,--but when received into the stomach and digested, would bring on bitterness. "And it shall," says he, "render thy belly bitter, but in thy mouth it shall be sweet as honey." The whole image is taken from Ezekiel, except that, though there is mention of sweetness in the mouth, yet there is no reference, or but an obscure one, to bitterness in the belly.

The book, being thus taken and swallowed, the meaning of the symbol is explained in the clearest and most express words; namely, that on St. John was imposed the gift of another and still more noble prophecy, which should retrace the path of the former, to be received from Christ, and to be brought to the knowledge of the Church. "And I took," says he, "the little book from the hands of the angel, and ate it up, and it was in my mouth sweet as honey, but when I had eaten it, my stomach was embittered."--"And he said unto me;" (this is the meaning of the symbol,) "Thou must prophesy again before many peoples, and nations, and tongues, and kings [37]."

Such was the inauguration of St. John. Then follows the prophecy, which begins with an act of his, relative to the temple of God. And therefore, by the image of a double court, one measured, and the other rejected on account of the profanation of the Gentiles, demonstrates that there would be in order a double state of the Church.

THE MEANING

Of the Interior Court measured by the Reed of God

The inner court of the temple, with those who worship therein, to be measured by the Divine reed, denotes the primeval state of the Church, examined, and accurately proved to be holy, according to the rule of the Divine word.--Not yet in truth, as it was afterwards, (when we arrive at the times of the outer court,) varying from measure, without symmetry, from the contagion of idolatrous worship, but serving God for some ages, regularly, through one only Mediator, Jesus Christ.

For it appears to me that a measure of this kind was intended, even under the type of the angelical dimension in Ezekiel; because it is said to him, c. xliii. from v. 7 to 10, and in the following verses, "But thou, Ω son of man, show the temple to the house of Israel, that they may be ashamed for their iniquities, and let them measure the pattern." See the passage. But if any one should think differently, and had rather refer the type of dimension to the signification of building, as what is displayed in architectural engravings, or graphically, may be the measurement by God, according to the prophets, that will still correspond to the same sense. For what then will this court denote, measured by the Divine reed, but the state of the Church so represented to be the workmanship of God, built on the foundation of the apostles and prophets, Christ himself being the chief corner-stone? opposed to the following court, which God did not acknowledge for his

A Key to the Apocalypse
building, and therefore John is prohibited from measuring. Whether you interpret it in the latter or the former manner, the substance, as you see, will be the same. But he that shall interpret it in a different sense, unless I am mistaken, can bring no example of his interpretation from Scripture.

How appositely indeed the situation of the altar in this court may adumbrate the frequent sacrifices of martyrs, under that state of the Church, will appear, both from the circumstance itself, and from the contemporary vision of the red dragon fighting with Michael for the offspring of the woman, when we come to the interpretation thereof.

Of the Outer Court with the Holy City trodden under foot by the Gentiles, and on that account to be omitted and rejected from measurement

The outer court trodden under foot by the nations, and rejected from the divine measurement, designates the holy city of God, or the Christian Church, soon after the end of the times of the regular court, (to which it immediately succeeds) to be given up to new idolatries, and its affairs having been confirmed by the entire demolition of the Gentile worship under the first court, it was now to be profaned by the contagion of renewed idolatry, as of revived ethnicism; in one word, the anti-christian apostasy which was to flourish in the Church for forty-two months of years [38]. Concerning which, in the history of the Beast, in a vision of a like nature contemporizing with this court, we shall fully and particularly treat.

But let us consider the words of the text in the interpretation of which we are now engaged. "And there was given me, says he, a reed like a rod; and the angel stood, saying, Arise, and measure the temple of God, and the altar, and those that worship therein. But the court, which is without the temple, leave out, and do not measure it, for it is given up to the Gentiles, and the holy city shall they tread under foot forty-two months."

In order that we may rightly understand the meaning of these words, it is to be understood that TO ἹΕΡΟΝ (by which name I embrace the whole edifice of the temple,) was distinguished by a double court, the one interior, in which the Nah, or temple itself, together with the altar of burnt-offering before its doors was situated, and was open to the Priests and Levites only; the other exterior, which is called (2 Chron. c. iv. v. 9.) the great court, and by Ezekiel, more than twelve times, the court without, or the outer court. This was the court of the Israelites, or of the Israelitish people, and therefore not improperly called the court of Israel, though that part belonging to the men, was more especially called so by the Jews. The first court was known by the names of the temple and the altar of sacrifice. "Rise, said he, and measure the temple of God (Ναὸν) and the altar of sacrifice." Where the Θυσιαστήριον does not mean the altar of burnt-offerings only which was there situated, but the space which surrounded it, that is, the whole space of the altar and sacrifice; as is to be collected from the words immediately connected with it, "and those who worship therein;" that is, in the place of sacrifice. How, likewise, Θυσιαστήριον is taken c. xiv. v. 18, and c. xvi. v. 7, vide Beza. Whence the old lexicon in Greek and Latin interprets Θυσιαστήριον altarium, sacrarium, altar, sacred place, and vice versâ, the glossary of Philoxenus, sacrarium Ἡρῶον Θυσιαστήριον. Temple of a hero, place of the altar. But this Θυσιαστήριον, together with the area of the temple (i. e. τοῦ Ναοῦ) I learn to be rightly comprehended within the name of the interior court, from the description of the tabernacle, where, in like manner, the whole enclosure which surrounded the dwelling-place, and altar of burnt-offering is reckoned under the denomination of one court, as appears Ex. c. xl. v. 33. So much of the first court which John is ordered to measure; but the latter court is designated clearly enough by its name--"The court which is without the temple, that is, by an ellipsis of the former substantive,--the court which is exterior to the enclosure of the temple and altar, and since the Gentiles admitted without right and justice were stabled in this, it is ordered by no means to be measured, but to be cast forth, and considered as profane. But you will say, it is not the outer court, but the holy city which is to be trodden down by the Gentiles. I answer, that the outer court and the holy city mutually explain each other, since the outer court was the place for the holy city or people of Israel to meet in for divine purposes: Nay, in the wilderness, the tabernacle having only one court, (which it was not lawful to enter ordinarily, unless for the Priests and Levites), there was no outer court, beside the camp of Israel, or the holy city. Therefore the sense is the same as if it were said, "The court which is without the temple cast out, and do not measure it, for it is given up to the Gentiles, and they shall tread it under forty-two months. For the relative it, a substantive is substituted, and that of the same kind, so as to point out the subject intended by the antecedent. "The holy city, says he, shall they tread under forty-two months." The change of the substantive for the relative often occurs both in this book and elsewhere, namely, when either the substantive which precedes, is repeated in the place of the relative, or its synonyme is substituted instead of the relative. An example of the latter kind you have here, and Acts c. xxv. v. 21. And indeed what else shall we say could be given to the Gentiles to have the power of occupying, so as to trample under foot? And what could the Gentiles trample on, but that which was given them? so that these words, not less than the court and holy city, seem mutually to explain one another.

Footnote:

37. By those words, "Thou must prophesy again," (by which the type of the eaten book is explained,) it is intimated that the following system of visions goes over again the Apocalyptical time from the very beginning. But if any vision of that prophetic system is to be sought for from the commencement of the period or Apocalyptical time, it is certainly agreeable to reason, that the first vision of the system should challenge the foremost place, both because it is first, and because it is the sum and compendium of all that follow.

38. There is an allusion to the profanation of Antiochus, which is described Ps. lxxix. Vide 1 Macc. c. vii. v. 17, and Ps. lxxix. 1, 2, 3. "Ω God! the heathen are come into thine inheritance, and made Jerusalem a heap of stones," &c.

THE ICHNOGRAPHY

Of the Holy Place, that is, of the Temple, and its Courts
Figure of the Temple
AAAA The Inner Court.
γ δ The Altar of Burnt-Offering BBBB The Outer Court. α β The Temple.
Aγ Aδ The Place of Offering Sacrifice. The Θυσιαστήριον. a The Holy of Holies. β The Holy Place.

To these two courts, (of which only, and not of more, the Scripture makes mention,) a third was added in after ages, namely, in the temple of Herod; with another wall built in the circumference of the temple, which was called that of the Gentiles and unclean persons; but this was not accounted sacred, nay more, on the columns erected, there was inscribed in Greek and Latin letters, "Let no stranger of another tribe pass through into the holy place." Josephus de Bello Judaico, 1-6. cvi. Greek 18.

THE MYSTERY

Of the Two Witnesses prophesying in Sackcloth

Two witnesses or prophets sent by God, clothed in sackcloth, are to preach, while the Gentiles are treading under foot the court of the people of God, or the holy city. These are the interpreters and assertors of Divine truth, who should deplore that foul and lamentable contamination of the Church of Christ, by continual complaints, and whom God would raise up as unceasing monitors to the Christian world, committing whoredom with the Gentiles, and as guides to his saints preserving the faith. After the example of those illustrious pairs, under the Old Testament, Moses and Aaron in the Wilderness, Elijah and Elisha under the Baalitical apostasy, Zorobabel and Jeshua under the Babylonian captivity. From their number, condition, power and actions, these Apocalyptical witnesses seem to be manifestly described, as likewise the state of the church in which they prophesied, agreeably with that of Israel, under the images of Babylon, the Wilderness and Gentilism, or Baalism. Let the reader examine with his own eyes what I have said of the description of the witnesses in the following table:

Moses and Aaron. Elias and Elisha. Zorobabe1 & Jeshua

"Having power over the waters, to turn them into blood. and to smite the earth with every plague."

"Having power to shut heaven, that it should not rain."

"These are the two olive-trees, and two candlesticks, which stand before the Lord of the earth."

"Whoever would hurt them, fire proceedeth out of their mouth, and devoureth their adversaries." Numbers xvi. 2 Kings i. Zech. iv.

Now let us come to the text. "And I will give power, (says he,) to my two witnesses, and they shall prophesy 1260 days, clothed in sackcloth." Where it is first to be remarked, that the whole prophecy which follows, from this comma to the sounding of the seventh trumpet, as the nature of the subject demands, was not exhibited to sight in a vision, but dictated to John by the angel sustaining the person of Christ, the observation of which renders the genius of the allegory or type much more easy to be perceived. "To my two witnesses." He calls them two with reference to the type, which is, as I have observed, of pairs; as if he had said I will give to my Zorobabel, and Jeshua, to my Elijah and Elisha, to my Moses and Aaron:--To which is to be added, that he calls them witnesses: Now witnesses by the law ought to be two, to establish every word. Add that they may be called two on account of the number of the tables of God, which the witnesses of the Old and New Testament, as of two Testaments, might apply in their prophecy [39].

"That they should prophesy clothed in sackcloth," that is, by woefully lamenting the trampling down of the Holy City, in consequence of the introduction of Gentile worship, by affording testimony to the truth of God, and by exhorting to repentance, "For 1260 days"--which indeed Are contained in forty-two months, and these it is plain are not days of hours; both from those three days and a half, part of those days a little after, assigned to the death of the witnesses, and which the things predicted to be done in them, prove, cannot be taken for days of hours; and because the beast (whose duration is the same), is contemporary with the company of 144,000 sealed: the company of the sealed is contemporary with the six first trumpets, and the affairs of the trumpets cannot possibly be run through in so very short a time as 1260 horary days, or three years and a half. But why, you will say, should the profanation of the Gentiles be measured by months, and the prophecy of the witnesses asserting the pure worship of God in days? Namely, because the worship of idols and every sin and error is under the power of darkness and night, over which the moon presides; on the other hand, true religion may be compared to the light and the day, the presidency over which belongs to the sun. Therefore (Acts c. xxvi. v. 18.) the mission of Paul to convert the Gentiles from idols, is said to be, "to turn them from darkness to light, and from the power of Satan unto God." With the same meaning also it is said "what fellowship has light with darkness?" Now months are directed by the motion of the moon the queen of darkness, but days and years by that of the sun who presides over light. For the same cause, as we shall see hereafter, the blasphemy of the beast will be reckoned in like manner according to the motion of the moon, by months, but the residence of the woman in the wilderness by days and years with reference to the motion of the sun. "These are the two olive-trees and the two candlesticks, standing before the Lord of the earth." That is, they are like Zorobabel and Jeshua [40] whom the Lord anciently anointed over the Jewish church, ruined under the Babylonian captivity, at length to be restored and superintended by these witnesses in a similar manner, under the bondage of the Gentiles. For the allusion is to "those two olive-trees," which Zacharias saw growing on each side of the golden candlestick, and supplying oil to its lamps, (Zach. c. iv.) of which the angel being asked what they meant, "these, said he, are the two sons of oil, or the anointed ones, which stand before the Lord of the whole earth, pointing out the two heads of the church, then in subjection to the Gentiles.--Zorobabel, the general, and Jeshua, the high priest, of whom he had prophesied a little before. For the candle then with its seven lights, designated the temple, and by its type the church of that time, whose instauration and conservation, the two holy ones were to take charge of, not by force, not by strength, not by any human aid, but by the power of God alone, operating in a certain invisible and wonderful manner, as those olive-trees, standing on each side of the candlestick, supplied oil to its lights in a very extraordinary and imperceptible way. But why, you will say, is mention here made by John, not of one as in Zacharias, but of two candlesticks, to which likewise and not to the anointed ones, the two prophets seem to be compared? I confess that I am here at a stand, nor have I yet found a sufficiently prompt and clear reason for this difference. In the mean time I think there lurks a Hebraism in the words, and it is as if he had said:--These are the two olive-trees, at or near the two candlesticks, standing before the Lord of the earth; so that the comparison of the witnesses may be only with the olive-trees, but the addition of the candlesticks may be judged only to pertain to the description of those olive-trees. For the copulative in the Hebrew has sometimes the force of the preposition עם, that is, with, near by; as (1 Sam. c. xiv. v. 18.) "Because the ark of God was at that time, and the children of Israel;" e. with the children of Israel. Vide Lex. Schindleri. But there will still remain a difficulty about the two candlesticks. May it be said, that the one only in Zacharias may here be reckoned for a double candlestick on account of the double rank of lights on each side of the stem; and the two olive-trees pouring in oil secretly on each side? There is, likewise, in Zacharias the mention of seven and seven and twice seven infusers, but what the meaning is does not sufficiently appear. But may we not suppose that this duplicate alludes to the private designation of the Christian church? as being compounded of two people, of Jews and Gentiles; or what, perhaps, is nearer the truth, because, at the time, in which the witnesses clothed in sack-cloth, were uttering their lamentation, it was to be divided together with the Roman empire into that of the east and west.

However it may be, it is certain that the candlesticks signify not the prophets or presidents of the churches, but the churches themselves, because in chapter i. the angel interprets the seven candlesticks, as so many Churches. "The seven candlesticks, (says he,) which thou sawest, are the seven Churches. [41] "

"If any one wish to hurt them, fire proceedeth out of their mouth, and devoureth their enemies, and if any one wish to hurt them, so must he be killed." The witnesses do not revenge themselves by the sword or daggers, if they are ever injured by their enemies, but out of their mouth proceedeth the vengeance; that is, they transfix their enemies with the shafts of the Word; whilst they are denouncing the wrath of God impending over the violators of his ministers, or imploring vengeance with their prayers and groans. For the fire which is here reported as proceeding out of the mouth of the witnesses is the word of vengeance; agreeably to that saying of the Lord to Jeremiah (v. 15.). "Behold I will make my words in thy mouth fire, and this people wood, and it shall devour them." Moses, indeed, and Aaron, and afterwards Elijah, the former against the conspirators in the sedition of Korah, the latter against the ministers of Ahaziah the King, the worshipper of Baal, literally called down fire from heaven, but the fire of our witnesses is to be interpreted mystically, since by the instruction of the holy spirit, our Egypt, and consequently the wilderness, is to be understood spiritually. Moreover, what the prophets denounce in the name of God, they are said to execute, as what the Lord says to the same Jeremiah, (c. i. v. 10.) "I have set thee over the nations and kingdoms, to root out and to pull down, and to destroy, to build, and to plant." Let not any one now be surprised that fire or the divine vengeance is said to be poured out of the mouth of the witnesses, with whom however the only power is that of denouncing or imploring it from God. It is thus the witnesses revenge their own injuries. That which follows shows by what means also they revenge the reproach brought upon the temple of God.

"These have power to shut heaven that it rain not;" (viz. that mystical rain fall not) "in the days of their prophecy. That is, they are endued with the power of the keys, by which they can shut heaven on those new Gentiles, contaminators of the Christian worship, that the grace of Christ's blood, sealed to them by baptism may not distil upon them for the remission of sins, so long as they shall persevere in being the cause of the mournful prophecy of the witnesses by their idolatries and superstitions. I will speak more plainly. They expel by the word of God those new idolaters from the hope of eternal life promised to the pure worshippers of God alone; until, mindful of the stipulation in their baptism, and having rejected the services of Satan, they shall have returned to the worship of the one God, through the only Mediator Jesus Christ, and thus put an end to the mournful prophecy of the witnesses. In the same manner also, Elijah did not bring rain again upon the Israelites, when they were already almost half dead with drought, until the worship of Baal and his prophets were exterminated.

Of this power of the witnesses we have an example hereafter, (c. xiv. 9.) "If any one say they shall worship the beast and his image, and shall receive the mark on his forehead, or his hand, he shall drink of the wine of the wrath of God; of unmixed wine poured out into the cup of his indignation, and shall be tormented with fire and brimstone in the presence of the Lamb. And the smoke of their torment ascendeth up for ever and ever."

Lastly, "they have power over the waters, to convert them into blood, and to smite the earth with every plague as often as they will." Moses and Aaron exercised a power of this kind when they were about to conduct Israel out of Egyptian slavery. Whence I collect, that the power of the witnesses, represented by this type, does not refer to all the days of the prophecy in sackcloth, but to the end of them, or the time of the phials; when indeed, under the auspices of the witnesses or prophets, as of Moses and Aaron, the Christian people, by plagues described under the image of those of Egypt, are in like manner to be led forth out of the tyranny and slavery of the beast. For the first plague of the phials smites the earth with a sore; by the second and third, the waters are turned into blood; the rest afflict with other and heavier plagues the adherents of the beast, or the Gentiles abiding in the court of the temple. The interpretation of all which we reserve for the proper place. Here it may be sufficient to have referred this last power to the effusion of the phials.

"But when they are about to finish their testimony, the beast which ascendeth out of the abyss, shall make war upon them, and shall overcome them, and shall slay them."

We have hitherto treated of the office and power of the witnesses; the fate now follows which they shall experience at the end of their prophecy, the description of which is wholly taken from the history of our Lord's passion. For the Lord Jesus, in like manner, when he was finishing his preaching, which lasted about as many days as the prophecy of the witnesses, was killed by the Roman president, a legate of that beast, which warred with the witnesses, (but in the shape of its sixth head.) The third day after, when there was a great earthquake also, he rose again; and a little after, namely, on the fortieth day, being received up in a cloud, he ascended into heaven. All which things God wished to represent in this slaughter of the witnesses or prophets; that as in the nature of their office they had borne a resemblance, as was stated before, to those illustrious pairs; so in suffering and death they should become conformable to Christ their Lord, that faithful Witness; which ought to be their consolation and their glory in the midst of their troubles.

But let us throw light on the text. "When," says he, "they shall be finishing their testimony," (for so ὅταν τελέσωσι should be translated, not by the preterite, when they have finished,) "the beast who ascends out of the abyss, shall make war upon them and shall kill them." That is, when at length, a part of the Holy City, or of the Christian world, having acknowledged the impurity of Gentilism, repenting, and cleansing the temple of God among them, and the witnesses rejoicing, shall begin to put off their sackcloth, and to be discharged from their daily lamentation, though they shall not be yet fully discharged from it, the seven-headed Roman beast in his last state, (of whom see ch. xiii.) indignant that the preaching of those hitherto-mourning persons should have prevailed, will make war upon them, conquer, and kill them: Of which, the first symptom of the lamentation of the witnesses beginning to come to an end, took place at the commencement of the Reformed Church, and has been continually repeated up to this present time. The other, respecting the war and slaughter, I suspect to be yet future. Our Brightman, indeed, supposed that it had been long ago fulfilled in the war of Smalcalde, under Charles the Fifth. Others accommodate it to the recent destruction of the German Churches. And who would not much rather wish that so sad a misfortune for the Church had already passed, than that it should remain to be apprehended? But the interpretation is not to be governed according to our wish; nay, the error will be greater on this side than the other; since the expectation of future calamity is more conducive to piety, than too credulous a security respecting it, as if already past. Two things persuade me that this last slaughter is .yet to be dreaded. The first is, that those sorrowful times, of the Gentiles treading under foot the Holy City, or the Christian Religion,--that is, the forty-two months, as long as the beast shall be reigning,--cannot be said to have completed their period; nor, therefore, the days of the witnesses lamenting in sack or hair cloth, contemporary and coeval with those months. The other is, that this destruction of the witnesses (as we shall in a short time see), is immediately antecedent to the overthrow and ruin of the great city, that is, of Rome, which the series of the phials will not permit to be at so short a distance, as we are not yet carried beyond the fourth of them, (though, in the present agitation of affairs, it is to be hoped, that is now passing,) as we shall then be instructed. But we will show, by-and-by, that the ruin of the city relates to the fifth, of which it is very probable that this slaughter of which we treat, will be the forerunner; especially since it is usual for our general Christ to contend with his enemies, and to bestow a victory upon his followers, only by the method of the cross. It does not follow, however, that because this should be the last slaughter, and even yet future, that any thing can certainly be determined of its severity, above all which preceded it. For perhaps it deserved a singular mention and description, not so much on account of its severity, (certainly, not of its duration,) as because it was a sign that the sorrows of the witnesses were then about to be immediately concluded, and of the impending ruin of the Roman city, and therefore alone was selected out of all the slaughters by which the beast would wear out the saints. In like manner, for instance, as the surrounding of Jerusalem by the army of Cestius Gallus, a little before the fatal siege of Titus, was predicted as a sign of its ruin then impending before the doors. For as our Saviour said to his apostles, inquiring about the signs of the time of its destruction, "When ye shall see Jerusalem encompassed with armies, then know that its desolation draweth near." So here it should seem to be intimated by the overthrow of Babylon; when you shall see that slaughter of the witnesses for three years and a half, then know that the desolation of the great city approacheth.

But the destruction by which the witnesses are predicted to be overthrown, must I think be understood in a very general sense, in which it may comprehend death, metaphorically or analogically so called. In this notion, that is said to die, which in whatever state it was constituted, either political or ecclesiastical, or in any other, ceases to be what it was. Whence likewise he kills, who inflicts on any one such a death. For as in the sacred style, to live is oftentimes to be, to die, is not to be. In which sense, we are said to die to Satan and sin, when we cease to be any longer their servants; and to live to Christ, when we begin to be his.

And the mode of opposition seems to require that as the resurrection of the witnesses to life, after the slaughter was perpetrated, should be of this kind, so the slaughter itself should be. But that is clearly analogical, because no resurrection properly so called, will take place before the advent of Christ, under the seventh trumpet; but this takes place while the sixth is still running on. [42]

The death of the witnesses then in war, if we explain it according to this rule of interpretation, will appear to he their overthrow and dejection from that office and station in the Church, reformed by the force of their preaching, which they had obtained for a while, whether that may be joined with corporeal death or otherwise; so that the prophetic life which they had lived till that time, should from thence continue no longer, and that they should no more exercise their offices. By which, at the same time, it necessarily follows, that the columns being withdrawn, and the false prophets of the beast substituted in the place of the prophets of Christ, the whole polity of the reformed Church, as widely as this may happen, should fall to the ground. Which, whether it will come to pass sooner or later, He only knows, in whose hands are the times and seasons.

In the mean time, lest any one should possibly be deceived, there is one thing to be accurately attended to, that this last war of the beast is not of the same kind with that which he had hitherto waged against the assembly of the saints, (of which indeed we shall speak in the history of the beast, c. xiii.) "that it was given him to make war upon the saints, and to overcome them;" but altogether of a different character. For why should that be related as peculiar to the last times of the beast, which if not from his first rise, at least from his acme, had been common to him? The war

Joseph Mede

which the beast waged against the saints universally, is one; that which he wages in his last state, is another; namely, with the prophets who had begun to lay aside their prophetic lamentations with their sackcloth; that is, with the heads of the Church, reformed from his party. This is still more manifest from the different event of one war from the other; the former, indeed, prosperous, the latter very unfortunate. By the former, the beast obtained power over every tribe and tongue, and nation, &c.; by the latter he draws down upon himself a sudden and fatal destruction, as we shall see in the text. "And their dead bodies shall lie in the street of the great city, which is spiritually called Sodom and Egypt, where also our Lord was crucified." That city surnamed great, is Rome, so called, not so much with a view to its size, as because it was the queen of other cities, according to that saying of the angel, c. xvii., "The woman which thou sawest is that great city which hath dominion over the kings of the earth." In like manner, by the name of the great king, (by which God is called, Ps. xlviii. v. 3, and Matt. c. v. v. 25, and which title was of old peculiarly suited to the kings of the Assyrians and Persians,) is intimated the king of kings, who has power over other kings. For which reason, throughout the whole Apocalypse, by whatever name Rome is otherwise called, whether of Babylon, or of the harlot, she is always distinguished by this title, great; as that great Babylon, that great harlot. Add that in the whole Apocalypse, this title is bestowed on no city besides, unless at last, after its fall, to the new Jerusalem, descending from heaven, in whose light from thenceforth the Gentiles should walk. Which whoever could suppose was intended here must have need of hellebore. But neither Jerusalem in the time of St. John, nor any other Jerusalem, except that, is ever to become "the great city," or the head or queen of the other cities of the world. It is added, "which is spiritually called Sodom and Egypt:" Egypt, on account of its tyranny; Sodom, on account of its fornication; that is, spiritual fornication. But here (as the reader should diligently observe) is a key to the allegory, (of which kind many occur in this book,) by which, in truth, the Holy Spirit means to intimate once for all, that whatever is any where exhibited in these visions of Egyptian plagues, or of the destruction of the Sodomites, is wholly to be interpreted πνευμαρικῶς, that is, mystically; since Rome, or the state of the Roman commonweal, the subject of all those plagues, was a mystical Sodom and Egypt. Then all references, too, to Egyptian plagues in the description of the trumpets and phials, as well as in this history of the witnesses; and of the destruction of the Sodomites in the judgment of the beast, c. xix. v. 20, and c. xx. v. 10; of all which the sense is to be opened by this key. Hence it may even be demonstrated, that the subject of the trumpets is the Roman empire; because of those plagues some are Egyptian. Now to what can Egyptian plagues be applied, but to Egypt? and this by the authority of the Holy Spirit is Rome.

Respecting the great city, then, the meaning is plain, but what the Πλατεῖα of the city may be, of which mention is here made, is not so easily to be known. For it seems, it cannot be taken for a street, or for what we call in Latin platea, or forum, or for any other place within a city, for the following reasons: In the first place, Christ our Lord, who is said to have been crucified in this Πλατεῖα, was not crucified either in any street or forum of the city of Rome, or Jerusalem, but without the gate of the latter, (Heb. c. xiii. v. 12,) in a province thereof only, by Pilate the governor. Therefore the Πλατεῖα of the great city is not any street or broadway within the walls of either of the cities, but a place without the city. Πλατεῖα, secondly, being put in the singular number, it is very probable that it designates a thing of that kind, of which a city has one only, and not many. But there are many streets in every city; at least in every one of consequence. Thirdly, it is supposed, that the bodies of the witnesses lie where they were conquered in battle; but it is not usual for troops to be gathered together within the walls of a city; but if not in the enemy's land, at least in the region and provinces subject to the city. Fourthly, "the people, tribes, tongues, and nations," might see "the dead bodies of those who were slain for three days and a half," and not suffer them to be buried. It seems, therefore, that they did not lie in any way or street of the great city, but were either dispersed or spread abroad throughout the provinces, to which, consequently, the signification of τῆς πλατείας ought to be accommodated.[43] And if any one should say, that the army of the beast, by which the witnesses were routed and slain, might be composed of various people and tongues, and therefore might easily see the carcases of those whom they had slain, we must recur to the former; it is not customary for such armies to be gathered together within the walls of a city. For, undoubtedly, the subject is so to be explained, especially where no appearance of allegory can be pretended, that there should not be any absurdity in the literal sense. What else, then, can we say of this passage, but that by the expression of Πλατεῖα, the whole region and territory, subject to the dominion of the city, was pointed out, and that such a signification may be drawn either from the Hebrew חוץ, to which it often corresponds in the version of the Septuagint? namely, according to the custom and use of the Hellenistic language, which is wont to apply a Greek word answering in one signification according to its original use, to a Hebrew word signifying many things, in some other signification; as might be proved by many examples, if there were a question of this custom. חוץ signifies with the Hebrews whatever is altogether external, either without the house, as streets and ways in cities; or without the city, as the circumjacent country or land. Job c. v. v. 10, where in the Hebrew it is לצ ינפ חוצות, the Chaldee renders it, "Who giveth rain on the face of the earth, and sendeth waters on the surface of the province, or on the region of the people." Or from a notion of width, that it may be the same as πλάτος τῆς γῆς Is. c. viii. v. 8, "And the stretching out of his wings (that is, of the Assyrian) shall fill the breadth of thy land, Ω Immanuel!" and Apoc. c. xxix. v. 9, of Gog and Magog: "They came up upon the breadth of the earth, (ἐπὶ πλάτος τῆς γῆς,) and encompassed the beloved city." Now it makes for this interpretation, that בחר another word which the Septuagint translate πλατεῖαν, and בחר which signifies breadth, or πλάτος, has exactly the same letters, and each is called by the same word in the Chaldee, פתאה Or lastly, by the notion of breadth, which is the original meaning of the word πλατεῖαν, the Holy Spirit meant to intimate the amplitude of the dominion of that great city, by which it surpassed all cities, and even at this day surpasses them, as if ἐπὶ τῆς πλατείας was used for ἐπὶ χώρας τῆς πλατείας, on the extensive country, &c. The word Πλατεῖα is an adjective, used substantively, and therefore something ought to be understood, and it may be either one thing or another, to explain the interpretation, nor do I know whether that signification of street is often found among the ancient Greek writers.

But now it can no longer be obscure to one by whom this interpretation is approved, either in what manner Christ may be said to have been crucified in the Πλατεῖα of the Roman city, or when the carcases of the slain witnesses were to be cast out; namely, not in the city of Rome, but in the Roman domain. I know, indeed, that many of our writers, in order to arrive at the same conclusion, understand here, under the name of the city, the whole dominion of the city. But what then, I pray, will be the meaning of Πλατεῖα? For of those two, of which it seems almost necessary it should be one, it can be neither; not dominion, as that is designated under the name of the city; not any province, though a great city has many; for Πλατεῖα means something unique and singular, as it is put in the singular number. And this may suffice for our remarks on the Πλατεῖα τῆς πόλεως τῆς μεγάλης. Let us now proceed to the remainder.

"And (some) of the peoples, and tribes, and tongues, and nations, shall see their dead bodies for three days and a half, and shall not suffer their dead bodies to be put into monuments."-- Whether this is to be taken in the sense of inhumanity or of kindness, is doubtful, and not to be decided except by the fulfilment of the prophecy. For it may be taken either as done by enemies, adding this for the sake of ignominy, to the slaughter which they had perpetrated, that they would deny sepulture to the bodies of the dead: Or by friends and favourers of the witnesses by this means consulting the interests of those who were soon to revive. For, however it may be held on other considerations, an act of the greatest cruelty, not to bury the dead, and to cast them out unburied, and especially among the Jews, as the greatest ignominy; yet to prohibit those who were so dead, as not to create a despair but they might again be restored to life, from being immured for a short time in the cloisters of the sepulchre, ought to be placed to the account of kindness. If the first is to be understood, some marks of infamy or ignominy seem to be intimated by this type by which the followers of the beast, not content with having made away with the witnesses, would inflict on them in addition. But if the latter, it may be some assistance from the reformed nations, out of fear of whom, as of a multitude, much the largest

and therefore, while the wound was yet recent, and their affairs not yet confirmed, not to be provoked with impunity to desperation, or at least, by exertion and secret favour, it should come to pass, that they should not deal with the witnesses as if there were no hope of their revival.--Achmet, from the doctrine of the Indians, (Apotelesma, 130,) "If any one in dreams should seem to be buried, the sepulchre refers to the full certainty of his death. If he should seem to observe some deficiency of those things which pertain to sepultures, that deficiency must be placed to the account of hope. If now you should be disposed to inquire what appears in the text which would lead rather to one interpretation than the other, I would introduce this observation into the argument on the subject, that since he announces what is here suggested in a different mode, and in different words, and since he treats of enemies in the following verse, he wishes them to be understood, in this and the latter instance, not as the same, but as different persons. In the one case, indeed, as the enemies, in the other as the friends of the witnesses. For of the enemies, in the following verse, exulting and sending presents to one another, he says, "They that dwell on the earth," but of those who would not suffer the dead bodies of the witnesses to be put into graves, "they of the tribes, and people, and tongues," partitively, as if it would note certain persons different from the others in disposition. Let the reader judge.

"For three days and a half." That is, as it appears for three years and a half, for the things which are there foretold, as to be performed, prove that it cannot be understood of horary days. For who can believe that the short space of three days and a half are sufficient either for disseminating the report of the slaughter of the witnesses through the world, or for sending messengers with gifts backwards and forwards among the nations. It is obvious that it would not be sufficient even for preparing them. To this must be added, that half a day, or twelve hours, is wholly inadequate for measuring acts of this kind. For these sort of things are accustomed to be marked, not by hours, but rather by months, or at least, by entire days. In the meanwhile it is to be observed, that the time is here to be computed, not from the date of the witnesses being killed, but from that in which they shall lie dead and inanimate, after they have been slain. But how long that war shall last, and how much time will be given to killing the prophets, the fulfilment of the prophecy only will explain. "And they that dwell on the earth shall rejoice over them, and be merry, and shall send gifts to one another, because these two prophets tormented them who dwelt on the earth." Of the custom of sending gifts in cases of public joy or of great rejoicings, vide Esther, c. ix. v. 22. "And after three days and a half, the Spirit of life from God entered into them, and they stood upon their feet, and fear fell on those who beheld them."

Such as the death of the witnesses was, such will be their awakening or resurrection from the dead; namely, their restitution to their former state; and that, not so much by any exertion or human assistance, as by the finger of God, who is wonderful in his works. For this is implied in the words, "The Spirit of life from God entered into them." Achmet says, (Apotelesm. vi. and vii. of the Doctrine of the Egyptians and Persians,) "If any one in dreams thinks he sees the resuscitation of the dead, it signifies the liberation of the conquered and the termination of wars." Apot. vi. Deliverance from Calamities. Vide Ezek. ch. xxxvii.

"And they heard a great voice from heaven, saying to them, Come up hither. And they went up to heaven in a cloud, and their enemies beheld them." Not only will the witnesses be restored to their former place and station, but they will be even elevated to a higher degree of honour and power. For that is the signification of being carried up in a cloud, and ascending to heaven. Vide Dan. c. vii. v. 13, and c. xix. v. 1. Whence in the interpretation of dreams which the Arabian I have so often quoted, Apomasar or Achmet, has collected from the ancient records of the Egyptians and Persians, we read, "If a king seem to himself to be seated in the clouds, and to be carried wherever he will, his barbarian enemies shall be reduced into subjection to him, over whom he shall preside with supreme command." Also, "If a king should seem to himself to have flown, as it were, to heaven, where the stars are, he shall possess eminence and distinction above other kings." Also, "If a king should seem to be carried upward to be seated in heaven, he shall reduce under his authority a larger region than that which he possesses." Apot. 162. 164.

These I bring forward for the purpose of showing, that the parable I speak of is applied in that signification by the prophets, in which it is understood according to the use of the East. The ministry of the witnesses, then, will not be despised as before, nor they themselves treated as men of an abject and contemptible kind. So that what our Saviour said of himself, Luke, ch. xxiv. v. 26, "Ought not Christ to have suffered these things, and then to enter into his glory?" may acquire its force and truth in the example of the prophets likewise. And who knows whether the reformed Church may not undergo the reproach brought upon Christ on this behalf by the subduction of the witnesses for a time, because they had not treated them according to the dignity of their embassy, while they enjoyed it. It is too well known what is the sin of the reformed Churches in this case; and as, while the prophets of Christ were strenuously engaged in purifying the temple of God, some in the mean time contaminated that most holy work by pillaging its treasures, and embezzling its oblations, not having left a maintenance in some places, to the great disgrace of true religion, by which its ministers might be sustained honourably, and according to the dignity of their order, much less, a superabundance, that they might lay aside for the improvement of the reformed affairs, the necessities of a saored war, the aid of afflicted brethren, and for other pious uses: Was not this the kind of prevarication for which anciently the Jewish temple was profaned by Antiochus Epiphanes, and the religion of the true God given up to be trodden under foot, in like manner, for three years? "A host," says Daniel, "shall be given to him against the daily sacrifice, on account of prevarication, and it shall cast down the truth to the ground, and it shall practise and prosper," ch. viii. v. 12. See the history, second Book of Maccabees, from the beginning of the third chapter to the fifth, and judge. But I will not press the matter any farther. This only will I add,--perhaps this increase of honour and power to the witnesses by their resurrection, will be brought about by the command of the Supreme magistrate, (which, perhaps, may be that voice from heaven,) as a compensation for the infamy and ignominy with which the followers of the beast had disgraced them when dead, supposing that to be signified by the prohibition of sepulture.

"And in that hour there was a great earthquake, and a tenth part of the city fell, and there were slain in the earthquake (the names of) seven thousand men." At the time at which the witnesses or prophets returned to life, and ascended into heaven, there was a great earthquake, that is, a great commotion of the nations, and revolution of political affairs, by which, in fact, a way was opened to the witnesses, and a facility given them of returning to life, with such an increase of dignity and power. By that commotion of the nations, "a tenth of the city fell, and there were slain seven thousand names of men." That we may attain as nearly as possible in a future event to the meaning of these words, two things are to be pre-established and proved. First, since there is no misfortune attending the fall of the beast, but what is contained in some one of the phials, the same overthrow of the beast is here described as at the effusion of the fifth phial. The proof is, that the subject is the same in both plagues; in the former, the seat or throne of the beast; in the latter, the great city. That the great city is Rome, the seat of the beast, is so plain that it need not be proved. It is still farther confirmed, because the slaughter which is here described, so nearly precedes the full abolition of the beast at the seventh trumpet, that nothing is related to have intervened but the conclusion of the second woe; but now, at all events, the total destruction of the beast is the work of the last phial, the conclusion of the second woe, or of the plague from the Euphrates, of the sixth phial. Therefore the destruction of the great city, which immediately precedes that conclusion, agrees with the fifth phial. Another thing to be previously established by us is, that the ruin of the great city is that very destruction of Babylon, which is celebrated in the eighteenth chapter. This is proved, because it is certain from that same chapter, that the destruction of Babylon, or the Roman city, goes before the complete demolition of the beast and the august reign of Christ, beginning with the seventh trumpet. Now the destruction of the same city, which is here related, so nearly precedes that kingdom, that the Spirit, with the mention of no destruction beside, as intervening, passes at once to that kingdom, and the description of the seventh trumpet. It necessarily follows, that the same destruction of the city is described in both places. For who can bring his mind to believe that the Holy Spirit would have altogether passed over that very great desolation, and have introduced the mention of some smaller overthrow, by no means to be compared with it?

This being the state of the case, it follows, that the interpretation of the passage is to be guided by the above rule, and is to be proved, as it were, by a touchstone; and therefore a meaning of these words is to be sought for, of such a nature as may agree with the description of that Babylonian destruction. Let us now see by what means this may be done. Philip Nicolai, a theologian of the Augustan confession, [44] a learned and acute man, thinks that by the Δέκατον τῆς πόλεως is to be understood the decarchy of the city, or the ten kingdoms, subdued to its dominion, which indeed, in this concussion of the nations, revolted from Rome, to whose government they had been subject for so many years; and from thenceforward its commands were not to be obeyed. This, in truth, is what is said in another place. That "the ten kings who had delivered up their power to the beast, when the words of God were fulfilled, should hate the whore, and make her desolate, and naked, should eat her flesh, and burn her with fire." But this notion of the word Δέκατον, however it had in the first place presented itself to me, while reflecting on the meaning of this passage, and though it pleased me very much from the appositeness of the event, yet afterwards, when I examined the matter more closely, appeared a little strained, and unusual; so that I fear it will not easily be approved by those who would desire a simple and unforced interpretation. I seek, therefore, for another. And first it suggested itself to my mind, that the tenth, perhaps, was the name of a tribute, either that which the high priest receives from the whole kingdom of the beast, or that which the city itself receives from its estates by the right of dominion. This tenth of the city, in that commotion of affairs, was to fall, that is, to fail, and therefore I inferred, that the principality of the city would be wholly extinguished; namely, despoiled of the territory bestowed on it for a patrimony, and its high priest driven from thence by force; that it would lose the prerogative and dominion which it was accustomed to exercise, to so great an extent over cities and people; since it would no longer be that which had procured for it prerogative and dominion, the metropolis of the kingdom of the beast, nor the seat of the false prophet. For it is well known, that tribute is the symbol of dominion, and that in this name, most of the provinces under the empire of ancient Rome paid the tenth part of their products every year. Which likewise may be proved to have been customary in the kingdoms of the east, both from the first of Maccabees, c. x. v. 31, and c. xi. v. 35, and from that summary of royal right, 1 Sam. c. viii. (for observe, what is said of tenths is not to be taken of sacred tenths or tithes: They were royal, accustomed to be paid to kings as viceroys of the gods,) which Aristotle also confirms in the second book of his OEconomics. It ought not, then, to appear strange, if any one should here affirm that under the name of a tenth, a representation so common, might be signified some kind of tribute belonging to the city. But there is no need to go back so far, since in Italy that mode of tribute has not yet been abolished, and besides, the Roman pontiff has long since renewed the image of -it in his ecclesiastical empire, by annually requiring a tenth part of ecclesiastical benefices. But to this interpretation it is an objection, that it seems it ought then rather to be called Δεκάτη than Δέκατον. Besides the word ἔπεσε, it fell, by which some effect consistent with an earthquake must be designed, is not sufficiently suited to an interpretation of this sort. Nay, if it could be established, yet it would seem to express the fall of Babylon, with which we presuppose it to be identified too obscurely and faintly, and not in a suitable manner.

At last, then, until any one shall suggest something more certain, and consonant to the text, I am brought to this conclusion, that I conceive by the tenth of the city, a part of the city is indeed to be understood, but not a part of the present city, but the whole of it, which is the tenth part of the ancient one. That this is the fact, and that not more than the tenth part of the ancient city of Rome, as it existed in the age of St. John, remains at this day, may appear from the following reasoning. For Lypsius affirms, that ancient Rome, such as it was in the age of John, with respect to form, was nearly round, but not however exactly so. Its semi-diameter, from the golden milestone placed at the top of the Roman forum, to the extremity of the building, was about 7000 paces, that is, 7 miles, its circuit at length was 42 miles. Since then it was not exactly round, let us diminish its semi-diameter, in order to measure its area by one mile (as much as in a hexangular figure, according to a perpendicular to the side, it ought to be diminished). It will then be 6, which multiplied by 21, the half of the periphery, will give 126 for the area of the city.

But modern, or pontifical Rome has only 13 or 15 miles for its circuit, as they know, says Lypsius, who have measured it. Its form, as may be seen from its ichnography, is an oblong, nearly quadrangular, in a proportion almost double. To measure which, let a rectangular parallelogram be constituted, whose perimeter may be 15, its length double the breadth; of which form, in fact, the sides will be 22 and 5, which multiplied into each other, will give an area of 121. Now the number 126 contains 10 times the number 121. The latter area, then, is the tenth part of the former, and consequently, modern Rome the tenth part of ancient. Q. E. Δ. Any one who is not much accustomed to reasonings of this sort, may apply the judgment of his eyes to the following diagram.

Diagram comparing Ancient and Modern Rome

We cannot, indeed, examine every thing here according to line and rule, but it is wonderful how near we can approach to it. I define the circumference of the present city by the walls by which it is surrounded, for beyond them, contrary to what was formerly the case, it is not at this day inhabited; but the whole contents, whatever they may be, are included within the walls; those walls which Hadrian the First, and Leo the Fourth, pontiff, erected, as it were, by a fatal instinct, as the boundary to that which had just been made the seat of the pontifical kingdom. For so Blondus relates, that the walls which now exist were built by Hadrian I. for 100,000 pieces of gold, collected from Tuscany. Those, as is remarked by others, Leo IV. afterwards, about the year of our Lord 850, either repaired or finished; and having added the Transtiberian or Leontine city to it, completed the city in the form and circuit in which it is now seen. And though it has much of the space included within the walls void and desert, yet since the walls are reckoned among the principal works of the city, the city itself cannot be considered as less extensive than its walls. Ampler, indeed, it might be, if, as the old one formerly was, it were extended every way beyond the walls by contiguous buildings.

That I may at length draw to a conclusion, the sum of what I have said reverts to this; that the Holy Spirit means to say, or to intimate, that so much of the Great City as remained at this earthquake, should become a ruin at the time, viz. a tenth of the city; for there was to be no more remaining up to that period. Nine parts were to fall many ages before; and we in truth have seen them fall, partly by the destructions and devastations which the barbarians brought upon it at so many different times, partly by decay from great age, and partly overthrown by lightning, as we have pointed out under the fourth trumpet. The tenth part was reserved for the pontifical Roman fate, being constituted the head of a new empire, and the mother of Christian harlots. This part the earthquake, which is connected with the resurrection of the witnesses, will entirely demolish.

Nor was it perhaps necessary that we should interpret the Holy Spirit as having spoken so rigidly as we have done, of the tenth part of the city, according to geometrical miles. It would have been sufficient, if, as formerly, he had spoken by his influence on Isaiah, c. vi. v. 13. of the destruction of the Jewish people, "A tenth of it shall be preserved, and be brought back into the land." So here we may understand, not so strictly a tenth, as some very small part, about a tenth of the ancient amplitude of the Roman city, which should remain as the seat of the beast for the last destruction.

It is added, "And there were slain in the earthquake seven thousand names of men." Here, if by names of men we understand heads of men, or individual men, the number seems too trifling, and not consistent with the magnitude of the slaughter, which the Holy Spirit elsewhere intimates. For in the destruction of Babylon, will there not be a far greater number slain than seven thousand men? And is it likely that the effusion of the fifth phial on the throne of the beast should terminate by so very small a massacre of men? In order to satisfy this doubt by some other means: First, it is to be observed, that by the name of the city is here to be understood, not the citizens and inhabitants, but the buildings and walls, that is, the royal seat of the beast; and so a double destruction of Babylon is described in these prophecies; first, of Babylon as the royal city of the beast, that is to say, of the Roman city at the fifth phial; afterwards of Babylon, as to the citizens or Roman state, which consists of the Pope, with the senate of empurpled Cardinals, and the other crowd of citizens, especially of ecclesiastics, who, after Rome has been destroyed and burnt, betook themselves to a habitation in some other place, and who are to be reserved for the last phial: at whose effusion it is said, over and above other destructions of nations and states in every part of the world, in that earthquake which was far the greatest of all that had ever taken place, even "that great

Babylon came in memory before God, to give unto her the cup of the wine of the fierceness of his wrath," c. xvi. v. 19; which, notwithstanding the burning and destruction of Babylon, described in the xviiith and xixth chapters, certainly precede the full extermination of the beast, and false prophet, as is there manifest from the text. I know some unravel this knot in a different manner, by saying, that Babylon, of which mention is made in the last phial, is Constantinople, the metropolis of the Turks; but they will never persuade me, that the Holy Spirit, in the first and principal image of all, has used so remarkable a synonyme, and that we are to understand two Babylons, and not one only, and the same, though with a double reference. To come, then, to the point. It may perhaps come to pass, that the first destruction of Babylon, that is, the devastation and ruin of the city of Rome, may be effected without any immense or total slaughter of the citizens. And though "her smoke was to ascend for ever and ever," that is, she should be wholly converted into ashes, and levelled with the ground, never again to be inhabited, yet a great part of the citizens might escape from the overthrow of the city, either because they would in time consult their safety by flight, or from some other cause, which the event will make manifest.

And this is one mode by which the doubt may be satisfied about the too trifling number of those who were slain. Another is, if we should say that by "names of men" are possibly intended men of name, or renown. For a hypallage of this kind is not unfrequent in the Scriptures, that in the order of the nouns, that which precedes is used in the place of an epithet. As for example, "The silver of the shekels," Lev. c. v. for shekels of silver; the uncleanness of man, for a man of uncleanness, that is, an unclean man, (ib. c. vii.) the law of justice, for the justice of the law; Rom. c. ix. the riches of grace, for rich and abundant grace, and the like. A name, besides, is familiar for celebrity in almost all languages, especially the sacred, in which men of name are illustrious men; sons without a name, (Job c. xxx.) ignoble; in Chaldee, vulgar persons. Whence Beza, in his Annotations on the Ephesians, c. i. v. 21, and Philipp. c. ii. v. 9, speaking of the exaltation of Christ above every name; as also Heb. c. i. v. 4, understands name in the signification of dignity and worth.

If we follow an interpretation of this kind, (nor do I see what can be opposed to it,) the names of men will be dignities of men, ὀνομαστοί, men of name, illustrious men and excelling in dignity, of whom about 7000 (and what if they should be of the order of the false prophet, which they call ecclesiastics?) should fall in this concussion of things and nations. The number, however, of 7000, I conceive to be so intended that a few more or less may be understood, according to the manner of Scripture. How great a number of the Plebeians are to fall in this war it does not belong to the subject to declare, since that may be conjectured from the slaughter of the nobles, nor did the Holy Spirit wish to descend so far as to reduce the dregs of the slain to a calculation.

But still another interpretation may be given, which would not render it necessary to come to an enumeration of particular men; for instance, if we may interpret names of men as companies and societies of men, men accustomed to be called by their proper names no less than individuals, as are states, municipalities, parishes, villages, abbeys, and similar titles of human communities. For what are these things else, if we are desirous of forming the hypothesis, than names of men? for so is the political state of the Thebans called by Eschines Θηβαίων ὄνομα, and the Roman name is used for the Roman people [45].

What, then, if out of these titles of human communities, whatever they may be, and whether at Rome, or in what they call the state of the Church, about 7000 are to be slain in this concussion of the nations; that is, they are to sink under adverse power, which Scripture, according to its usual style, has called death.

But nothing is to be rashly pronounced concerning a future event, since the issue of things predicted is a commentary on the prophecy. These observations I have adduced that it may appear more clearly, as far as relates to words, that the interpretation may be more liberal than is commonly supposed, since the use of Scripture does not bind down the word name to any uniform and certain signification. For names of men are not to be found conjunctively any where else, than in the place now under consideration; nor are names to be found, singly of individuals, unless twice only, c. i. v. 15, Apo. c. iii. v. 4. The word is otherwise applied in a different signification. There remains, "And the rest were affrighted, and gave glory to the God of heaven." That is, by their consternation; by which, even unwillingly and ungratefully, they acknowledged the finger of God. For to acknowledge, by whatever mark, the wisdom, goodness, or power of God, is to give him glory. As they who detected by God confess their sins, are said to give glory to God, as Achan. Then follows, "The second woe is past, the third woe cometh quickly." The meaning is, that the great earthquake should be continued till the end of the second woe, or sixth trumpet; and the mournful prophecy of the witnesses was at length to finish with it; since after such a victory over the followers of the beast, and their ascent into the heaven of power and honour, they would no longer be clothed in sackcloth. If the second woe, or the plague of the sixth trumpet, be the overflow of the Turks from the Euphrates in ancient time on the Roman world, as we then interpreted it, it can scarcely be denied, but that the passing away of this plague, must be the drying up of the waters of the Euphrates at the effusion of the sixth phial, by which "the way of the kings from the east might be prepared," c. xvi. v. 12. From which coming of the kings of the east, (lest any interval should otherwise be left between the two trumpets,) the seventh trumpet seems to begin, and therefore that wonderful preparation of the dragon, the beast, and the false prophet, for the war to be waged at Armageddon, c. xvi. vv. 13, 14, together with its event at the last phial, v. 17, must be referred to the beginning of the same seventh trumpet. And indeed, it appears very probable, that the preparation for war belongs to the same trumpet as the war itself. But here a doubt arises, which requires solution, and therefore must not be passed over in silence. For since there is the same termination to the forty-two months of the beast as there is to the 1260 days of the mourning of the witnesses, and those days finish at the conclusion of the plague of the sixth trumpet, or of the second woe, it may not improperly be asked, why the months of the beast should not be extended farther, since, after this time, no small portion of the beast remains which is not to be put an end to, until the beginning of the seventh trumpet.

It may be answered, that this takes place because at that time the conversion of Israel, and the new kingdom begin, (for they are called kings from the East,) or because, in the duration of the beast, the empire of the Roman city is chiefly attended to. But that great city, the royal residence of the beast, is taken and overthrown in that earthquake; so far that the beast from thenceforth will have in some degree changed his form, since his metropolis being thus demolished, it can no longer be considered as the kingdom of the seven mountains, (which is the other signification of the seven heads.) There still remains in the text the sounding of the seventh trumpet, and the august kingdom of Christ in the great day of judgment. The interpretation of which we will defer to the end of the book, that we may exhibit all the prophecies relating to it in that place, at the same time and in one point of view.

Footnotes:

39. Why should not the two witnesses be considered as the Old and New Testament, which during the apostasy of 1260 years were to be neglected and vilified as we see they are in Popish countries; but in the hands of sincere believers, properly applied, would produce the effects described?--R. B. C.

40. As these witnesses prophecy for 1260 years, (the whole time of the apostasy) to whom can the allusion be made, but to two testimonies, which might be constantly produced by the faithful against the corruption of the times; and I know not where we are to look for them, but in the books of the Old and New Testament, combined in the Bible?--R. B. C.

41. If this was a difficulty to Mede, it is almost presumptuous in any other to attempt an explanation. But there have been two revelations of light from God, under two dispensations, and preserved by two Churches or holy societies--the Jewish and the Christian. In the time of Zachariah, there was only one revelation, one church, one candlestick, and if we may be allowed to apply the two olive-trees to two figurative infusers, rather than to two persons, we may suppose them in the first instance to have designated the law and the prophets. But in the time of St. John there were two revelations, two churches, two candlesticks, the one illuminated by means of the Old Testament, now combining the law and the prophets, the other by the New Testament comprising the doctrines of Christ and his apostles. Reference is made to Zachariah, because be described the one and prefigured the other. May not then the two witnesses be summarily intended for the law and the gospel, or rather for the Old and New Testament?-- R. B. C.

42. If these observations be just, (and there is every reason to believe that they are,) what are we to think of the witnesses? They cannot be living persons in succession throughout the period of 1260 years, because they die and revive metaphorically. Are they not, then, as I before observed, the twin parts of the true religion; that is, the law and the Gospel, contained in the Old and New Testament? Their death, therefore, will be the temporary dissolution of their acknowledged authority in some part of the world, by the success of infidelity for a short time; and their resurrection will be the reinstatement of their influence over the nations, in consequence of some signal revolution, which will carry conviction to the minds of men, and bow their necks to the yoke of Christ. Thus explained, the whole parable becomes consistent and intelligible.--R. B. C.

43. From hence, again, it appears obvious that the witnesses could not be two persons existing together at any one time, or in succession, because after death, such a description could not be applicable to their dead bodies; but rather two combined systems or modes of religious instruction, which might metaphorically be said to die and revive; that is, to be discarded for a while, and afterwards restored to just influence and authority.--R. B. C.

44. Confession of Augsburg.

45. This is much the most probable supposition as applicable to the numerous titles of ecclesiastics under the Roman Catholic hierachy.--R. B. C.

THE MEANING

Of the Red Dragon with Seven Heads fighting with Michael about the new-born Child

The first vision of the little book, of which we treated in the eleventh chapter, ran through the whole Apocalyptical course, from the beginning to the end, and that, as we elsewhere observed, to point out its connexion with the seals and trumpets. Now to that vision the remaining prophecies of the same interval, and of the affairs of the Church are to be accommodated, in order to complete the system of the little book. Of which, "the war of the red seven-headed dragon with Michael," comprises the same period as the measured court of the ecclesiastical state, in which the dragon, inhabiting the Roman empire, raged with dire persecutions against the Church with child, and travailing to bring forth Christ [46] as king over the Roman world, and for nearly three hundred years waged war against the Spirit of Christ, powerfully operating in his servants. But the woman at length, after throes in delivery, spoliations, and butcheries, gave birth to such a Christ [47], brought forth a King "who was to rule all nations with a rod of iron," and the dragon, being dispossessed of the Roman throne, "there was" in that world "salvation and power, and the kingdom of our God, and the power of his Christ."

This summary of the whole matter being premised, for the sake of clearness, let us come to the particular explanation of the text

"And a great sign (he says) was seen in heaven," whither John was called in the beginning to behold, and where he had seen all the foregoing visions. I do not think any other sense of this circumstance is to be sought for. For it is manifest even from the end of the preceding chapter, that John had hitherto beheld what passed in heaven. "A woman clothed with the sun, and the moon under her feet, and on her head a crown of twelve stars." A sign, and a very beautiful image of the primitive Church in a state of pregnancy, resplendent on all sides with the faith of Christ, the Sun of Righteousness, and treading under her feet the elements of the world, (whether the shadows of the Law, or the darkness of Gentile superstition;) glittering, lastly, with the insignia of apostolical origin. Many are inclined to consider the moon as a symbol of terrestrial and mutable things, which the Church of Christ looks down upon as beneath her. Though this may be true, yet never, I believe, in the whole Scripture, is the moon celebrated under this allusion. But the interpretation of prophetic symbols is not readily to be sought for elsewhere, but in those properties, by which, in some place or other, Scripture bears testimony to it. Now it is certain that most of the feasts on which they performed their holy rites, in typical worship, were described according to the changes of the moon; as the new moons, the passover, pentecost, the feast of tabernacles; nay, that the calculation of the whole ecclesiastical year, depended on its revolution. To which, perhaps, that passage in the 104th Psalm, v. 19, may refer: "He appointed the moon for seasons," לְמוֹעֲדִים that is, for feasts. Why, then, may not the symbol of the moon be referred to the Mosaic worship? which the Church, in truth, by the revelation of Christ, beholds as prostrate, and placed under her feet; according to that observation of the apostle to the Colossians, ch. ii. v. 14, in which he asserts that "Christ had blotted out the hand-writing of ordinances which was against us, and had taken it away, having nailed it to his cross." Moreover, as God may be said to have created the sun as the greater luminary, for the dominion of the day, and the moon, the lesser luminary, for the dominion of the night, why should not the symbol of the moon, appointed to the presidency over the night, signify what is the display of the power of darkness, or blindness, that is, the worship of Satan and his demons in idols? So that indeed the whole matter may be transferred to baptism, in which the Church, illuminated, and from thenceforth to be clothed with Christ, tramples under foot the worship of idols, with a renunciation of Satan and his angels, his service, and his pomps. For all these things the ancient formula of renunciation expressly contained; and besides, the abjurors turned to the West, as to that part of heaven from whence the night arises, as, on the contrary, the professors of faith in Christ, and in the true Triune God, turned to the East, as the quarter from whence the sun, after the night has passed away, brings back the day. (Dionys. Arcop. de Hierarch Eccles. ch. ii. Cyril Hierosol. Catech. i. Mystagog.--Greg. Nazian. Orat. xl.--Hieron. to ch. vi.--Amos. Ambrosius. Of those who are initiated into Mysteries, ch. ii.) Moreover, with a regard to the same figure (as was also observed above), the duration of the apostasy, or of Christianity defiled by idols, is described by months, according to the motion of the moon, but that of the woman and the witnesses persevering in the faith of Christ, by years and days, with reference to the motion of the sun. To which interpretation I should in preference accede, I am somewhat in doubt, and whether to one only, or to both. In truth, the apostle to the Galatians, ch. iv. seems to call both, as well the Mosaic tutorship as the worship of Gentile idols, promiscuously the elements of the world, and the Church of Christ rejoices that both are subdued under her feet. Let the reader use his own judgment.

"And being with child, she cried out in pain, and labouring to be delivered." The Church, whenever she is regarded universally and abstractedly as an imaginary person, is a mother, but when with respect to individuals, who are produced in her continually, she has offspring which she is said to bring forth to God. This is so obvious in the prophets, that it is unnecessary to add a word more respecting it. Vide Ezekiel, ch. xvi. to v. 21, also ch. xxiii. v. 4, Isa. ch. liv. Hosea, ch. ii. v. 4, 5. The allegory, then, is not to be disturbed by the unreasonableness of any one, because he would distinguish the mother from her offspring, which, however, in another sense, coalesce in one and the same Church. Kimschi on Hosea, ch. ii. v. 2, 3, "The synagogue or congregation is compared to a mother by way of universality, but the several individuals to children."

Those pains and torments on account of which the woman in childbirth cried out, were those severe persecutions which the primitive Church endured at the time of her delivery. For it is well known that tribulations and distresses are compared to the pangs of childbirth. Whence those words of Isaiah, ch. lxvi. v. 7, "Before she travailed she brought forth; before her pain came she was delivered of a male child." The Chaldee has this paraphrase: "Before tribulation come upon her, she shall be redeemed; before trembling come upon her as the pains of a woman in labour, her King shall be revealed, that is, the Messiah." But Jeremiah himself interprets this image, ch. xxx. v. 6, 7, "Ask now and see, if a man do travail with child? Wherefore do I see every man with his hand on his loins, as a woman in travail, and all faces are turned into paleness? Alas! because that day is great, and there is none like it. It is even the time of Jacob's trouble, but he shall be saved out of it." See also what our Saviour calls ὠδῖνας, Matt. ch. xxiv. v. 8, 9, Mark, ch. xiii. v. 9, "These are the beginning of sorrows," ὠδίνων, &c.

"And there appeared another sign in heaven, and, behold, a great red dragon, having seven heads and ten horns; and upon his heads seven crowns. And his tail drew the third part of the stars of heaven, and cast them upon the earth." This is the sign or image of the heathen Roman empire worshipping the dragon; inasmuch as his emblems universally are seven heads and ten horns; seven heads both on account of the seven hills on which the city was built, and on account of the seven orders of kings or dynasties which would successively rule the empire of that city; but the ten horns are so called on account of the ten kingdoms, which were to rise in the time of its last head (upon which they grew,) which interpretation is not mine, but that of the angel, ch. xvii. where there will be a more convenient opportunity of treating on these matters, if any thing requires to be added. In the mean time, another character of the Roman empire is here subjoined, for it is said to have drawn "a third part of the stars of heaven with its tail, and cast them on the earth;" that is, to have subjected a third part of the princes and dynasties of the world to its empire. For so much, namely a third part of the globe known in the age of John, the Roman dominion circumscribed within its boundaries,

Now the tail, according to the doctrine of the Indians in Achmet, generally signifies attendants and followers of power, Apot. 152; but what more the tail of the serpent may imply, will be seen *by-and-by. And these, indeed, were the characters of the Roman empire universally; but the representation of a dragon determines the worshipper of the dragon and the enemies of the woman's seed specifically, that is, as heathen, and the adversary of the Christian name; and since he is red likewise, it points him out as cruel, and crimson with the blood of the saints. Add that, under the type of a dragon, reference seems to be had to Pharaoh, the dire and malignant enemy of the ancient synagogue, travelling in Egypt, as the Roman of the Christian Church in childbirth. For he also, in a similar manner, and on the same account, is clothed with the image of a dragon, Psalm lxxiv. v. 13, 14, "Thou hast divided the sea by thy strength. Thou hast broken the heads of the dragons, (that is, of the Egyptians) in the waters. Thou hast broken the heads of Leviathan (Chaldee, of Pharaoh). Thou hast given him to be meat to the people inhabiting the wilderness." Isaiah, ch. li. v. 9, "Awake, awake! put on strength, Ω arm of the Lord! Awake, as in the ancient days, in the generations of old. Art thou not he that hath cut Rahab, and wounded the dragon?" Ezek. c. xxix. v. 3, "I am against thee, Pharaoh, king of Egypt, the great dragon." In all these passages the Hebrew word is ר which the Septuagint, Symmachus, and Jerome, interpret the dragon; and, indeed, the Syrian interpreter always calls the dragon in the Apocalypse by the same word. For the confirmation of which, Drusius says, that it is the Arabic language in which the dragon is called Thennin. And Exod. ch. vii. "Aaron threw down his rod before Pharaoh, and it became לתפין a serpent, or dragon:" It signifies, indeed, elsewhere, a whale or grampus, but then as a marine dragon, whose form in some respects it resembles. But why, you will say, is so much stress laid upon this word? Why, in order to show that in the resemblance which Satan first abused, in subverting Adam, it is the custom of the Holy Spirit, under the type of that disgraced and accursed animal, to designate the kingdoms infested by the devil, and hostile to his church, the seed of the woman.

"And the dragon stood before the woman, who was about to be delivered, that when she should bring forth, he might devour her child." That is, as Pharaoh did to the ancient Israel springing up in Egypt, and as afterwards Herod did to Christ, the Son of Mary, our Lord, so the Roman dragon laid wait for the mystic Christ, whom the Church was about to bring forth, that he might oppress him immediately after his birth.

"And she brought forth a male child, who was to rule all nations with a rod of iron" (or an iron sceptre). That is, she brought forth a mystic Christ, or Christ formed in his members, not the Son of Mary, but of the Church, according to that of the Apostle to the Galatians, c. iv. v. 19. "My little children, of whom I travail in pain again, till Christ be formed in you." For since the words are a periphrasis of Christ, it is necessary that some Christ should be intended by them, as in the prophetic types is frequently the case, not truly, but analogically spoken; "who," says he, "was to rule all nations with an iron sceptre," that is, with power produced by the force of iron, or war, as he was about to have dominion over those who were not originally his citizens, but either enemies, or foreigners, whom it would be necessary to subjugate before he governed. The words are taken from Ps. ii. v. 9. not according to the present Masoretic reading, but the ancient one of the Septuagint, and of the apostles. Of which authors, I think I can collect, that this is the meaning, from c. xix. v. 15. where in like manner as in the Psalm, they are applied to Christ our Lord, to whom they primarily belong. "Out of his mouth," says he, "went a sharp sword, that with it he might smite the nations; and he shall rule them with a rod of iron." Here the words are applied to the mystic Christ, or the Christian man, the offspring of the church among the Gentiles, who is represented under the type of Christ his Head, and to whom the Lord promises that he would sometime give a power of a similar nature with his own, under the name of the Church of Thyatira. "He that overcometh," says he, "and keepeth my works unto the end, to him will I give power over the nations, and he shall rule them with a rod of iron; as the vessels of a potter shall they be broken to pieces; as I also have received of my Father." It will be some assistance here, to attend to the words of Andrew, in which, according to the opinion of Methodius, he comments upon this place. "The Church," says he, "without intermission, by those who are initiated in baptism, generates Christ, as to be formed in them, to the complete fulness of spiritual growth. The male child is the people of the church, by whom Christ, as God, by the hands of the Romans, strong as iron, rules the nations." He alludes to the type of the fourth kingdom in Daniel, in which I do not agree with him, (for how could David have alluded to that?) otherwise he is not wide of the mark, as will soon appear.

"And her child was caught up unto God, and to his throne." A hendiadys [48] for the throne of God. The son of the woman was caught up to the throne of God, that is, was elevated to the Roman throne, where, with that power with which it was declared that he was about to rule, he did rule the nations. Christ, the Son of Mary, was indeed truly raised to the throne of God; but the mystical, or supposed Christ, whom the apostolical Church brought forth analogically, since the throne of the higher powers is, as the apostle calls them, Rom. c. xiii. the throne of God, the terrestrial heaven. "For there is no power," says he, "but of God." Whence, in the divination of dreams, "If any one should appear in a dream to be carried up into heaven," they interpret it of a royal exaltation. It is well known, likewise, in the sacred language, that magistrates are called מיהלא, that is, gods. "God standeth in the congregation of the mighty, he is a Judge among gods." Ps. lxxxii. 1. "I have said ye are gods, and ye are all the children of the Most High." v. 6. As those then are said to sit in the seat of Moses, who teach the doctrine delivered by Moses; so those may be said to sit on the throne of God, who exercise his functions in the earth. When, therefore, the offspring of the apostolical Church is said to be caught up, or taken to the throne of God, it is the same thing as to be elevated to such a height, as to sit as it were next to God, which, I say, is true of royal eminence. Now this was fulfilled, when the Christians under Constantine the Great, and his successors, became possessed of power, after the Dragon was cast out.

But you will say, since the mystic Christ is said to be appointed to rule the nations over which he presided, in the same manner as Christ the Lord, with an iron sceptre, in what warfare, or by what battles (if this be the signification of the iron sceptre), did the offspring of the apostolic Church subjugate to himself the Roman world? I answer, by a double warfare. The first, spiritual, wonderful, and divine, against demons, the princes and gods of this world, which, indeed, with an army of celestial angels fighting with him against his enemies, he manfully waged, of which we shall treat in the sequel; the second, strictly corporal, when he had just attained the throne, which so many illustrious victories prove partly of Constantine over Maxentius, Maximinian, and Licinius; partly of Theodosius the Great against others, as well as Eugenius and Arbogastes, the standard-bearers of demons, before the contumacy and pride of the Gentile worshippers of the Dragon, rebelling against Christian government, was fully broken, subdued, and laid to rest.

Joseph Mede

But before we leave this subject, one thing still remains to be observed, namely, that not immediately as the offspring of the woman was brought forth, was he raised to the throne of God, but as soon as he came to maturity in the kingdom. Therefore she is said to have brought forth a son, who was to rule, that is, not immediately, but when he came of age. As Christ, the Son of Mary, our Lord, (to whose image this mystic Christ, the offspring of the Church, is in all things conformed), was in like manner, not as soon as he was born, but when he had arrived to a proper age, raised to the throne of God, and took possession of the kingdom, there to sit till he had reduced his enemies under his footstool.

"And the woman fled into the wilderness, where she bath a place prepared for her by God, that they should nourish her there, one thousand two hundred and sixty days;" of which, as it is afterwards repeated, and somewhat more fully described, we will defer the explanation to that place.

"And there was war in heaven. Michael and his angels fought against the dragon, and the dragon fought, and his angels: And they prevailed not, neither was their place found any more in heaven." It was said, that the mother having brought forth, as soon as her child was safe, escaped the snares of the dragon. But how it came to pass, that he who had so diligently watched her, should yet have failed in his attempt, now at length begins to be related. We learn that this happened by the aid, and under the auspices of Michael, who went strenuously to oppose the dragon, as he lay in wait; and when at length he became his superior, threw him down from heaven to earth. Thence the son of the woman not only escaped unhurt, but was raised to the throne of God, and she withdrew into a secure place from the fury of the dragon. "And there was war in heaven." Namely, while the woman was bringing forth, not after she had brought forth, as many suppose. For it is certain from v. 14. that this war was carried on before the flight of the woman into the wilderness. But the woman did not flee into the wilderness before she had brought forth, and before her son was caught up to the throne of majesty, v. 5 and 6. "Michael and his angels fought with the dragon," not alone, but with the assistance of the martyrs and confessors of Christ their King, by whose grace they fought; of whom, therefore, it will soon be sung in the hymn of victory, that "they overcame him by the blood of the Lamb, and for the word of his testimony, and they loved not their lives unto the end;" which cannot be said of angels only. "And the Dragon fought, and his angels," that is, demons, with the assistance likewise of their worshippers, the Roman tyrants and their ministers.

But who, you will ask, is Michael? Not, I think, Christ himself, but, as it appears from Daniel, unless I am mistaken, one of the chief princes, or seven archangels, nay, the first, c. x. namely, that great angel, who is said by the same author, to stand up on the part of the people of God, c. xii.; and whom, therefore, Christ, the great General in chief, and the King alike of angels and men, employed in opposition to the fury of Satan and his followers against his people. For the angels are sent forth for the salvation of those who are the heirs of God," Heb. c. 1. [49] and who protect and defend them according to a mode of acting secret and unseen, against evil spirits, who operate on such men as are enemies of God, and his Christ, although they do not appear in a visible shape. So in this war, in which we are treating of the primitive Church of Christ against the Roman worshippers of the dragon, the angels took part under Michael their leader, either by confirming the holy martyrs and confessors of Christ against the threats and power of tortures, and in diminishing their pains in their last agonies, and sometimes taking away entirely even the sense of pain; or by breaking and debilitating the attacks of their spiritual adversaries, and by throwing in the way of their persecutors, who acted under their influence, sometimes obstacles, and impediments, arising on a sudden, and so stifling their attempts; sometimes by infusing terrors and other alienations of mind, so that suddenly desisting from their undertakings, they even unwillingly granted to the Church a truce, and breathing time; until at length, after a war of three hundred years, when Christ saw that his people were sufficiently tried, and he determined to give a full victory to his angels, when the offspring of the woman was placed on the imperial throne, and the Christians were possessed of power, the kingdom of the devil being vanquished, fell with a wonderful ruin. For this is what he says,--"The devil prevailed not, neither was a place found for him any longer in heaven;" that is, routed and chased with all his forces, he was cast out of heaven, ("Prevailed not," is a Hebraism, of which hereafter.) "And the great dragon was cast out, that old serpent which is called the devil, and Satan, who deceived) the whole habitable world;" (that is, impels it to idolatry, and had hitherto been seated in the Roman empire;) "he was cast out to the earth, and his angels were cast out with him." That is, he, with all his demons, hitherto worshipped as gods, were hurled down from the summit of divinity in which they gloried, to the depth of execration and contempt. As what we read to have been done formerly in the liberation of Israel from the tyranny of the Egyptian Pharaoh, to whom the dragon bears a resemblance, that "God executed judgment on all the gods of the Egyptians," (Ex. c. xii. v. 12; Num. c. xxxiii. v. 4,) the same found a place here likewise, at least, according to the words. The Jews have a tradition, that it took place there likewise. Vide both Targums, R. Salomon, R. Aben Ezra, with R. Moses, Ben Nachman, &c. Nor is there ground for any one to pervert the clear words of Scripture to any other sense, especially since Isaiah appears to allude to it, c. xix. v. 1.

"Prevailed not," for was conquered, is a Hebrew figure, as I observed; by which adverbs of denying signify the contrary of that to which they are applied. As in this very vision it is said a little farther, "They loved not their lives unto the end;" that is, they reckoned their lives of no account, or they gave them up for Christ. For this mode of speaking among the Hebrews is not diminution, but augmentation. So Prov. c. xii. v. 3, "A man shall not be established by wickedness;" that is, he shall be utterly removed and eradicated. Id. c. x. v. 2, "The treasures of wickedness profit not;" that is, they are hurtful, they are destructive. Id. c. xvii. v. 21, "The father of a fool shall not rejoice;" that is, he shall be affected with sorrow. And 1 Cor. c. xvi. v. 22, "If any one love not the Lord Jesus Christ, let him be anathema;" that is, whoever hates and curses him. Vide Burtorf Thesaur. Gramm. lib. 2, c. xix. So here,--the dragon and his angels prevailed not, is the same as they were completely overcome.

But I have already given a fuller history of this victory in the interpretation of the sixth seal, with which this fall of the dragon contemporises; nay, it is the subject of that seal, as far as it regards the remarkable change of the Roman empire. But what I have said of the offspring of the woman placed on the imperial throne, and of the Christians then possessed of power, is clear and manifest from the song of triumph which is subjoined--"And I heard a loud voice in heaven saying, Now is come salvation, and strength, and the kingdom of our God, and the power of his Christ, for the accuser of our brethren is cast down, who accused them before our God day and night."--"And they overcame him by the blood of the Lamb, and by the word of their testimony, and they loved not their life unto the death." Which words, as they are very clear, and delivered without any veil of allegory, so they are a key to the interpretation of the whole vision. For, from hence it may be clearly perceived, in the first place, what the elevation of the offspring of the woman to the throne of God would be, namely, the introduction of "salvation and might, and the kingdom of God, and the power of his Christ," to the Roman throne; and likewise by the conquest of what enemy, he should come to the kingdom; namely, by the overthrow of that accuser, who calumniates and traduces the brethren clay and night before God; and lastly, what kind of forces Michael and his angels should employ in this battle against the dragon and his satellites, namely, the holy martyrs and confessors, "who overcame him by the blood of the Lamb, and by the word of his testimony, because they loved not" (that is, they gave up) "their lives unto the death." And, indeed, it is utterly impossible that the elevation of the offspring of the woman, the overthrow of the dragon, and the introduction of the kingdom of God, and of his Christ, should not correspond with one and the same event, since the flight of the woman into the wilderness begins from all as from one termination of affairs. But why is Satan here called by the name of Κατήγορος, or Accuser? It is to be understood that this arose from the usage of the Hebrews, by whom he was anciently called by the same name, which they made their own. For they call him רוגטק, Kategor. R. Juda, in the book Musar, as cited by Drusius, says, Kategor is Satan, the wicked adversary or calumniator, who is an adversary to man, and calumniates him before the blessed Creator. Maimonides in Pirke Avoth, (where in a sentence of R. Eliazar, both this, and the word Paraclit of a contrary signification, likewise derived from the Greek, occur,) says, He is called Paraclit, Παράκλητος, or the Intercessor, who intercedes with the King, for a good blessing for man; the opposite to whom is Kategor; for he it is who traduces man to the king, and endeavours to destroy him. And, indeed, if ever Satan deserved the name of accuser or calumniator on any other occasion, strictly deserved it during the time of this childbirth, and the war attending it. Witness the many calumnies and reproaches with which the dragon-worshippers overwhelmed the Christians, during this whole time, objecting to them Thyestoean feasts, Edipodian incests, adultery, promiscuous concubinage, homicides, conspiracies against princes, pestilence, famine, fires, and whatever public calamity took place. But there rather appears here to be a reference to the book of Job, where Satan, by calumniating and accusing him, was the cause of Job's being permitted by God to be proved by him with temptations and tribulations. Which here, likewise, the Holy Spirit intimates, was done by him after his accustomed manner. The intelligent reader will understand what I mean. Then follows in a song of triumph--"Wherefore rejoice, ye heavens! and those who dwell therein," (that is, holy angels, and blessed spirits, by whose exertions this victory has been obtained.) "Woe to the inhabitants of the earth and of the sea," (that is, to the terrene world,) "for the devil is come down to you, having great wrath, (and therefore prepared to contrive some new mischief,) knowing that he hath but a short time."

For though from the time when he was cast down by Constantine the Great, from the Roman throne, the worship of the dragon continued for a short space among the people; yet when he foresaw that not long after he should be expelled likewise, and that the whole Roman world would be sprinkled with the baptism of Christ, in the progress of events; being wholly inflamed with anger and fury, he took counsel how he might bring the victory of the Church into hazard, by whatever means he could employ; and if lie should fail in the attempt, even when cast out, he might subvert it by some new contrivance. In both of which designs we shall see that the most wicked spirit was not wanting to himself.

Footnotes:

46. Query if this be the right interpretation?--R. B. C.
47. Is not Constantine intended?--R. B. C.
48. ἐν διὰ δυοῖν, i. e. one thing divided into two by a conjunction.--R. B. C.
49. Rather "to minister to those who shall be heirs of salvation."--R. B. C.

THE MYSTERY

Of the Woman dwelling in the Wilderness
    The woman delivered of a child, when the dragon was overcome, from thenceforth dwelt in the wilderness, by which is figured the state of the Church, liberated from Pagan tyranny, to the time of the seventh trumpet, and the second Advent of Christ, by the type, not of a latent, invisible, but, as it were, an intermediate condition, like that of the Israelitish Church journeying in the wilderness, from its departure from Egypt, to its entrance into the land of Canaan; a state, therefore, safe from the fury of that red dragon, who resembled Pharaoh, but not yet arrived at that pitch of glory, to which it should finally arrive, when the rest of her enemies should be subdued, as by the possession of Canaan. A state, indeed, which was externally better than the servitude of that heathen tyranny, (out of which, as from Egyptian slavery, the Christian people emerged by the power of Christ,) as from thenceforth endued with a power, under the auspices of Christian emperors and kings, of worshipping Christ freely, as the Israelites in the wilderness of worshipping Jehovah; with temples, likewise, as the tabernacles of Christian worship, magnificently built, with an ecclesiastical polity, constituted by kings, with sacred revenues, tithes, and oblations, but unhappy by its apostasy of various kinds, not less than Israel in the wilderness, with the calf, Baal-peor, Balaam, Korah, &c. Nor, perhaps, should that circumstance be passed over, that the forty-two months of the Christian woman's residence in the wilderness answers to the number of resting-places of Israel in the wilderness. Vide Numbers, c. xxxiii.

The reason and tendency of the type being thus explained, let us illustrate the text particularly, and apply it to the event
    "And when the dragon saw that he was cast down to the earth, he persecuted the woman who brought forth the male child. And there was given to the woman two wings of a great eagle, that she might flee into the wilderness, into her place, where she is nourished for a time, and times, and a half, from the face of the serpent. And the serpent cast forth water out of his mouth after the woman, like a river, that he might cause her to be carried away by the flood."
    This was the first attempt of Satan, when he was cast down, but not yet entirely cast out, remaining, on the contrary, a short time below. That he might, if it were possible by any means to do so, overwhelm the woman, who, when her offspring was possessed of power, was departing to a station in the wilderness, before she should retreat thither wholly secure from his fury. For she did not immediately, as she began to escape, arrive in the wilderness, but after some space of time and delay had intervened; as Israel consumed some time in the journey which he had undertaken from Egypt. But the words here used are so to be understood, that they may appear in some way to be referred to what was said above of the same flight of the woman into the wilderness, either in this, or in a similar sense. "When the dragon saw that he was cast down to the earth, he persecuted the woman who had brought forth the male child." For since (as was observed above) "there was given to the woman," after the birth and exaltation of her offspring to the throne, (by two wings of a great eagle furnished to her, as if for flight) "to depart into the wilderness, where she was to be nourished for a time, and times, and half a time; he cast out of his mouth after her a flood of water, that he might cause her to be carried away with the flood." So, likewise, Pharaoh persecuted the people of Israel, departing into the wilderness out of his dominion, by a flood of another kind.
    The great eagle is the Roman empire. Its two wings, the two Cæsars of the now divided empire of the West and East, under whose protection and authority the church departed into its eremitical state. For it is well known, that the Roman empire, as soon as it had received the Christian faith, became bipartite, and was borne up as it were on the two wings of the Cæsars. The eagle being the ensign of the Roman empire, renders this interpretation obvious to any one. But what forbids us from confirming the interpretation of the prophetical type by an apocryphal writer? This is Esdras the prophet, for under this denomination does Clemens of Alexandria quote him, (Strom, book 3d, a little before the conclusion) according to whom, the type of an eagle signifies the fourth kingdom, the twelve feathered wings as many first Cæsars. Vide c. xi. and xii. But tell

A Key to the Apocalypse

me, Reader, would you not also say, that here is a reference also to that saying of the Lord concerning the departure of Israel out. of Egypt. Exod. c. xix. v. 4. "Ye have seen," says he, "what I did to the Egyptians, and how I bare you on eagles' wings, and brought you unto myself," that is, into the wilderness. But there is something else in this verse which requires to be expounded. Why is the time of the woman's inhabitation in the wilderness, which was reckoned a little before by days, here changed into years, or a time, and times, and half a time? I seek no other cause of this alternation, than that it might be the key to a similar notation of time in Daniel, and might inform us that the Church was now arrived at those very times, which he described by the period of a time, times, and half a time. And, indeed, without this index, that designation of time would have been very uncertain, and inexplicable. For from what source, or by what indication, could it have been known, that time denoted a year? or if so, that times did not mean more than two years? But now, from this communication it is clear, that the period may be resolved into 1260 days, and therefore, signifies a year, two years, and a half.

These difficulties having been explained in this manner, let us now examine what that water was which the dragon vomited out of his mouth like a flood, that he might. overwhelm the woman while she was preparing to take her journey into the wilderness. The gushing out of water is language and doctrine according to Prov. c. xviii. v. 23. "The words of a man's mouth are deep waters, the well-spring. of wisdom is a flowing brook." Whence the word נָבַע, which signifies to burst forth, and gush out as a fountain, is applied to doctrine, as Ps. lxxviii. v. 2. "I will open my mouth in parables, I will utter, or pour forth, things hidden from the foundation of the world;" which is alleged of the doctrine of our Saviour, Matt. c. xiii. v. 35. So Prov. c. i. v. 23. Wisdom is said to preach in the streets; "I will pour out my Spirit upon you; I will make known my words unto you." What, then, is the effusion from the mouth of the serpent, a venomous beast, but pestiferous doctrine, that is heresy? according to that verse of Prov. c. xv. v. 28. "The mouth of the wicked poureth forth evil things." Now the history of this time exhibits it as proceeding like a flood from the mouth of the dragon,--I speak of Arianism and its offspring. By this his flood the dragon had nearly caused the woman to be carried away. He intended it no doubt. And, in truth, it was wonderful that the Roman emperors, who had so recently given their names to Christ, and had not fully settled the Christian establishment, offended and alienated as they were at the horrid dissension in so primary a point of doctrine among Christians (only just respiring from persecution), at such deadly party feuds, tumults, and credulity, among the brethren, even equally to that of the Pagans, should not have cast off the faith.

"But the earth succoured the woman, and the earth opened its mouth, and swallowed up the flood which the dragon cast out of his mouth." That is, the multitude of Christians in the councils persisting in the orthodox faith, exhausted the diabolical inundation, as the earth does water, when it has long continued in a state of drought. For if water, (but of a poisonous and pestiferous nature) such as proceeds out of the serpent, represents heresy; the mode of analogy undoubtedly required that the substance which should have the effect of absorbing and removing the same, should be figured by the earth, as that whose property it is to exhaust an inundation of waters by its aridity.

Which, indeed, happens in this matter so much the more agreeably to the explanation of the subject, because elsewhere likewise in historical and simple expression, the earth is commonly used for the inhabitants of the earth. Vide Gen. c. xli. v. 37. 1 Sam. c. xiv. v. 25. Deut. c. ix. v. 28. and elsewhere at large.

Of the Ten-horned Beast blaspheming God, and of the Two-horned Beast, or False Prophet, his Founder and Hierarch

A new scene of evils invaded the woman, as soon as she had entered the bounds of the wilderness; for she immediately encountered a double sort of beast, less formidable indeed in appearance than that of the dragon, or serpent; whose figure only she dreads, professing to be nothing but a Πανθῆρ, or a lamb, but being truly an agent of the dragon, who has been cast down, and in his stead prepared to bring troubles on the offspring to which she should give birth in the wilderness.

"And the dragon was wroth with the woman, and departed to make war with the rest of her seed, (viz. with those which she should produce in the wilderness,) who keep the commandments of God, and hold the testimony of Jesus Christ."

"And he stood on the sand of the sea." That is, when the dragon saw that he who was now expelled from the Roman empire, that he had not succeeded in overwhelming the woman, as she was hastening into the wilderness, by the inundation of Arianism, but that she nevertheless had arrived there in safety; and besides, that he should no longer be suffered to possess the sovereignty of the Roman world, as he had formerly done, in his own name, he now attempts it in another way, by tacitly substituting a kingdom dependent on himself, and for that purpose he stood on the sea shore, that he might form a new appearance of the Roman kingdom, thence to arise, subservient to him. The history of the double beast, prepared to transact the affairs of Rome, now follows; one ten-horned, and the other two-horned, connected by the strictest necessity with each other, and both reigning at the same time, and in the same part of the world. The first of which, that is, the ten-horned beast, you may call if you will secular; the other, or two-horned, ecclesiastical.

Of the Ten-horned Beast

The ten-horned, or secular beast, is that university of ten kingdoms, more or less, (into which the empire of the Cæsars, after the expulsion of the dragon, had settled after the Barbaric plague,) coalescing at length into one Roman republic, through the renewed impiety of the dragon.

"I saw," said he, "a beast ascending out of the sea, having seven heads, and ten horns, and upon his horns ten diadems, and upon his heads the name of blasphemy." The same beast is here described as that which afterwards, c. xvii. carries the harlot; the seven-headed Roman beast, under the state of its last head. "I saw," says St. John, "the type of that last state of the Roman kingdom, in which, acting under its seventh head, it was divided into ten kingdoms; and yet in the same manner, as it had done under its former heads, he blasphemed the great God Almighty by the worship of idols." For the number of seven heads is a particular mark of the Roman kingdoms, as well as the furniture of ten horns. The name of blasphemy is the mark of idolatry. The diadems, or crowns, placed on the horns, (which are on the last head only,) point out that the kingdom is exhibited under the government of its last head, which will be amply confirmed by the remaining description of the beast.

"And the beast which I saw was like a leopard, and his feet as those of a bear, and his mouth as the mouth of a lion." That is, this kingdom, partly in respect of its regimen, and its state, partly in respect of its disposition, was so composed, that it represented the three monarchies, anciently pourtrayed by these beasts in Daniel, in a certain blended association. Since it was Greek in the remaining appearance of the body, it stood on feet in their march and action, like the Persian kingdom; with its mouth, like that of Babylon, it issued its edicts to be performed. For the leopard is the type of the kingdom of the Greeks, the bear of the Persians, the lion of the Babylonians. First, then, that kingdom was plainly like the Grecian in its body, for instance, a kingdom like that divided into many parts, Dan. c. vii. v. 6. and c. viii. v. 8. 22. For the Greek was divided into four parts; this last Roman kingdom was separated into ten kingdoms, to which type is referred the bearing ten horns on the last head of the beast, which the angel afterwards interprets, c. xvii. are ten kings, or kingdoms, into which the Roman empire of the sixth head, having been dilacerated, coalesced into a new kingdom, under the seventh, for the purpose of carrying the harlot. That the ten horns were upon the last head only, that is, the seventh, and not, as commonly supposed, promiscuously on all, I thus demonstrate. While the head flourishes, the horns flourish, and when it falls, the horns also arising from it must necessarily fall. On the first five heads, then, there could not be horns, because those five heads, as the angel says in c. xvii. were already fallen; neither could there be on the sixth, because while that was reigning in the age of John, (as the angel expressly affirms,) the time of horns was not yet come, for says he, "The ten horns are ten kings, which have not yet received their kingdom." They are reserved, therefore, for the last head. Away, then, with such painters as distribute the ten horns according to their fancy, on seven heads, giving single ones to some, and two to others, out of their liberality, which, how inconsistent it is, and remote from the groundwork of the text, yea, and plainly repugnant to the interpretation of the angel, there is no one, who, having been already informed on the subject, shall seriously weigh it in his mind, that will not be induced to confess. Therefore, it is to be taken as true and certain, that the seventh head alone in the scale of heads, raising themselves one after another, towered over the rest, the highest in situation, the last in place.

Now then I proceed to explain the remaining appearance of this last beast. By the feet on which the body rests, and on which it is moved, and walks, and of which those before answer the purpose of hands and arms to beasts, in holding, seizing, and fighting; by the feet, I say, it alludes closely to the Persian empire; since, as they relied on the councils of their Magi in the management of their affairs, so the Roman kingdom in its last state is governed by the authority of idolatrous monks and clergy, like those Magi. To which that future saying refers of the other falsely prophetic beast, "that it exercises all the power of the ten-horned beast before him." For the feet are to be considered here, not as the lowest and most dishonourable parts of the body, but of the same kind as they are in beasts; not merely the instruments of walking, but also of fighting, and seizing their prey, in which, and in bears especially (I speak of the fore feet), the chief strength of the body consists. Nor are the feet to be here understood as that part only which makes an impression on the ground, but that which comprehends the thighs also, and arms, as well as the smaller part commonly called the foot.

Lastly, the ten-horned beast issues edicts to be observed with a Babylonian mouth, by commanding the worship of deities and idols, with pain of death, and burning alive, denounced against those who refuse it, in the same manner as Nebuchadnezzar did to those Jews, who would not adore the golden image which he had set up, sixty cubits high, to his god Bel. Dan. c. iii. At the same time, I do not wish, by this interpretation of mine, to excite a prejudice against that of others; namely, of those who may think that regard should be had rather to the natural disposition of those beasts, whose qualities or fierceness the ten-horned beast might express. Let every one judge for himself. "And the dragon (who had been cast down, and stood on the sea-shore,) gave him his power, (that is, his strength or forces,) and his throne, and great authority."

Power, Δύναμις, signifies, with the Hellenists, forces or army, according to the use, as it appears to me, of the Hebrew חיל, by which is denoted both strength and bravery, and an army likewise. The Seventy say, in Exod. c. xiv. v. 28. of the army of Pharaoh overwhelmed in the sea, "The waters covered, πᾶσαν τὴν δύναμιν, all the host of Pharaoh," and c. xv. v. 4, "he hath cast, τὴν δύναμιν αὐτοῦ, his host into the sea." And so in various passages, not only in these, but in profane writers. From this notion spring those expressions, Κύριος δυνάμεων, the Lord of hosts, and Matt. c. xxiv. v. 29. δυνάμεις τῶν οὐρανῶν, the powers of the heavens, or the celestial hosts, shall be shaken. So, in the next verse, the Son of man is said to be about to come in the clouds of heaven, μετὰ δυνάμεως καὶ δόξης πολλῆς, with power and great glory, which is explained in the following chapter, us "coming in his glory, and all the holy angels with him." So in this place, the dragon or Satan delivered to the ten-horned beast, τὴν δύναμιν αὐτοῦ, that is, his forces, or his army. But the forces of Satan are his angels or demons, and idols, the receptacles of demons. These forces he delivered over to this last beast, to be worshipped and reverenced, together with his throne, and great authority; that is, in one word, all that power from which he had lately fallen, when conquered and overthrown by Michael, and the holy martyrs and confessors of Christ. So that, indeed, the dragon, or Satan, in this beast of the last state of the empire, recovered in some measure the ancient dominion which he had exercised in the red one; but in a form so dissimilar from the former one, that the seed of the woman in the wilderness did not immediately perceive it. For the dragon did not now make his advances as before, in the form of a dragon, that is, did not profess himself to be what he was, the sworn enemy of the Christian name. For if he had done this, the seed of the woman would have known him immediately, and been upon his guard against him, as his deadliest foe, from that innate antipathy which God had denounced from the beginning of the world should subsist between them. "I will put enmity between thy seed and her seed." But, in truth, when he had assumed the form of another beast, having no affinity with the serpent, it was not so difficult for him to impose upon the seed of the woman, that is, the Christian Church, rejoicing in its late victory, and now secure from the dragon, and to allure it to adopt his customs. Which, indeed, the arch impostor so covertly and deceitfully did, under the mask of a beast not friendly to him, that the Church did not acknowledge till late, that she had been deceived by her ancient enemy, and led to venerate the dragon under this mask. For who would have suspected that the dragon lay hid under the figure of a leopard, or (what is the same) of a Πανθῆρ [50], that is, under the appearance of an animal, which, while other beasts, attracted either by the beauty of his skin, or the sweetness of his smell, love to approach and behold, the dragon alone is said to abhor and avoid? Or, to explain the matter a little more clearly, who would have supposed, that under the empire of the Christian religion, the destroyer of idols assuming worship for herself, heinous idolatry, and long since exploded heathenism, would be restored with the utmost labour, and promoted by laws and edicts?

"And I saw one of its heads, (namely, the sixth,) as it were, wounded to death, (which was done in the battle with Michael and the holy martyrs [51],) and his deadly wound was healed," by the medicine of this vicarious power. That this seven-headed dragon, (or the Roman empire, possessed by the ancient serpent, that is, the heathen empire,) was the beast with the sixth head, may be shown by what is afterwards said of these heads. Five in the age of John had fallen, one (which is the sixth) then ruled the Roman states, and chiefly because this beast of the last dynasty immediately succeeded the fifth, on the same throne. The dragon, I assert, is here said to have given up his throne to the beast of the last dynasty, or the seventh head. Therefore he was the immediate successor, or the beast of the last head. Nor let any one be disturbed, that during the continuance of the sixth head, it appears seven-headed in the vision. For though the heads performed their parts, not at the same time, but in order, and successively, yet the beast is exhibited with all its apparatus of heads and horns, under every state, that it may every where designate the same Roman kingdom, though under different successions of dynasties.

But to return to the text, in which, in the Complutensian edition, according to the testimony of Irenæus, Aretas, the Syrian paraphrast lately published, and among the Latin authors, Primasius does not acknowledge the words "I saw," but joins the words, "one of the heads," with the word "gave," as in this sentence, "The dragon delivered unto him his power and throne and great authority, and one of its heads mortally wounded, that it might be cured." I suspect also that the Latin Vulgate read it so formerly, on account of the words "de capitibus suis," instead of "ejus." But whether this reading is to be preferred to the other, I will not hastily affirm, but only that it appears to be very ancient, so that I wonder it was not noticed by R. Stephen. But whichever it may be, the received reading, if rightly interpreted, and as the subject actually requires we should interpret it, evidently gives the same sense. "I saw (says he) one of the heads, as it had been wounded to death ," namely, not at the time the apostle saw it, but before it emerged in this form from the sea, ὑπερσυντελικῶς, or in the preter-pluperfect tense, as in ch. v. ver. 6, he had said, he "saw in the midst of the elders and of the animals a Lamb standing, as if it had been slain," not slain at the time he saw it. What is added, however, about the healing of the wound, that he saw done, either while the beast was just emerging from the sea, or as soon as it had arisen from thence? For that healing was not, (as is still believed by many,) some subsequent fate, but the very nativity of the last beast. From each of the remaining heads, it had passed to the turn of the successor without a wound; but in the transition from the sixth to the last, the beast sunk under a deadly wound; from the cure of which I say, and not before or sooner, the ten-horned beast, or that of the last state, took its beginning, and did not deduce its origin any higher. That this is the case, the whole series of the following narration evinces. For whatever evil the beast is related to have perpetrated, whatever worship and adoration was paid to him by the inhabitants of the earth, all is said to have been done after the cure of his wound. "I saw (says he) one of his heads as if it had been wounded to death, and the wound of death, or the deadly wound, was healed, and all the world followed, wondering after the beast,"--namely, that just healed," and they worshipped the dragon," &c. Then likewise "was given to him a mouth speaking great things, and blasphemies," &c. And "he opened his mouth against God," &c. All those things were done after his cure; but before that, no evil deeds are predicated of the beast, no mention of subjection or honour paid to him by the nations. Whatever is commemorated before, partly relates to the form of the beast, partly to the occasion and manner of his rise. And why, I beseech you, should we represent to ourselves an antichristian beast, of whom for some time, no facts are related, no persecution recorded? Nay, if we follow the reading of Irenæus and the Complutensian version, by expunging "I saw," there will be no longer a place for such an interpretation. "And all the earth wondered after the beast;" that is, with the utmost approbation and consent, they went over to the party of the beast. "And they worshipped the dragon, which gave power to the beast, and they worshipped the beast, saying, Who is like unto the beast? who is able to make war with him?" That is, they did not simply worship the beast as a beast, but also as a vicegerent of the dragon. Therefore they did not venerate the beast alone, but the dragon himself likewise, under the mask of the beast. For to worship the beast, unless so far as idolatry discharged the functions of the dragon, in the sense in which it is here used, would not have been more impious than to obey any kind of mundane power.

The beast, in truth, denotes a kingdom. To adore the beast, then, according to the usage of the Hebrew and Oriental languages, is the same thing as to be subject to him, which the explanation subjoined to the word worship, not obscurely points out. "They adored (says he) the beast, saying, Who is like unto the beast? who is capable of contending with him?" As if he had said, They devoted themselves willingly to the obedience of the beast, as to one who so far excelled others in power, that there was no one that would resist or make war with him. In which also, ver. 12, the earth itself, not merely its inhabitants, is said to have worshipped the beast; that is, to have yielded to his dominion. "And he caused (says he) the earth, and those that dwell therein, to worship," &c. So in the benediction of Jacob, Gen. c. xxvii. v. 29, "Let the people serve thee, and nations worship (or bow down to) thee. Be lord over thy brethren, and let thy mother's sons bow down to thee." For this meaning of the words τοῦ προσκυνεῖν, vide Gen. c. xxxvii. v. 7, and c. xlix. v. 8, in the benediction of Judah; so also Isa. c. xlv. v. 11. But to be subject to the beast according to his religious constitution, as it refers to the seven-headed dragon, is blasphemous, and impious towards God. Whence, they who so adore the beast, are said to adore the dragon in adoring the beast.

"And there was given to him a mouth speaking great things and blasphemies, and there was given him power to continue forty-two months."

Hitherto of the constitution and state of the beast. It is afterwards explained in what things he exercised the power committed to him by the dragon; viz. in two,--in blasphemy towards God, and the persecution of the saints. The whole description is taken from the prophecy of Daniel, ch. vii. where he treats of the same subject, as here, that is, the Roman beast in the last state. But the circumstances which are there related to Daniel by the angel, rather succinctly, are here more diffusively laid open, as in an interjected explanation.

"There was given to him (says be) a mouth speaking great things." The mouth speaking great things is Daniel's; but here the great words are explained by "blasphemies;" under which name, it will presently be asserted, idolatrous worship was designated, as a matter of the highest affront to God.

Moreover, he says, that the beast should so blaspheme for forty-two months; that is, of years, throughout the same space of time, as the Gentiles should trample down the outer court of the temple, or the holy city. And not undeservedly, since that profanation of the Gentiles runs in a parallel line with the same impiety as this blasphemy of the beast, and both point out a subject of the power of darkness and of night, and therefore to be measured, not by years or days, but months, according to that of the moon, which presides over the night. And, indeed, unless the Holy Spirit had intended the designation of time to be referred to the blasphemy, why has he inserted it in this place, immediately after the mention of blasphemy? The months are not to be reckoned from the beginning of his cruelty, or warfare with the saints, but of his blasphemy. As if the word ποιῆσαι signified some certain act, or state of the power of the beast, (of which kind some suppose that to be, which is here called the power of acting or doing.) it must then altogether be referred to the act of blasphemy. But τὸ ποιῆσαι seems rather to be applied in the senses of lasting or remaining, as it is elsewhere used with words of time. For thus, Acts, ch. xv. v. 33, ποιήσαντες δὲ χρόνον τινὰ, "when he had spent some time;" and ch. xx. v. 3, ποιήσας τε μῆνας τρεῖς, "and there abode three months." 2 Cor. ch. xi. v. 25, νυχθήμερον ἐν τῷ βυθῷ πεποίηκα, "a night and a day I have been in the deep." Add James, ch. iv. 13, "to-day or to-morrow we will go into such a city," καὶ ποιήσομεν ἐκεῖ ἐνιαυτὸν ἕνα, "and continue there a year." Drusius remarks that עשׂה is thus used, Eccles. ch. vi. v. 13, and "facere" in Latin, Seneca, Epist. lxvii. "Quamvis paucissimos unà fecerimus dies."-- "Though we have passed very few days together." In the marble tablet, "cum qua fecit annos ix." "Where, when he had continued nine days." In Alfenus, i. e. "Is servus fugerat et annum in fugâ fecerat." "That slave had fled, and passed a year in flight;" that is, spent, continued, finished, transacted.

According to these examples, why should not "ποιῆσαι μῆνας 42," signify lived so long, remained, continued blaspheming? The force of which expression, those who did not understand, seem to have inserted in the text the word "πόλεμον war," which is extant in some of the copies. Now, as I said before, that by the name of blasphemy in this place, was designated, as by way of eminence, idolatry, or spiritual fornica. don, may be evinced by a twofold, or even a threefold argument. First, because Babylon, the metropolis of this beast, means the mother of harlots, and with her the kings and inhabitants of the earth are said to commit whoredom. But the beast of which we treat, is nothing else than the community of those kings and inhabitants. Secondly, it must be a blasphemy of the same kind, which should suit with the state of the head, immediately preceding nay, of all the other heads for on all "were written the name of blasphemy," ver. 1. Add that this beast of the last state, was born and composed from the renewal of the impiety of his predecessor of the sixth head. But what blasphemy could be ascribed as common to them all, except idolatry alone? Assuredly none [52].

The use of Scripture adds force to these observations, by expressing the idolatry of God's ancient people by this name. To understand which it must be known that there are three words in Hebrew, translated by the Greek interpreters and the Latin Vulgate in the acceptation of blasphemy, נאץ, and חרף, in none of which you may not discover the sign of idolatry. In the word גדף, Ezek. c. xx. v. 27, "Yet in this your fathers have blasphemed me. When I had brought them into the land, for which I lifted up my hand to give it them, then they saw every high hill, and all the thick trees, and they offered their sacrifices," &c. In the word חרף, Isa. c. lxv. v. 7, "Which have burned incense on the mountains, and blasphemed me on the hills." And certainly חרף answers precisely to the Greek βλασφημεῖν, for both signify to treat with contumely, or to reproach. Whence, 2 Kings, c. xix. v. 22, "Whom hast thou reproached and blasphemed?" it is joined with גדף, as synonymous; as also Ps. xliv. v.16. The Seventy are in the habit of rendering both by ὀνειδίζω, π9αροξύνω, and the Chaldee also by its own חרם. Moreover, let me add this likewise, that it was usual with the Jews, not only of the age of Isaiah, but also of a lower age, to understand the worship of idols by the nomenclature of reproach or blasphemy. This may even be collected from the paraphrases of the Hagiographists, where, Ps. lxix. v. 10, instead of the words, "The reproaches of them that reproached thee are fallen upon me," the Chaldee has, "The rebukes of the impious who rebuke thee, while they make their idols partakers of thy glory, are fallen upon me."

With respect to the word נאץ, which is another of the two, to which βλασφημεῖν answers, according to the Seventy; in Forster it is, to attack with contumacy, reproaches, and reviling words. Jerome always translates it in the Psalms, as often as it occurs, (and it occurs five times,) according to the true interpretation of the Hebrew, blasphemare. With others it is, to despise, or to irritate by contempt, so that the most accurate signification of it seems to be, to provoke to anger by reproaches and contumelies. By this expression, I say it may be shown from Deut. c. xxxi. v. 20, that idolatry is designated, as well as by the former. "When they shall have eaten and filled themselves, they will turn to other gods, and will serve them וְנִאֲצוּנִי, and will provoke me." So, indeed, the Vulgate uses the sense of blaspheming, though not the word. For what else is Deo detrahere, to detract from God, than to blaspheme him? But in other places it does express the word, as Jer. c. xxiii. v. 15-17, "From the prophets of Jerusalem is profaneness gone forth into all the land."--"They say לִמְנַאֲצַי unto those that blaspheme me, (the discourse is about idolaters,) the Lord hath spoken, There shall be peace to you, and to every one who walketh after the imagination of his heart," &c.

To these quotations may be added, if you please, by way of illustration, that the profanations of Antiochus, by which he polluted the temple of God, and his sacrifices, are called blasphemies, 1 Macc. c. ii. v. 6, and 2 Macc. c. viii. v. 4. Also, that Kimchias interprets that of Gen. c. iv. v. 26, "Then was the name of the Lord profaned by invocation [53]." Then men turned away after idols, and the invocation of the divine name was polluted and profaned. Whether he has translated rightly or not I do not inquire, but so he has rendered and understood it. Hence according to the scholastic doctors there are three species of blasphemy; one, when something is attributed to God which does not belong to him; another, where something is taken from him which does belong to him; a third, when what is appropriated to God, is attributed to a creature, as in idolatry. For as an adulterous wife brings a reproach upon her husband, so the Church, prostituting herself to idols, does upon God; since idolatry is spiritual adultery.

"And he opened his mouth in blasphemy against God, to blaspheme his name, and his tabernacle, and those that dwell in heaven."

What he had before said generally about blasphemy, he here pursues in detail, and distinguishes a triple idolatry of the beast: For first, he blasphemes the name of God; that is, in the worship of images. "By giving the incommunicable name to stocks and stones." Wisdom, c. xiv. v. 21. Or the name of God means the person of God, (may we be permitted thus to speak,) which is then blasphemed, when any thing besides God is worshipped with divine honour. Secondly, his "tabernacle;" that is, the human nature of Christ, in which the Deity hypostatically dwells. Ὁ γὰρ λόγος σὰρξ ἐγένετο καὶ ἐσκήνωσεν ἐν ἡμῖν, John, c. i. v. 14. And according to the same Evangelist, c. ii. v. 19, "Destroy this temple, and in three days I will raise it up. But he spake of the temple of his body." Has not that passage in the Hebrews, c. ix. v. 11, a reference to this "In a greater or more perfect tabernacle." This tabernacle, I say, the beast blasphemes, when he believes the body of Christ to be made every day out of bread, by the transubstantiation of the mass, and therefore worships the bread instead of Christ, the tabernacle of God; nay, looks up to the propitiatory sacrifice offered for the living, and the dead, as crucifying Christ anew. He blasphemes the celestial inhabitants likewise, that is, the angels and saints, who dwell in heaven, whilst in their names he invokes the demons and idols which he worships [54].

What a reproach is this to the blessed spirits! nay, an affront to Christ their Lord: In derogation of whose prerogative and glory they are constituted, even against their will, mediators and intercessors with God, patrons and presidents of mortals in the manner of the heathen. See what we have already said, at the end of the sixth trumpet, out of the theology of the Gentiles on demons and their offices. And the beast, not content with this alone, degrades the blessed spirits besides, with his disgraceful and wicked fables and miracles; so that you may doubt whether he offends more by the worship which he wishes to display, as addressed to them, or by the injurious nature of his fables.

Thus far of blasphemy, then follows the other part of the impiety of the beast, by which he exhibited himself as the vicegerent of the red dragon,---the persecution of the saints. For in addition, "it was given to him to make war upon the saints, and to overcome them." So Daniel, "He made war with the saints, and prevailed against them." With the saints, that is, with the seed which proceeded from the woman in the wilderness. Now, though the whole domination of the beast may be a kind of warfare against the saints, (according to what was said at the beginning, "that the dragon went away enraged," under the mask of this beast, "to make war with the rest of the woman's seed, who keep the commandments of God, and retain the testimony of Jesus Christ,") yet a war of another kind is here to be understood, as appears from v. 10, where something is said of retaliation to be at some future time rendered to the beast. "If any one lead into captivity," &c., and "If any one kill with the sword, he must be killed with the sword." The war, therefore, is one which is waged with slaughter and blood. Add that we are at present engaged in the description, not of the ecclesiastical, but of the secular beast, with which war of any kind can scarcely agree.

But the beast did not carry on this war immediately from his commencement; but after he had arrived at his acme, during the twelfth age from the birth of Christ. His first expedition threatened the Albigenses and Waldenses, and by whatever other name the true worshippers of Christ were called; of whom so great a destruction was made, that throughout France alone, if P. Perronius, in his history of the war, has made a right calculation, there were slain about a million of men. For not only was this war carried on by burnings alive, by the loss of goods, by exile, and other kinds of punishment, but that nothing might be wanting to the true appellation of war, in such an inhuman persecution, whole armies were raised against them, and those crusading expeditions, first undertaken against the Saracens, being now turned against the Christians, of that chaste and pure religion which refused to adore the beast, it raged cruelly for about seventy years, with incredible fury and inhumanity.

The histories of this butchery are to be met with, to which I refer the reader. I choose to subjoin the words of Thuanus, a most illustrious historian, but of the opposite party. He says, in the Preface to the History of his own Time, "Since exquisite punishments were of little avail against the Waldenses, and what was unseasonably applied as a remedy aggravated the evil, and their number every day increased, a regular army was at length raised, and a war of no less magnitude than that which our people had formerly waged against the Saracens, was resolved upon against them; of which the issue was, that they were brought to their senses, rather by being slain, routed, every where despoiled of their goods and dignities, and dispersed on every side, than by being convinced of their error. Therefore, they who had defended themselves in the beginning by arms, being at last conquered by arms, fled into Provence, and the Alps bordering on the French domain, and there found retreats for their life and doctrine. Some departed into Calabria, and remained there for a long time, and even to the pontificate of Pius the Fourth; part passed over into Germany, and fixed their habitations among the Bohemians, in Poland and Livonia; others turning to the West, found refuge in Britain."

Now in this war the memorable fact happened, that those Albigenses who were conquered at Morell with a great slaughter by Simon Montfort, the leader of those who were signed with the cross, seem to have seized on this prophecy of the saints conquered by the beast, as an argument for consolation and constancy. [55] For when the Bishop of Toulouse, interposing to prevent the slaughter, admonished the remnant, who remained in tents, by sending to them a religious person, that, convicted by such a scourge, of God's being angry with, and pronouncing a judgment upon them, they might at length, (having laid by their hard-heartedness) be converted to the faith which they call Catholic; but they, on the contrary, retorting that the conquered were the people of Christ, by this kind of shield frustrated the attack of temptation, and all to a man fell bravely, being slain by a band of soldiers rushing in upon them.

After this war against the Waldenses and the Albigenses, there was a cruel conflict carried on in various ways against different portions of their remains in different places, as well as against other associates of the same pure religion in every part of the world, until at length, notwithstanding all this, after the year 1500, whole kingdoms, principalities, and republics, with their reformed churches, seceded from the dominion of the beast to the party of the saints; against whom war was afterwards carried on, and continues to this day, nor will it finish until the beast shall come to an end.

Now if any one would diligently measure in his mind the whole series of this butchery, comprehended in little more than 450 years, and would refer the number of the slain to calculation, I am either deceived, or it will appear marvellous, that the persecution of the beast not only equalled, but surpassed the ten heathen persecutions.

We just now observed, that the number of the Albigenses and Waldenses who were slain, was estimated at a million of men. From that time to the Reformation of the Church, no one has undertaken the calculation of those who were taken off, partly by the flames, partly by the sword, partly by other tortures, though the number is known not to have been small. From the origin of the Jesuits to the year 1480, that is, in little more than thirty years, Baldwin on Antichrist remarks, that nearly nine hundred thousand were destroyed. In Belgium alone, and that only by the hand of the executioner, the Duke of Alva, that cruel champion of the Roman see, boasted, that under his authority about thirty-six thousand souls, by his orders, had been taken off in a few years. Vergerius testifies, who well knew the fact, that the Inquisition, as they call it, of heretical depravity, in the space of hardly thirty years, made away with a hundred and fifty thousand Christians, by divers kinds of afflictions. Sanders confesses, that an infinite number of Lollards, and Sacramentarians, were delivered to the flames through the whole of Europe; who, however, he says, were not given up to slaughter by the pope and bishops, but by political magistrates. So, indeed, in consistency with the prophecy, the fact ought to be; for of the secular beast it is said, "that he made war with the saints, and overcame them;" and of the ten kings, c. xvii. that "they should carry on war with the Lamb, and the elect, and faithful;" but of the ecclesiastical beast, not indeed that he himself killed with the sword, "but caused that whoever would not worship the image of the beast, should (by that image) be killed with the sword," as we shall see a little below. Then follows, "And power was given him over every tribe, and tongue, and nation."

Now what was this power, but that of waging war with the saints? as if it would extend itself as widely as the Roman domain, for the subject of discourse is not perhaps of dominion, but of the amplitude of persecution. If any one prefer the other interpretation, the sense will be, that such was the authority of the beast, that no tribe, tongue, nor nation, resisted his impiety. But we must not understand this of individuals, (many of whom were found in every age who preserved their faith to the Lamb) but of whole tribes, tongues, and nations, that is, of the political governments of mankind. Of which it is very true, that none is to be found which the beast had not detained for many ages in servile obedience to his impiety; so that those who dwelt dispersed here and there, through the provinces of the beast, and were in reality Christians, constituted alone at that time the undefiled and virgin Church, as that which had, alas! no state, republic, principality, nor kingdom, of its confession of faith. But here it is to be kept in mind, that the form of the beast was that impiety which supplied the place of the dragon, in whose communion those many kingdoms of the Roman dominion, as we have observed, coalesced to form one beast. Those, therefore, who embraced this are said to yield to the power of the beast, as all tribes, languages, and nations, did.

"And all they that dwell on the earth shall worship him, whose names are not written in the book of life of the Lamb, slain from the foundation of the world."

Now, lest any one, fascinated by so universal and catholic an assent to the laws of the beast, should presume that it was done piously and rightly, and that the example of so many nations and people might be followed by them without danger, or even when broken down and debilitated by the cruelty of persecution, he might violate his faith given to the Lamb, and yield to the worship of the beast; the Holy Spirit denounces, in a declaration plainly to be feared, in what situation and number they are to be esteemed by God, who exhibit themselves as complying with this monster of impiety; that they are not to be considered as in the roll of the Lamb who was slain, but to perish eternally as exiles from the kingdom of God. To this formidable admonition is subjoined an apostrophe, in order to excite attention. "If any one," says he, "has ears to hear, let him hear." As if he said, Ω pious worshippers of Christ, incline your ears, and retain in your inmost souls what is now proclaimed beforehand of the very unhappy lot of those who follow the beast; and it is not a thing of small moment, but the hinge upon which your salvation turns. Those words, therefore, ought to be referred to what precedes, and not to what follows, in the same manner as it is clear, the same address is more than once to be referred in the epistles to the churches. Vide c. ii. v. ult. c. iii. v. 6. 13. 22.

"If any one leadeth into captivity, he shall go into captivity; if any one killeth with the sword, he shall be killed with the sword."

A consolatory reflection for the pious, against whom the beast, when they refused to obey him, proceeded with war, imprisonment, and the most inhuman punishments. The time will come, when God, the just avenger of his people, may demand retribution for so many butcheries, suchenormous cruelties, and may execute vengeance on the raging beast.

And "here," says he, "is the patience and faith of the saints." That is, let not the saints, relying on this equity of the Divine Power, and on his justice in ordering human events, be disturbed at what they are about to suffer, or faint in their minds, but courageously contending against the beast, firmly and patiently wait for the vengeance which will certainly, and in an accumulated degree, proceed from God.

Hitherto we have treated of the secular beast. Now the apostle proceeds to the description of the other beast seen by him, namely, the ecclesiastical beast, or rather the false prophet, who exercises the lieutenancy of the former beast, and of his blasphemies.

Of the other Two-horned Beast, or False Prophet

The two-horned beast, or pseudo-prophet, is the Roman pontiff, with his clergy, having indeed two horns like the Lamb, of whose power of binding and loosing on the earth he boasts himself the vicar, but uttering idolatries and butcheries of the saints like a dragon. For this beast was the author and founder of that ten-horned beast, which supplied the place of the dragon in tyranny and blasphemies, under the mark of the Christian profession. Of whom, therefore, as he exercises the power in the office of hierarch, so likewise is he the pontiff of the same, no less than of his clergy, (with whom he privately constitutes the pseudo-prophetic beast,) he conducts himself as head and monarch, exhibiting that seventh and last head of the Roman commonwealth, in the city on seven hills; who, indeed, by signs and miracles, which it was given to him and his clergy to do, or pretend to do, by the thunder of excommunication, as of celestial vengeance, brought in by degrees the kings, lately risen in the Roman world, out of the dissipated empire of the Cæsars, to submit their necks unanimously to him and to the government of Rome, now otherwise subdued, so as to introduce an image of the ancient, and now demolished heathen empire. Which went on so favourably for him, that not only the Roman beast, wounded in his Caesarean head, evidently revived in that image, but the image itself likewise, at the nod of the false prophet, fell upon those who exclaimed against his appearance, and chastised them with the secular sword, as the false prophet did with the spiritual.

"And I saw (says he) another beast ascending out of the earth, and it had two horns like a lamb, and it spake as a dragon."

He saw another beast, namely, the pseudo-prophetical or pseudo-ecclesiastical beast, which consisted, as we have said, of the Roman pontiff with his clergy. For the pontiff alone, and by himself, though he may be called the false prophet, does not, however, constitute the beast, unless with the addition of his clergy, since the beast denotes an assembly of men, delighting, like an animal, in a certain order of its members, and not a single person. But he saw him ascending from the earth; that is, not like the former, risen from the sea, or the dominions of the world; that is, from a more noble kind of origin, but sprung from the lowest condition of human affairs; or rather, not born as the secular one, during a tumultuous conflict of armies and people contending with each other, but growing up quietly, and without noise, like herbs and plants springing from the earth. For the sea, though it signifies a conflux of people into one dominion, signifies also an army in war. "And it had two horns like a lamb," that is, the bipartite power of binding and loosing, delegated by Christ to Peter, and so far, indeed, similar to that of the Lamb, inasmuch as lie said, "As my Father sent me, so send I you." This power, in fact, the beast assumes, and says that he acts therein as the vicar of Christ, hut he speaks as a dragon; even as the red dragon, whom Michael had a little before overthrown, and expelled from the Roman empire; whilst in truth, like him, he patronizes the worship of deities and idols, by his authority, and, in a similar manner, causes the true and pure worshippers of the Lamb that was slain to be exterminated by persecution and butcheries. For "he exercises all the power of the first beast before him." The two-horned beast executes that delegated power of the dragon committed to the first beast, and consisting in idolatrous worship; as a hierarch, whose office it is to preside in offering sacrifices. "Before the beast, or in his sight," is the same as with him, or for his sake; as if one should say, this two-horned beast belongs to the ten-horned beast, for the purpose of sacrifice, so that it ought not to appear wonderful if he speaks as a dragon. For thus the לפני of the Hebrews; to which ἐνώπιον, in the sight of or before answers, is sometimes equivalent to the dative of the person to whom something is given, or in whose favour it is done, as, instead of that which is said 1 Sam. ii. 18, "Samuel was worshipping before the Lord," it is in ch. iii. "worshipping the Lord." But the Roman pontiff, in an especial manner the head of the latter beast, exercises the supreme administration likewise of the former beast: "And causet4 the earth, and those that dwell therein, to worship the first beast, whose deadly wound was healed." That is, in general, whatever the first beast is, whatever obedience is offered by the nations to his impiety, is wholly to be referred to this hierarch as its parent, by whose exertion, in fact, it should come to pass, that the earth and its inhabitants should worship the first beast, which arose out of the sea, and whose deadly wound was healed. In what manner, and by what means and contrivances he effected this, he particularly explains in the sequel. "For (says he) he doth great wonders, so that he maketh fire to descend from heaven on the earth, in the sight of men."--"And he deceiveth those that dwell on the earth, by the miracles which it was given him to do, in the presence of the beast, saying to those that dwell on the earth, that they should make an image to the beast which had the wound by the sword, and yet lived." For he doth, καὶ ποιεῖ, the Vau of the Hebrews; and, therefore, καὶ in Scripture is not only a conjunction copulative, but also disjunctive, rational, causal, or dinal, or explanatory, as the sense requires; and this it may be sufficient to observe once for all. The pseudo-prophetic, or pontifical beast, is the occasion of constituting for the nations that ten-horned beast, by which the power of the dragon revived. For he persuaded him, by the same signs and miracles, to agree with him in fabricating an image of the beast slain in its sixth head; which at length, being formed at his suggestion, that wound, received in its dragon state, appeared by the introduction of a new idolatry and tyranny, according to the similitude of the former, to be cured; and the beast who worshipped the dragon, to be renewed; for the Roman beast is the image of the last head of the beast slain in its sixth head. He said to the inhabitants of the earth, that they should make an image of the beast which had received the wound from a sword; that is, the image of him in the condition in which he was when he received the wound; "and he lived;" that is, thus at length the beast revived, or was restored. For those words do not refer to the description of the beast whose image was to be fabricated, as the words of the false prophet who was speaking; but they are those of the angel relating or exhibiting the consequence of that advice; namely, that in this manner the slain beast revived. As if he had spoken more fully as follows: "Saying to the inhabitants of the earth, that they should make an image to the beast which had the wound from a sword. They did so, and he revived." As 2 Kings ch. xx. v. 7, Isaiah said, "Take a lump of figs;" and they took them and laid them on the ulcer, and he recovered, viz. Hezekiah, or the ulcer. Now this is what was said in the description of the secular beast, that the dragon delivered to him his forces, and great authority, and therefore his deadly wound was healed. That is, the dragon impressed the form of his worship and power on the beast of a different religion; whilst he substituted his angels or demons, not, indeed, as formerly, to he worshipped under those titles in which they proclaimed themselves enemies to Christ our Lord, but under the shelter of the Christian religion, in the names of saints and good angels,--and, shame on the blasphemy!--even of Christ himself. For he who worships idols, under whatever name he may invoke them, worships demons.

Nay, that nothing might be wanting to the complete image of the beast that was slain, that is, of the dragon, what some of the emperors who worshipped the dragon had done before, the pontiff himself took care should be offered to him; even divine honours, and an authority peculiar to God; so that "he sits in the temple of God," as St. Paul says, "exhibiting himself as God." Which though John, or the angel unfolding the history to him, does not here specially treat of, yet he means to

Joseph Mede

have comprehended under the general name of an image, as a part of that similitude under which he is compared to the slain beast.

And thus far of the fabrication of the image; now we proceed to the wonders applied in favour of his party. "He doth great wonders, so that he even causes fire to descend from heaven on the earth." Not unwillingly here should I accede to the opinion of Graser, if it could by any means be confirmed from the writings of the Hebrews, that this assertion of drawing down fire from heaven is used as a proverbial hyperbole, to the exaggeration of that which preceded it, as if one had said, he does great wonders, nay, of such a kind and so great, that they appear to be not far removed from the miracles of Elias himself, by which he maintained the worship of the true God. For the Jews, says Graser, commonly attribute so much to that miracle of Elijah, that they use it proverbially for all stupendous facts, by which the dignity of God is elucidated. But whoever is not pleased with this exposition, let him follow the Complutensian reading confirmed likewise by other copies. "He does great wonders καὶ πῦρ ἵνα ταταβαίνῃ, and that fire should descend from heaven on the earth;" and so, as the summary of those things which are afterwards more diffusively explained, may be proposed in these words; the sentence may be interpreted of a two-fold species of means, which the false prophet should employ, to induce the inhabitants of the Christian world to form anew the image of the beast, which was slain in his sixth head; that is, by the display of miracles, and by the thunder of excommunication, by one of which he seduced the minds of the nations into error, by the other he subdued the contumacy and pride of the disobedient. Now each of these, whichever way they are regarded, is treated of in the following words in order. Of the wonders in these words,-- "And he seduces the inhabitants of the earth by the wonders which it was given him to perform, saying to the inhabitants of the earth, that they should make an image of the beast, which was wounded by the sword," and those which follow to ver. 16. Of excommunication in these words,-- "He causeth all to receive a mark in their right hands, or in their foreheads, that no one might buy or sell, but he who had the mark, or name of the beast, or the number of his name."

A mode of speaking by synecdoche, by which, from the interdiction of commerce with others, the censure of ecclesiastical anathema is intimated. Nor is that assimilated improperly to celestial fire or lightning; for what, I beseech you, is to devote any one to the eternal fire in the name of God, but to call down fire from heaven? especially since the punishment to proceed from God in the lake of fire and sulphur, or Asphaltites, in which Sodom and Gomorrha were burned by fire rained down, is more than once represented in this book. Nay, the apostle Peter speaks of that conflagration, 2 Pet. c. ii. v. 6, that "God had set it forth as an ensample to those who should hereafter live ungodly; that is, by an ellipsis of the former substantive, common in the Hebrew, an ensample of the punishment of those who should be ungodly hereafter. And Jude, here expressing more clearly the intention of Peter, says, "πυρὸς αἰωνίου δίκην ὑπέχειν;" that is, "to bear the similitude or type of eternal fire." For so, in a sense similar to this, the collation of the words of the two apostles with each other, and the nature of the thing itself, will persuade an attentive reader, that the words of Jude ought to be interpreted. And on this occasion likewise, permit me to add, that it was a memorable and melancholy omen to the Jews, then rejected by God, which Josephus relates to have befallen them in the very beginning of that fatal war, the defeat sustained by them at the passage of Jordan from the country of Jericho; namely, while some were thrown into the river by the enemy, others not being able to bear up against their force, voluntarily leaped into it; so that the lake Asphaltites was filled with carcases rolled down by the descending flood; in which case, says he, the plague, though very great in itself, yet appeared still greater in its nature to the Jews.

But to proceed to the event of the prophecy. As to the wonders, it is a notorious circumstance, that a universal idolatry has prevailed in the kingdom of the beast for about twelve ages, to the present time, as well as the primary species, consisting in the worship of dead saints, of relics, and angels, as the next in order, the worship of images, and afterwards that latest blasphemy of a god in bread, by a great assemblage of wonders, by supposed cures, and miraculous visions, by the coercion of demons in appearance only, and by other surprising effects of different kinds, was first recommended, as it were, to unhappy Christians, and afterwards enforced and confirmed. All which things, indeed, the two-horned beast, or Roman pontiff, with his pseudo-prophetic attendant, is said to have done; inasmuch as they either contrived them or approved them by their authority when contrived by others; or they obtruded what were really the operations and tricks of evil demons, for true and divine miracles, in order to seduce the Christian world. For this is the very thing which the apostle Paul predicted to the Thessalonians, "that the appearance of the man of sin should be according to the working of Satan, with all power, and signs, and lying wonders, and with all deceivableness of unrighteousness."

The examples of thunder, or the pontifical anathema, by which he maintained his authority in decreeing and commanding, are in truth so obvious to every one, that I may be wholly spared the labour of introducing them here from the annals of the Church. One I wish to notice as very remarkable, and which so nearly relates to the image of the fabrication of which we are treating, that it may alone be sufficient to establish the truth of this prophecy. In that controversy or war about images, which arose among the Greeks about the year 720, and which was agitated for 120 years with great fervour, and persecution of idolatry, it can hardly be described into what peril that image of the slain dragon, then rude and imperfect, and not having received the finishing hand of the artificer, was brought. Nor in that controversy, as is commonly supposed, was the worship of images alone, but also that of dead saints and relics strenuously opposed. Leo Isaurius (says Theophanes, Hist. Miscell. Lib. xxi. ch. 23) not only erred with the impious concerning the affectionate adoration of venerable images, but also concerning intercessions of the most chaste mother of God, and of all the saints, whose relics, likewise, that most wicked man abominated, like his teachers the Arabians, (that is, the Mahometans.) The same writer says of Constantine, whom, as a term of reproach, the patrons of idols called Copronymus, (same chapter,) "This most mischievous, unmannerly, savage man, &c. first departed from God, and his undefiled mother, and all the saints." So this paltry Greek idolater blasphemes the pious emperor. Again, Lib. xxii. c. 42, "He every where opposed the intercession of the holy virgin, and mother of God, and of all the saints, as useless, both in his writings, and unwritten declarations, through whom every favour flows down upon us, rejecting their holy relics, and rendering them hateful. If at any time he was told of any extraordinary thing to be applied to the health of souls and bodies, or according to custom to be honoured by those who live piously, he immediately threatened death against those who did thus, as acting impiously; or, at all events, proscription, exile, torments. And that scrap most acceptable to God, as it was accounted a kind of treasure to the possessors, was taken away to he rendered hateful from thenceforth." Let the reader see likewise, c. 54. So also in c. 48, "As often as any one who fell down, or was sick, uttered the usual outcry of Christians,--Help, mother of God or was apprehended keeping vigils, &c. he was condemned as an enemy to the emperor, and was denominated immemorable." Nay, still under Theophilus, the last of five emperors who contended against images, it appears that the worship of saints was opposed by that hymn of Theodorus, in which the Constantinopolitan Church was accustomed every year, (Ω sin and sorrow,) to cherish again the memory of idolatry, at length victorious. For there the eighth ode says, "The sacred relics of the saints, and their images, that savage Lezius, together with John, (who was patriarch of Constantinople under Theophilus,) those deserters of piety nu-piously asserted were on no account to be venerated." What, then, did the Roman pontiff do in this case? He succours the image of the beast, in the greatest danger of being broken, and when he cannot succeed by letters and threats, he has recourse to fulminating arts. He strikes Leo the Isaurian, the leader of the Iconoclastes, with an anathema; he absolves his subjects in Italy from the oath of obedience, and deprives him of the Exarchate of Ravenna, and the rest of his dominion, as far as he is able. By which act, as he gave courage to the idolatrous faction in the east, so he opportunely terrified the kings of the west, from attempting any thing of a similar kind. By the same thunder, the Lateran Synod of 280 bishops, under Alexander the Third, ordained that the Albigenses, and their defenders, and supporters, should be blasted, and actually did blast them. The same thunder likewise, the great Lateran Council decreed, should be called down on the temporal lords, who, when required and admonished by the Church to purge their territories of them, neglected to do it; that is, that they should be bound by their metropolitans, and other provincial bishops, under the bond of excommunication, and if they contemptuously neglected to discharge this duty, their vassals should be denounced by the Roman pontiff, absolved from their allegiance, and their lands given up to be occupied by Catholics."

"And it was permitted him to give life to the image of the beast, that the image of the beast might both speak, and cause as many as would not worship the image of the beast to be killed."

If the image had not been endued with a vital power, the slain beast would not have revived by its fabrication. For the dragon-worshipping beast, which it was to resemble, was not an inactive beast, but was accustomed to exert himself very strenuously, and to attack those who opposed his inclination. Of the same kind, therefore, must that image be, in which he afterwards revived. Hence it is said to be given to the false prophet, not only that he should entice the Christian people to make an image of the beast, but that he should bestow life on it, by which, and by edicts of a similar nature, he might order what was necessary for the maintenance of his dignity, and might punish those who were disobedient, and who refused to submit to his religious constitution, by the sword, or by a secular death. And indeed the whole power which the image has, as a secular idolatrous beast, of warring with the saints, he exercises only as delivered to him by the pseudo-prophetic beast. For the matter is so managed, that those whom the pseudo-prophetic beast has condemned for heresy, (as they call it) or for dishonouring the image, he gives at last to the secular beast the power of killing; of which he possesses none himself, but that dependent upon ecclesiastical judgment. And this is what they call delivering over to the secular power, every where to be met with in the histories of the bestial executions. The pseudo-prophetic beast, indeed, as he would wish it to appear, does not himself kill, but yet he delivers those condemned by his sentence to the secular power, as to an executioner, to be killed.

"And he causeth all, both small and great, rich and poor, and free and bond (that is, of whatever rank, state, and condition) to receive from him [56] a mark upon their right hand, or upon their foreheads. And that no one might buy or sell, but he that had the mark or the name of the beast, or the number of his name." What is meant by the interdiction of buying and selling, (to begin with the last in order,) I have just now shown, namely, to denote the papal excommunication, under which those who fall are excluded from the custom and commerce of citizens. So the canon of the Lateran Council under Alexander, of which mention was made a little above, issued against the Waldenses and Albigenses, prohibits expressly under an anathema, "That any one should presume to receive, or maintain them in their houses, or to carry on any business with them." And the Synod of Tours, in France, prohibits under a similar denunciation, "Where the followers of that heresy, (as they call it) were known, that any one should presume to grant them a place of refuge in their territory, or to afford them protection; but prescribes that no communication should be held with them in buying and selling."

And what? Does not the false prophet here likewise speak like a dragon? For the dragon Diocletian published a similar edict. That no one should sell or supply any thing to the Christians, unless they had first offered incense to the gods, of which Beda thus sings in the Hymn of Justin Martyr:

> Non illis emendi quidquam
> Aut vendendi copia;
> Nec ipsam haurire aquam
> Dabatur licentia,
> Antequam thuriticarent
> Detestandis idolis.

> No power to buy or sell,
> Not even water from the well,
> Could wretched Christians have;
> Unless to idols dire,
> With frankincense and fire,
> They hateful glory gave.

This synechdochical mode of speaking perhaps the Holy Spirit used, to intimate that the papal anathema, though it boast of an abscission from the internal and invisible communion of Christ, has not really any power beyond that of excluding the person from the internal and visible commerce with other citizens.

Now, as to what is said of the mark or character. The mark of the beast is not properly any thing but the name; therefore it is called the mark or name of the beast, and in the following chapter, the mark of his name. Now there is an allusion here to the ancient custom, by which slaves were wont to be marked with the names of their masters, and soldiers with that of their general; (the former chiefly on the forehead, the latter on the hand;) therefore, in a like manner, the followers of the Lamb, in a subsequent chapter, who form a contrast to the attendants on the beast, are inscribed on the forehead with the names of the Lamb and the Father. In the same sense, .in both examples, to indicate to what lord each assembly belonged, and for whom it fought; that the former professed themselves the servants of the beast and his image, the latter of Christ and his Father.

What relates to number, is to be understood rather as an appendix of the name or mark of the beast, than the mark itself; and, indeed, it is the number, not so strictly of the name of the beast, as of the beast itself, as it is also immediately after called. But it is only called the number of the name on this account, because it would be contained in the letters of the name of the beast, referring to numbers, God so disposing it. And yet it does not follow, because the number agrees so intimately with the name, that therefore the number of the beast is to be confounded with the name. For the method of opposition (or contrast) requires, that, as in the assembly of the Lamb, the character of the name is distinguished from the number of the assembly, so likewise it should be in the bestial assembly. Add, that the character of the name and the number are altogether of a different kind, I say, as to signification, if we direct our interpretation according to the analogy of other places. For the character of the name is one thing as to the Lord, to whom those who bear it devote themselves, and the number is another, which points out from what ancestry or origin those who are celebrated by it derive their race. As the number twelve, and that formed from the multiplication of twelve, exhibited as well in the virgin assembly as in the structure and dimensions of the New Jerusalem, is a symbol of its apostolical origin and character.

But not to dwell longer on these generalities, let us see at length what is that name of the beast

A Key to the Apocalypse

in which his number, also marked by the Holy Spirit, is contained. It is, in truth, what some suspected, while the Apocalypse had been recently written, that word so often repeated, Λατεῖνος. For it was by this name [57], after the division of the empire, and the ten kings had arisen in its provinces, and not before, that the Roman false prophet, with the rest of the inhabitants of the West, was called by way of distinction, and that by those to whom the Apocalypse was addressed,--the seven Churches of Asia. For the Greeks, and the rest of the Orientals, with whom, in the dilaceration of the empire, the name had remained, wished themselves only to be called Romans; but us, with our pontiff, and under him, his bishops, kings, and dynasties, by a kind of fatal instinct they called Latins. And this very name, with its letters cast up in the manner of the Greeks and Hebrews, completes the number noted by the Holy Spirit; but it is a mystical number;--by which is indicated of what lineage the beast is, and how falsely he boasts himself the successor of the apostolic choir, when he is really that of the dragon.

"The number of the name of the beast is 666;" which, if you endeavour to deduce from the compounds of 12, the symbol of the apostolic race, you will labour in vain, for you will never from thence be enabled to make 666, by whatever mode you may multiply: But on the contrary, from the power of 6, which is the number of the red dragon, that is, the beast of the sixth head, you will do it very easily, since the whole may be made up from sixes, how great soever it may be of units, tens, and hundreds; as if the seed of the dragon had pervaded the whole body of this last beast, and all its limbs. "Here is wisdom," says the Spirit. "He who hath understanding, let him compute the number of the beast, for it is the number of a man, and his number is 666."

That this ought to be computed according to the mode which I have described, I seem to myself to collect from the analogy of the virgin company, whose number 144, in contradiction to that of the beast, is wholly apostolical, arising from 12 multiplied into itself. The rule of contraries is contrary. And there, indeed, the Holy Spirit has expressed both, as well as the name inscribed, as the number of the company inscribed, but here he has left the name to be conjectured from the number. To settle the matter in few words. To receive the mark of the name of the beast then, is to devote oneself to his power, and to confess his dominion; but to be of his number, is to embrace his impiety, derived from the dragon, namely, the Latin idolatry. Whence it will not perhaps be unworthy consideration, that though no one can receive the mark of the beast's name, or be subject to his power, but he must of necessity receive his number also, at the same time, that is, partake of his impiety; it is possible that a person may admit the number or impiety of the beast, but may reject his mark or name.

This is what has taken place among the Greeks for a long time past, who, although they embrace the same form of impiety, engrafted from the dragon, or the Latin idolatry, and that originally confirmed among themselves, under the auspices of the Latin pontiff, in the second Council of Nice, who was labouring there likewise to erect the image of the slain dragon, yet they have refused now for 700 years to be subject to the Latin pontiff, or to bear his name, as before they seceded in consequence of a schism, they had been accustomed to do.

Of the Virgin Assembly, or one hundred and forty-four thousand of the Sealed of the Lamb

The virgin assembly of the followers of the Lamb of Sion, and the same selected company of Israel, adopted from the Gentiles, of which mention was made at the beginning of the seventh seal, (for it is described by a double vision, as we there observed, in order to connect the prophecy of the seals with that of the little book) signifies the Church faithful to the Lamb, a virgin under Babylon, in the midst of a world of nominal Christians, who followed the beast; the kindred and undegenerate progeny of the twelve apostles, apostolically multiplied; as alone according to the example of the heavenly choir, instructed to celebrate the Lamb and the Father with an evangelical song, in a chaste and holy manner; which by a sad fatality, not one of the beast's party was able to learn. Yet a people not addicted to any one seat, as the people of the beast, but accompanying the Lamb wherever he went, warning finally the worshippers of the beast frequently and sharply of the duty of evangelical worship, and of the manifest severity of God against idolaters; and at length denouncing to all, if they would not perish eternally, to withdraw themselves as quickly as possible from all connexion with it. This is a summary of the vision. Let us now elucidate the text according to this rule.

"And I looked, and lo, a Lamb stood upon mount Sion, and with him a hundred and forty-four thousand." From the number 144, or twelve times twelve thousand, it appears that the same assembly is here described as was sealed at the introduction of the seventh seal; viz. that legitimate and undegenerate offspring of the apostles, bearing this number twelve as a mark of its origin. Let the reader reconsider what we there remarked.

Now, mount Sion was the throne of the kingdom of David, and the same as what is called the city of David, because he built it, when taken from the Jebusites, externally with new walls, and internally with a royal citadel, streets, and squares. Therefore here it is parabolically applied, and it

Joseph Mede

will designate that place on the earth which Christ, having conquered the dragon, made the dwelling-place of his kingdom, or his Church, that is, the world denominated Christian. In this world the virgin Church has its mansion, and therein still preserves its faith and chastity undefiled, when the beast appeared to have contaminated, and trodden down all things, with his adulteries and slaughters, and to have left nothing sound and uninjured.

"Having (the name of the Lamb and) his Father's name written on their foreheads."

The name of the Lamb is improperly omitted from some copies, as the Vulgate, Primasius, Andrew, Aretas, the Complutensian edition, and the Syriac translator allow. That it was the true reading is not to be doubted, but that the subject itself requires it to be so read, will clearly appear in the progress of the interpretation. For here is an allusion (as we also noticed in the history of the beast) to the ancient custom, by which both the slaves of masters, and the soldiers of the emperor, were distinguished, being anciently inscribed with their name or mark; and the slaves, indeed, principally on their foreheads, (witness Rhodigian's Book, v. 33.) but the soldiers on their hands. Vegetius, lib. ii. 5, says, "The soldiers, inscribed with permanent marks on the skin, and inserted in the rolls, were accustomed to take an oath." But Ætius says, lib. viii. 12, "They call them brands, which are inscribed on the face, or some part of the body, as those of soldiers are on the hands. But of the inscription of soldiers, Lypsius will give us more ample information, lib. i. de Mil. Rom. dial. 9. "Under the princes," says he, "they punctured with a sharp instrument youths just taken, and branded them on the skin." These were real stigmas, and impressed on the hands of soldiers. They were inscribed with the name of the emperor. Hence Augustin calls it the royal mark, and Chrysostom σφραγῖδα, the seal. This is to be derived from the circumstance, that anciently the name of the emperor used to be inscribed on the shields, spears, and standards, and in imitation of that on the skin; or else from sacred rites, for those whom they consecrated to God, or initiated, they branded with marks or stigmas."

Now then to the point. They bear the name of the Lamb, and his Father, on their foreheads, who do not break the faith by which they gave themselves up to the Lamb, as their emperor and Lord, and to his Father in baptism, and who do not relapse to the worship and pomps of Satan, and his angels, which they had once abjured. For thus in ancient times, (in order to throw a greater light on what has been here said) was the form of renunciation in baptism couched in most Churches. "I renounce Satan and all his works, and his pomps, and all his worship." In many, and those, the most ancient liturgies, was added, "and his angels." In others, "and all his inventions, and all who are under him." In others, in the same sense, "and his world." All which things may be expressed readily in the apocalyptical sense,--"I renounce the dragon, and all his forces;" that is, as Cyril of Alexandria explains the form of baptism, "I bid farewell to the multitude of demons, and I reject all their pomp and worship."

The Roman Church was here a little more terse than others: for in it there is mention made only of Satan, his pomps, and his works; where, under the name of Satan as chief, it understands his angels also; of pomps and works, the idolatrous worship, and all its apparatus.

That the sacrament of baptism, by which we solemnly profess faith to the Lamb, and the Father, and by which we receive their name, and are called Christians, is the Lord's seal, the fathers every where declare, and that from the highest antiquity of the Church. Hence that of Origen, "We bear the immortal laver on our foreheads; when the demons see it they tremble." Augustine also calls it, "the royal mark, the mark of the Emperor, the mark of the Redeemer." They also maintain that this seal may be cancelled, and as it were, obliterated by idolatry and superstition. Tertullian on Spectacles, c. 4, treating of baptism under the name of a seal, says, "When, upon our entering into the water, we profess the Christian faith in the words of his law, we call God to witness by our declaration, that we have renounced the devil, and his pomps, and his angels. What will be the chief and principal instance in which the devil, and his pomps, and his angels, are to be understood, but idolatry?" and c. 24, "Do we not abjure and break the seal in breaking his testimony?" Of the same kind also is that in the Book of Idolatry, c. 19, "There is no agreement between the sign of Christ, and the sign of the Devil." In like manner Augustine Tract. 7 on John, "He has lost the sign of Christ, he assumes the sign of the devil." Christ will not have such a communion. He will possess solely what he has purchased. With these Isidore agrees, Origin β. 18. c. 59. On the execration of spectacles, "He denies God, who undertakes such things, and has become a prevaricator to the Christian faith, who desires that afterwards, which he renounced long ago, at his baptism, that is, the devil, his pomps, and his works. All therefore who have received the mark of the beast, have denied, abjured, rendered of no avail, and accounted, as if they had never received, the mark of Christ, and of the Father. Only those, a hundred and forty-four thousand, who had not gone over to the camp of the beast, but adhered firmly to the Lamb, show the Lord's mark on their foreheads.

One thing still remains to be noticed; viz. that though the sealed in both instances, namely, here as well as in c. vii. are the same, yet the reason for the sealing is not the same in both; and that in consequence of the different intent of the sealing. For there the subject of protection is treated of;

A Key to the Apocalypse

here, of service and fidelity. But there is no necessity on that account to seek any other sign absolutely different from that of baptism; for baptism answers to both, since, over and above that which is the sign of our profession, God superadds another, namely, that of his grace, by which he acknowledges those who are washed, as his own, and receives them into his protection.

The latter, then, is treated of in the first vision of the sealed ones, the former in the present, if I am not deceived. And it favours this construction, that Clemens Alexandrinus, according to Eusebius, lib. iii. c. 17, calls baptism τέλειον φυλακτήριον, perfect guardianship. Also that Nazianzen, Orat. on Holy Baptism, affirms, that it is called a seal, as συντήρησιν, because it is conservation. Lastly, that of Basil, Exhort. to Baptism, "Unless the face of the Lord be sealed upon thee, unless the angel acknowledges the mark upon thee, how shall he fight for thee, or defend thee from thine enemies?" Now let us proceed to what follows.

"And I heard a voice from heaven, as the voice of many waters, and as the voice of great thunder, and I heard the voice of harpers harping on their harps. And they were singing as it were a new song before the throne, and before the four living creatures, and the elders," &c. This indicates the voice and song of the heavenly angels, glorifying the Father, and the Lamb, as they are reported to have done, when first the Lamb took the book of fates to be unclosed. With regard to these angels, therefore, he says by and by in the 5th verse, "And I saw another angel flying in the midst of heaven;" that is, a different one from those precentors. For there is no mention made of an angel before this, unless we call those who sung together a chorus of angels. Now the voice like the sound of many waters, and of thunder, signifies nothing but the voice of a numerous and crowded multitude, of which kind was that frequently heard in the temple, while it was still flourishing, of the Levite choristers, sounding forth the praises of God with the voice, and with musical instruments, on account of the multitude of whom, and of the people joining with them, a sound was produced resembling the waves of the sea, and the noise of thunder. This is not conjecture, but a plain matter of fact, as is directly expressed in the Song of Victory, c. xix. where the metaphor is the same. "I heard, as it were, the voice of a vast multitude, and as the voice of many waters, and as the voice of mighty thunders, saying, Hallelujah!" Hence, in Ezek. c. xliii. v. 2, where it is simply in the Hebrew, "His voice, (that is, the voice of the glory of the God of Israel) was like the voice of many waters;" the Septuagint render it by a paraphrase, Φωνὴ τῆς παρεμβολῆς, ὡς φωνὴ διπλάιον τῶν πολλῶν, "The voice of his camp, as the voice of many redoubling the sound." The Chaldee has it in like manner, "The voice of those who bless his name, as the voice of many waters." And that passage from the same prophet, respecting the cherubim, c. i. v. 24, "I heard," says he, "the noise of their wings, like the noise of many waters, as the voice of the Almighty, the voice of speech as the voice of a host." Lastly, in this acceptation is what is said in the description of the person of the Son of God in the beginning of the Apocalypse, taken from Daniel; for what, according to Daniel, is "the voice of a multitude," is substituted by St. John "the voice of many waters;" what Daniel has, "His feet were like in colour to polished brass, and the voice of his words as the voice of a multitude," John expresses, "His feet were like fine brass, as if glowing in a furnace, and his voice as the sound of many waters."

Moreover, the song is new which is sung to God, after the appearance of Christ in the world, in which, to Him that sitteth on the throne, and to the Lamb together, and to them alone, redemption, and power, and riches, and wisdom, and strength, and honour, and glory, and blessing, are religiously and evangelically offered. The formula of this song is to be found, c. v. v. 12, 13, and that under the title of a new song. So that it is scarcely to be doubted but that reference is made to it here, since mention is no where else made of a new song in this book. "Worthy," say they, "is the Lamb that was slain;" that is, as it is before a little more explicitly said by the elders and living creatures, because he was slain, "to receive power, and riches, and wisdom, and strength, and honour, and glory, and blessing." "To Him, therefore, that sitteth on the throne, and to the Lamb, be blessing, and honour, and glory, and strength, for ever and ever.--Ἀμήν." This is the formula of the new song, which, if God should ever enable me more thoroughly to understand, I shall, perhaps, more diffusively detail by an explanation; for it is deeply imprinted on my mind, that the whole mystery of the evangelical worship is therein contained.

As to the reason of the term applied to it, it seems to be called new, either as different and distinguished from that which was sung before the mission of Christ, (for under this, according to the saying of the apostle, "Old things are passed away, behold all things are become new,") or, for the new benefit resulting from his advent, granted to none of the former ages of the world, but only to the last times; for which benefit, God was from thenceforth to be glorified, as well by angels as by men. And this reason for the expression will be confirmed both by that passage of Isaiah, c. xlii. vv. 9, 10, "New things do I declare--Sing unto the Lord a new. song," and that appellation which occurs so often in the Psalms, of a new song, not to be understood, as it appears, in any other sense than either such a one by which the Divine power is celebrated for some new blessing, especially that of deliverance; (as in Psalm xl. "He brought me out of the miry clay; and He hath put a new song into my mouth;") or, at least, one which is sung according to the manner of such songs, with no common joy and delight. That either of which would agree with the evangelical hymn is so plain, that there is no reason why I should endeavour to prove it.

"And no one could learn that song but the hundred and forty and four thousand, who were redeemed from the earth." In the whole Christian world, as long as the beast was possessed of power, no one knew how to sing the song of angels, except those who were of the number of that 141,000 attendants of the Lamb. Since these alone, without any spot of idolatry, glorify the Father and the Lamb on earth, as the blessed angels in heaven, and they do that very thing which the Church in the Lord's Prayer incessantly asks of the Father that it may be done by all: "May thy will be done, as in heaven, so also on earth." The idea, therefore, or perfect example, of worshipping the Divine Power lawfully and duly, cannot be sought from any other source than from the celestial inhabitants.--"These are they who have not been defiled with women, for they are virgins." That is, who have not associated with immodest women, or harlots. But who are these women? Certainly not those who are commonly so called, but in the language of the prophets, states, and those indeed nominally Christian, but devoted. to idols, of which the queen is Babylon the Great, called the Mother of Harlots, with whom the kings and inhabitants of the earth commit fornication. With such, those who are of the company of the Lamb have not consorted; that is, they have not contaminated themselves with idolatrous incest. "For they are virgins;" that is, free from all stain of idolatry. For the mode of analogy fully requires that these should be called virgins in the same sense in which the others, whether kings or people, are said to commit fornication with Babylon. Besides, since Babylon herself is spoken of as the mother of harlots, it follows that her daughters, the other states, must likewise be young harlots, with whom the inhabitants subject to them are polluted by spiritual fornication.

"These are they that follow the Lamb wheresoever he goeth." That is, most faithfully adhere to him, and do not desert him on any occasion; the metaphor being taken from those who never recede from a person's side, but accompany him in every place. Or thus: In whatever city, region, or territory, the Lamb has pitched his tent, there they attend upon Him; not like the rest of those who are called Christians, but will not seek for and follow the Lamb any where, unless he dwell at Rome, in the seat of St. Peter. "These were redeemed from among men, being the first-fruits unto God and the Lamb." That is, they were redeemed from the remaining profane crowd, that they might become a sacred property to God and the Lamb, like the first-fruits. For the Απ9αρ9χὴ, or Primitiæ, do not, as is commonly. believed, denote merely the first-fruits, but also, whatever in general is consecrated to God, as exempt from profane uses; for that expression in the Hebrew is תְּרוּמָה, under which name the Scripture comprehends, as well tithes, as whatever were the object of oblations, except burnt offerings. Whence Chrysostom calls the tithes which Abraham paid to Melchisedeck, first-fruits. And Irenæus also contends that the first-fruits, which he asserts that God even still requires of his creatures for himself in his Church, ought not to be less than a tenth, since Christ says he did not abolish the natural precepts of the Law, but extended them; and, in truth, Christians have not an inferior, but a greater hope than the Jews. (Iren. adv. Heres. lib. iv. c. 27 and 34, juxta Feverardent. ed.) Why, even Callimachus, in his Hymn on Delos, calls the tenths, accustomed to be sent to Apollo, ἀπαρχὰς δεκατηφόρους, first-fruits producing tithes. From all which circumstances it appears, that the word ἀπαρχὴ, not only denotes an oblation of first productions, which in Hebrew is רָאשִׁית or בִּכּוּרִים but also any other; and the reason of the name arises from this, that his own portion was to be given to God, before any thing was consumed for own purposes. Moreover, since the word does not include the definition of what part of the first-fruits was to be given, it came to pass that the ancient Christians chose to call their productions of the earth, or oblations of fruits, (though they thought they ought not to be less than the tenth part,) ἀπαρχὰς, or first-fruits, rather than tenths, as a voluntary, not a forced donation.

These observations, though not much conducing to my object, I nevertheless wished to introduce, that I might make it palatable, if possible, to those among us, who sometimes employ themselves in searching out the antiquity and right of tithes in the Christian Church, from the Fathers and the Councils. In the mean time, (to return to the subject from which I have made a little digression,) it must be confessed, that the more strict signification of first-fruits is not ill-suited to the place before us,--namely, that the virgin company may be called the first-fruits in respect to the multitude of palm-bearers who are afterwards to receive him in a much larger number. Let the reader's judgment be free.

"And in their mouth was found no guile," (ψεῦδος, mendacium, lie: So the Vulgate, Syriac, Complutensian, Aretas, and Andrew in the Palatine copy; in others δόλος;) "for they are blameless."

"There is found no lie." Of the kind of which there is found in the mouth of the beast's company, and of all idolaters, who profess that they worship the Lamb and the Father, yet really bestow the honour due to the Divine power on created things. For in truth, all idolatry is lying, since it worships for God what is not God. To which refers that passage of the apostle to the Romans, ch. i. 25, "They have changed the truth of God into a lie, and served the creature instead of the Creator," παρὰ τὸν κτίσαντα. Whence idols are called lies, as Amos ch. ii. v. 4, "Their lies (idols in the Vulgate) have caused them to err, after which their fathers walked." In the same manner, Isaiah ch. xxviii. v. 15, "We have made lies our refuge." So also Jerem. ch. xvi. v. 19, 20, "The Gentiles shall come unto thee from the ends of the earth, and shall say, Surely our fathers have inherited lies, (Chaldee, פלחו have worshipped vanity); and things wherein there is no profit. "Shall a man make gods unto himself, and they are no gods?" Hence, too, the Apocalypse, ch. xxi. v. 8, "Idolaters and liars;" and also ver. 27, "that worketh abomination and maketh a lie," seem to be placed on a level, or as synonymes. Moreover, since the idolatry of men of any description is a lie, then truly that of those, who at the same time pretend that they are the worshippers of the true Deity, is most properly deceit, or a fraudulent lie; so that if we attend to the hypocrisy of those followers of the beast, in opposition to whom the company of the sealed attendants of the Lamb is described, the reading which has "guile," will appear preferable to the other, which has "a lie;" though it makes no great difference in the matter itself. In the mean time, for a fuller explanation of this pas. sage, let the reader compare that of Zephaniah iii. 13, which is indeed very similar to it. "The remnant of Israel shall not do iniquity, nor speak lies; neither shall a deceitful tongue be found in their mouth."

"And I saw another angel flying in the midst of heaven (ἐν μεσουρανήματι), having the everlasting Gospel to preach to those who dwell on the earth, and to every nation, and tribe, and tongue, and people."

The description of the assembly being finished, the history of events in that state of the Church follows, which were to be transacted, as well by the assembly under the auspices of the Lamb, their leader, as by the Lamb himself, against revolters and rebels. Of those events the order is double. First, of a three-fold admonition to the followers of the beast, exhibited as the shout of so many angels; secondly, of judgments in the Parable of the Harvest and Vintage. The first of the admonitory angels is he who is called another; but another, as I observed with reference to the chorus of angels, a little before described, in the number of whom that evangelist was not included. And here it must be remembered, (what I have already noticed above,) that the angels, in visions of this kind, represent the rule of those over whose government they preside; and what is transacted by the joint operations of both, is said to be done by the authority of angels, as the leaders or directors of the action. Hence, therefore, there is room to suppose, that the flying so sublimely, (provided that also ought to be considered as within the purview of the parable) is the president, not of every rank of men, but of those of a higher condition, and of such men lie is about to make use in publishing the Gospel. Besides, that Gospel is called αἰώνιον, or eternal, and that, I think, not so much with respect to the future as the past, as that which was promised, ἀπ' αἰῶνος, that is, from the foundation of the age, or the beginning of the world, namely, "that the seed of the woman should hereafter bruise the serpent's head;" that is, by the coming of Christ, the kingdom of the devil should be destroyed, and the kingdom of God established. In which sense also, the apostle says, that it was "promised by God, πρὸ χρόνων αἰωνίων, before the world began," Titus, ch. i. v. 2. So then αἰώνιον will be here the same as ἀπ' αἰῶνος, and the everlasting Gospel mean the same as in the Hebrew, any מלש הרשב the ancient Gospel, as ἔρημοι αἰώνιοι, Isa. ch. lviii. τριβοι αἰώνιοι, Jer. ch. vi. v. 16, and Βουνοὶ ἀέννασι, Deut. ch. xxxiii. v. 15, are rendered, the "old waste places, the old paths, and the ancient mountains."

"Saying with a loud voice, Fear God and give glory to him, for the hour of his judgment is come, and worship him who made heaven and earth, and the sea, and the fountains of waters."

The first angel, announcing that the time of the kingdom of God was now at hand, in which his judgment would be exercised on idols and idolaters, and therefore it began to be exercised as soon as the demons were thrown down, and cast out from the Roman throne; on which account he exhorts the nations, and tribes, and tongues, and people, who had from that time submitted to the power of Christ, that mindful of what they had done, they should worship the one only true God, the Creator, as it is announced in the Gospel,--and keep themselves from idols. "Fear God," says he; that is, reverence him, and give him the glory,--the glory of adoration and religious worship, as is explained in the following words: "For the time of his judgment is come;" that is, the time when Christ by his cross spoiled principalities and powers, and announced, by his apostles and evangelists, to the nations whom he had suffered so long to walk in their own ways, that they must be converted from idols, or otherwise they would be punished with eternal death, at his return from heaven. Why, then, did Christians, who profess their faith in Jesus Christ, this judge and conqueror of demons, return again to the worship of idols and demons?

It is perhaps possible, that the time of judgment might be understood more strictly of the judgment of God, some time before displayed against the dragon and his followers, by which Paganism fell; but I would rather extend it more widely, and take it universally of the kingdom of

Christ begun and promulgated in the last times, in which idols are no longer to be endured; namely, according to that saying of our Saviour, in the Gospel by St. John, ch. xii. v. 31,--"Now is the judgment of this world, now shall the prince of this world be cast out." See also ch. xvi. v. 11. From which judgment, indeed, the apostle Paul also (in the same manner as the angel here) drew an argument for dissuading the Athenian pagans from the worship of idols, Acts, ch. xvii. v. 30, 31, "The times of this ignorance God overlooked, but now commandeth all men every where to repent, because he hath appointed a day in which he will judge the world in righteousness, by that man whom he hath ordained; having given assurance thereof to all men, in that he hath raised him from the dead." Similar to which is his admonition to the Lycaonians, ch. xiv. 15, "We preach unto you, that ye should turn from these vanities to the living God, who made heaven and earth, and the sea, and all things therein; who, in the generations that are passed, suffered all nations to walk in their own ways;" that is, before his judgment was manifested to them. We must supply: But now he promulgates his judgment to all; which the angel here expresses by saying, "The time of his judgment is come." But when? you will ask; and where, and with what ministers, did this angel perform his preaching? Certain preludes were issued as soon as superstition began to attach itself to the memories, and to hang round the relics of the martyrs in the Church, as appears by the history of Vigilantius, with whom, when opposing a superstition of this kind, many others, even some of the bishops of that time, agreed, as his adversary Jerome witnesses, who improperly attacks him on that account.

But this preaching most manifestly appears to have been fulfilled from the year of our Lord 720, in the Greek and Oriental Churches, where the evangelical angel indeed was flying, ἐν μεσουρανήματι, in the midst of heaven, that is, in a lofty and sublime place; for he employed one who was of the administrators of the Gospel, not a man of low and vulgar rank, but of the highest powers in the Christian world; for instance, the Constantinopolitan emperors, Leo Isauricus, Constantine Iconomachus, Leo the Arminian, Michael Balbus, and Theophilus; who all, but especially the first, protested most strenuously by their edicts and decrees in favour of a religious worship addressed to God alone, the Creator, in contradiction to the worship of the creature, not only that which was exercised in the veneration of images, but in reference to the saints, and their relics. Let the reader look back to the testimonies which I quoted upon this subject from Theopanes, when I was treating of the two-horned beast. But besides this, under the auspices of the second emperor, a council of bishops was convoked at Constantinople, in 338, and the adoration of images was charged with impiety, and condemned. You will acknowledge, Reader, if you are not tired of referring to it, that the very declaration of the Synod is the address of the angel, and grounded on the same foundation as his, according to our interpretation. But since it happened there, by the fraud of some who had indeed assented with the rest to the condemnation of images, yet favoured the invocation of saints, (for the votes were not equal against the latter and former superstitions,) that two canons, one relative to the worship of the blessed Mary, the mother of God, the other to the addressing the rest of the heavenly saints with religious invocation, were intermixed in the beginning with the decrees of the Council. As soon as the Emperor Constantine, with the Fathers of the sounder opinion, had remarked them, they immediately adjudged them to be erroneous, and took care, in testimony of their judgment, that they should be cancelled, and blotted out of the book. Of this fact I have a witness, if any one should doubt it; in the first place, the author of the refutation of that Constantinopolitan declaration, inserted in the Acts of the second Council of Nice; which, while it assumed that the first publication of it refuted itself, thus refers to those canons: "After this their publication," says he, "they rejected even the offer of intercessions acceptable to God, blotting it out from this their rescript." Then the acts of Stephen the monk and pseudo-martyr, according to whom, when the bishops, who were sent by the emperor to convince him, began to recite the decree of the Council, he immediately proceeded to object to the title of the Council as Holy, that it ought not to be called holy which proscribed holy things. "Have you not," says he, "torn in pieces the sacred shrine adorned with images? Have you not discarded this adjective Ἅγιος, Saint, from all the just, from all apostles, from prophets, from martyrs, and pious men? For it is established by you, Ω generous men! that when any one should approach one of these persons, and he should be asked by him whither he was going, he should answer, To the apostles, to the forty martyrs; or, whence he came, From the temple of the martyr Theodorus, from the temple of the martyr George. Are not these your doctrines? With what consistency then have you, who have proscribed holy things, convened a holy council?" These are the words of Stephen himself. Let us hear besides the describer of his acts (who lived at the same time), tragically exclaiming against the same persons, for undervaluing the worship of the mother of God. "To what a degree, Ω Christ, do I admire thy lenity, which cannot be expressed in words! In what manner may I explain the depth of your benignity, which surpasses all the power of words! Still do those audacious tongues continue to burst forth in such a manner, that they do not hesitate to utter that great and wicked saying, namely, that the virgin mother of God herself is a being of no utility after death, and destitute of all advantage, and cannot be an aid, or a patroness to any one." I add to these the testimony of Cedrenus. He relates, that Constantine issued an universal law, (without doubt, from the opinion of a council, whose Acts are not extant at this day, except the declaration only) "That no one whatever of the servants of the Lord should be called Saint, but that their relics when found should be despised, (that they might not be superstitiously venerated, Ω Cedrenus, even though they were real; and if false, be cast out of the temple;) nor their intercession invoked, for it was of no value." "The wretch added," says he, "that no one should implore the intercession of Mary."

Now the reader may agree with me, whether he does not think it clear from these testimonies, that there was something transacted in that council against the worship of saints and relics. I have dwelt so much the longer on the proof of this, because it is not so well known to every one as that against images. But we have not yet discharged our duty; that calumny about the epithet of Saint being denied to the just, as if in degradation and contumely, must first be wiped away. For it is evident from the declaration of the Synod, (which is extant at this clay in the Acts of the second Nicene Council) that the apostles and the just are every where honoured by those fathers with the title of sanctity. They are not therefore to be supposed to have absolutely prohibited that which they themselves have often done. But we may be allowed to conjecture, that, in the opinion of that age, the word ἅγιος (for of this word only are we disputing,) appeared to infer the honour of intercession; and therefore, that superstition might by all means be opposed, the use of it in common discourse about the temples, especially when they went there to pray, was interdicted. For ἅγιος seems to he derived from ἅγος, by which word is signified veneration, or a being worthy of veneration. Whence are ἅγιοι, σεβάσμιοι, and both from ἅζω, to venerate, to worship. Nay, that it manifestly refers to the worship of the dead, it is of common origin with ἐναγίζειν, to offer sacrifices to the dead, to perform funeral rites to deceased relatives; and with ἐναγισμὸς, the performance of such rites, sacrifices to the dead. Besides, (with the reader's good leave, and without a charge of trifling annotation,) it might be the case, that the word ἅγιος, among the Greeks, (as the examples of similar blunders on the part of the vulgar may sometimes be observed among us,) might seem to imply, though falsely, by whom our prayers are offered to God; that is, προσαγωγία, an usher and mediator with God; in the same manner as Gregory Nazianzen gives the title to our Lord Christ, according to the apostle to the Ephesians, c. ii. v. 18. Δι αὐτοῦ ἔχομεν προσαγωγὴν πρὸς τὸν Πατέρα. "Through him we have access to the Father." However it may be, it appears by the testimonies adduced, it was at the time supposed, that by the use of this word the superstitious feeling towards the saints who had departed this life, was supported and cherished. To resist which, by every means and effort, its use was interdicted, not, indeed, absolutely and universally, as their adversaries calumniously represent, but in giving that title to the temples only, which were named in memory of the apostles and martyrs.

This was done, as it appears, to do away the error of supposing, that either the places themselves, where God was approached through the intercession of martyrs, or of those whose names they bore, were entitled to veneration. Therefore, instead of the name of Saints, they thought fit to substitute that of apostles and martyrs, certainly not less honourable. It was indeed the province of him to judge on this subject considerately and advisedly, who had all the circumstances of the time, and the facts of the case, before him, openly and fully displayed. In the mean time, it does not detract at all from the virginity and purity of the Church, if she has sometimes judged with less wisdom in such cases as refer to the reason and mode of performing any act. It does not necessarily follow, that she who is chaste should always act or speak prudently. From nearly a similar cause, the word sacerdos, priest, as applied to evangelical presbyters; and sacrificium, a sacrifice, as applied to the sacrament of the eucharist; (not to name other words of this kind,) were ordered to be disused among many of the reformed churches. And that indeed not altogether rashly, if they had not substituted (in the opinion of some,) the word ministri, ministers, not a very appropriate term; by which all who discharge the sacred office are properly called according to the use of Scripture, but by which, however, priests are not distinguished from deacons. Should we not rather have called them by the apostolical name of presbyteri, presbyters, if we dislike sacerdoti, priests? But these are matters which belong to another place.

Moreover, not only in the East, but in the West also, though the Roman pontiff was enraged, the proclamation of this angel resounded, not indeed, as there, with the full blast of the trumpet, but still with a public and solemn denunciation. First in the year 790, in the Synod of Frankfort, under Charlemagne, composed of nearly 300 bishops, besides abbots, and others; where the worship and adoration of images were condemned, together with the second Nicene Council, which had established them, and which Pope Hadrian had by his legates managed and approved. And again in the Synod of Paris, in the year 825, assembled by the command of Louis, in which it is shown at length, both from Divine authority and from the opinions of the Fathers, that the adoration of images was a wicked and impious practice, and the Nicene Synod was reprobated, as guilty of this kind of superstition. Add to this, the commentary sent by Charlemagne to the pontiff Hadrian, the

Joseph Mede

champion of idols, after the Frankfort Council; and here likewise you may acknowledge the angel flying in the midst of heaven. Hitherto we have attended to the exhortation of the first angel: now let us listen to the preaching of the second.

The second angel denounces Rome for its filthiness, and the multitude of its idolatries; by which, in despite of the exhortations of the first angel, she had not only contaminated herself, but also had exhibited herself as the leader and chief of all the nations of the world, that they with her might do the same, and by which she was now converted from the city of God into Babylon; on this account become at length wholly obnoxious through her impenitence to the Divine sentence delivered against all idolaters, as no longer to be endured, but to be destroyed, and cut off by an irrevocable decree; and the preparation for that ruin was ordained to be continually and assiduously prosecuted from this proclamation.

And the assembly of the Waldenses and Albigenses were the attendants of this proclamation, partly in word, and partly in deed, as those who first of all mortal beings openly denounced the Roman Church for its idolatry, or mystic whoredom, to be the apocalyptical Babylon; and they likewise took the first step towards its ruin; since thus detected, immediately a great multitude of men began to abominate her, and privately to make a defection throughout all the provinces of her dominion; and, in addition, her authority from thenceforth, day by day, began to fall more and more into decay, and her ruin then to commence, which was not to stand still, till it should at length come down to the burning of the city. I will say in a word, from the preaching of this angel, a select force of holy soldiers began to be formed for the uninterrupted destruction of Babylon.

"Babylon has fallen. It has fallen." As if he had said, Now are the foundations laid for the ruin of Babylon; from this time shall the preparations for waging war against her be undertaken. It is an imitation of Isaiah, c. xxi. who expressly, in the same words, and on an occasion not different in kind, related the ruin of the ancient Babylon, not yet accomplished, but pre-announced, as here by the foundations being laid, it should most surely come to pass. For as chronology teaches, Isaiah uttered his prophecy at the very time when the Medes, who were hereafter to lay waste Babylon, having shaken off the yoke of the Assyrians, asserted their own liberty; and having built Ecbatana, under their new king, Dejoces, laid the foundations of that kingdom, which was to be fatal both to Nineveh .and Babylon.

"Because she made all nations drink of the wine of the excess of her fornication."

That is to say, she has deceived them with philtres, with medicated wine; θυμὸς here does not mean wrath or violent anger, but according to the Hellenistic use of the word, poison [58]; for they conceive it to be synonymous with the Hebrew חמה, which signifies sometimes wrath, sometimes poison. Hence, Deut. c. xxxii. v. 33. Sept. "Θυμὸς δρακόντων ὁ οἶνος αὐτῶν, καὶ θυμὸς ἀσπίδων ἀνίατος." "Their wine is the poison of dragons, and the incurable venom of asps." Also Job, c. xx. v. 16. "Θυμὸν δρακόντων θηλάσειεν, ἀνέλοι δὲ αὐτὸν γλῶσσα ὄφεως;" that is, "he shall suck the poison of asps, the viper's tongue shall slay him." Add Psalm lviii. 4. "Θυμὸς αὐτοῖς κατὰ τὴν ὁμοίωσιν τοῦ ὄφεως," "Their poison is like the poison of a serpent." Vide also, if you will, Deut. c. xxxii. v. 24; Job, c. vi. v. 4. Nay, wherever the signification of poison occurs in the Old Testament, you will not see it expressed more than once in any other way than this, or by the word χολῆς [59]. Now mention is twice made in the Apocalypse of οἶνος τοῦ θυμοῦ, or poisoned wine of this kind; of οἶνος τοῦ θυμοῦ τῆς πορνείας, the poisoned wine of fornication, in which, as I said, an amatory virus or philtre is meant, (according to which the same c. xviii. v. 23. φαρμάκεια, sorcery, a word suited to that meaning) and οἶνος τοῦ θυμοῦ τῆς ὀργῆς, the poisoned wine of indignation, which is the potion of those who undergo punishment; since by the former the Holy Spirit expressed the enticement to spiritual fornication from the custom of harlots conciliating love by philtres; by the latter, he alluded to the manner of the Jews, who were accustomed to offer to those who were to suffer death, a cup of wine, in which myrrh or some kind of aromatic bitter was mixed, for the purpose of bringing on a torpor. A potion of which kind, for this reason, is related to have been offered to our Saviour just after be had been affixed on the cross, but he refused to drink it. Matt. c. xxviii. v. 34. "They gave him wine mingled with gall," μετὰ χολῆς μεμιγμένον, that is, wine of wrath, for χολή and θυμὸς mean the same. Now, by the word χολή, the evangelist meant something bitter in general, according to the use of the Greeks, (by whom wormwood is also called χολή). This St. Mark shows to have been myrrh, "And they gave him wine mingled with myrrh." But myrrh in Hebrew מור, Syriac ארומ, took its name from its excessive bitterness. And hence it seems to follow, that the prophets in depicting destructions, so often make use of the parable of the cup; as that which according to national custom it was usual to present to those who were about to die.

Such was the proclamation of the second angel, whom the third soon succeeded. Whatever new admonition he superadds, let us listen to with submissive attention.

The third angel, going beyond the two former, admonishes the worshippers of the beast how horrible a danger impended over them, if they still persisted in being his followers; and therefore persuades them, renouncing all delay, immediately to withdraw themselves from his society; that by this means they might consult their own safety, for those who adhered to him afterwards could not possibly be safe. Which preaching, indeed, being the most remarkable of all, was fulfilled in the labour of Luther, and his associates and successors; the consequence of which was the illustrious Reformation of the Churches, which we now behold, not by individual men, as was done at the voice of the preceding angel, but by provinces and tribes, to the assertion and purification of religion, every where shaking off the yoke of the beast. "And a third angel followed them (that is, the two former), saying with a loud voice, If any one worship the beast and his image, and receive the mark on his forehead, or on his hand, he also shall drink of the wine of the wrath of God, which is poured out without mixture into the cup of his indignation, and he shall be tormented with fire and brimstone before the holy angels, and before the Lamb. And the smoke of their torment ascendeth for ever and ever, and they have no rest day nor night, who worship the beast and his image, and whosoever receiveth the mark of his name."

A terrible description of a terrible judgment, to which scarcely any thing similar occurs within the compass of the whole canon of Scripture. "The wine of the wrath of his indignation," is the potion of punishment accustomed to be given to those who are about to die, as we observed on ver. 8. Pure wine, that is, wine not diluted with water, strongly inebriates, and still more, if different kinds of wine are mingled together; of which kind, therefore, some would understand to be meant here, by those words κεκερασμένου ἀκράτου, that is, mixed wine; since he would otherwise speak of things that oppose each other. But I am inclined to think, that ἄκρατον κεκερασμένον may be the same with pure wine mixed with myrrh, gall, frankincense, or a similar drug of bitter flavour, which was used to be put into a cup, called by the Jews the cup of malediction, after the manner of the nation; and that there is an allusion to it in the lxxvth Psalm, v. 9. according to the Septuagint. "Ποτήριον ἐν χειρὶ Κυρίου, οἴνου ἀκράτου πλῆρες κεράσματος," "A cup in the hand of the Lord of pure wine full of mixture." When the Chaldee has, "There is a cup of malediction in the hand of the Lord, of strong wine full of a mixture of bitterness, so as to take away the use of reason from the wicked." For we said, that the potion was given to take away the use of reason from the dying person. But instead of what the Sept. has, pure wine, in the Hebrew it is חמר, red wine, which had not lost its colour by admixture with water. For there: were red wines in the Holy Land. The remaining part of the description is obvious.

It will be useful here, to observe the progress of this triple proclamation, and how the latter exceeds the former in importance. The first angel admonished only of one duty, that of worshipping God duly, according to the directions of the Gospel, and did not reprove the fault committed on this head. The second proceeding farther points at the crime of spiritual fornication, and that to be inevitably punished by death and destruction, but which it threatens at the time to Babylon alone, the chief leader and contriver of the crime, and not yet to the participators in it. But the third, the full measure of heinousness being fulfilled, denounces to the whole army of the beast, and to all who should continue in obedience to him, the most horrible and unspeakable torments, and that they would have neither end nor remission. Then follows, "Here is the patience of the saints, here are they who keep the commandments of God, and the faith of Jesus." As if he should say, This preaching will be the touchstone, to prove both the patience and obedience of the saints. Their patience indeed, if, acquiescing in the expectation of so terrible a punishment, of such as will compensate for all delay, they should by no means be disturbed at the daily successes of the beast; nor fall away in their minds in any degree to him by the rage of persecutions, with which he will assail the refractory, and those who are disobedient to his command; their obedience, truly "to the commandments of God, and the faith of Jesus," if, after having heard this threat, they without delay forthwith withdraw themselves from communion with the beast, and renounce his image, and mark. These are they "who keep the commandments of God, and the faith of Jesus;" that is, who rightly and evangelically worship God in the faith of Jesus Christ, and on that account are called, not undeservedly, by the name of evangelical.

The virgin church having thus discharged her triple admonition, the sanction of it succeeds against her enemies, under the type of the harvest and the vintage; which, when once finished, the blessed remuneration of the just is no longer delayed, as is proved by that denunciation from Heaven delivered before the description of both. "I heard a voice from heaven saying unto me, Write, Blessed are the dead which die in the Lord from henceforth. Yea, saith the Spirit, that they may rest from their labours, and their works do follow them."

I know that most refer this celestial declaration to former events, as for the purpose of consoling the saints, who are now about to suffer very grievous injuries from the beast, irritated by the preceding shout of exhortation. In which opinion I also concurred some time ago. But now, having weighed the matter more accurately, I incline to think, that it is to be referred rather to subsequent events, as an admonition of the near approaching resurrection and judgment under the seventh trumpet; the preparation for which would begin to take place in the following visions; so that the word ἄπαρτι, from this time, may be used not in respect of the subject exhibited in the preceding vision, but of that to be exhibited in the following one, which, without doubt, immediately precedes the resurrection of the dead and judgment. As if he had said, Now we are come to that state of things, that only one thing remains to be fulfilled, before the time in which the dead in the Lord shall rise to a blessed life. For so in the Gospel of St. Matthew, c. xxiii. ver. the last, our Lord says to the Jews, "Ye shall not see me ἄπαρτι, from thenceforth, until ye shall say, Blessed is he that cometh in the name of the Lord." That is, not from the moment of time in which he was speaking these words, but from the time of the Passover, which he was then about to celebrate; after which he no longer presented himself openly in the sight of the Jews. Now my reason for thinking this to be the case is threefold: First, that I do not remember any where in the sacred Scripture, that the day of death is pointed out as the day of recompense, but only the day of resurrection and judgment. Secondly, the denunciation from heaven, with a command to write, does not seem applicable, except to point out some remarkable turn of events. Undoubtedly a command of this kind is nowhere else to be found, except in the beginning of this entire prophecy. Lastly, there is an agreement in sense, if well-attended to, between this proclamation, and that at the sound of the seventh trumpet, ch. xi., where the time is said to be come, when "the cause of the dead," (namely, those who died for the sake of Christ) "should be judged, and God should give reward to his servants the prophets, and to the saints, and to those who fear his name, both small and great, and should destroy those who destroy the earth." So here, "Blessed are the dead from henceforth, who die in the Lord, that they may rest from their labours;" that is, they may henceforth lead a life secure from their ancient evils and calamities; (by which is intimated the extermination of enemies and tyrants;) "and their works do follow them;" that is, they shall obtain a most blessed reward for all their sufferings and all their good works.

Meanwhile, if this interpretation is admitted, I alter not the sense of the words, "those that die in the Lord," by understanding those with the last words of the foregoing sentence, "not of any who sleep in the faith of Christ, but especially of the martyrs, who poured out their lives for Christ," (for to such belongs the first resurrection,) so that I think with Beza, it may be rendered, who die on account of the Lord, or for the Lord's sake. As in the Epistle to the Ephesians, c. iv. v. 1, "A prisoner in the Lord," is a prisoner for the sake of the Lord, the same indeed as "the prisoner of Christ," c. iii. v. 1.

In which sense the ancients (as we may conjecture from Tertullian) understood 1 Thess. c. iv. v. 16, "The dead in Christ shall rise first;" that is, the martyrs, who were delivered up to death for confessing Christ. See Tert. de Animâ, c. lv. Moreover, it is to be noted, that the ablative in the Latin, and so likewise the dative in the Greek, which signifies in some places the instrument, and mode of acting, denotes also the cause for which, or on account of which, a thing is done. "He strikes in anger; he is impelled by envy," or the like. But since the Hebrews express this ablative or dative by the preposition ב, and in imitation of them the Greek Scriptures express it by εν, it follows from thence, that iv also signifies in the same place, the cause, on account of which a thing is done. Such a signification, indeed, with this particle, is not very frequent, but I have no doubt but diligent observation would supply more examples than occur to me at present. So much with reference to the heavenly proclamation. Now let us investigate the sense of this pair of visions, to which we observed it was a forerunner; and let us do this, as far as is allowable, in a future event, with the sobriety and modesty which become us. And first of the harvest, by which the primary step is taken towards consummation.

"And I looked, and behold a white cloud, and upon the cloud one sitting like the Son of man, having on his head a golden crown, and in his hand a sharp sickle. And another angel went out of the temple, crying with a loud voice to him that sat on the cloud, Put forth thy sickle and reap; for the time is come for thee to reap; for the harvest of the earth is ripe. And he who sat on the cloud thrust in his sickle on the earth, and the earth was reaped."

The word harvest embraces three things,--the mowing down, the gathering in, and the threshing of the corn. Whence it follows, that it constitutes a two-fold parable in the sacred writings, and of a contrary meaning. Sometimes in that of slaughter and destruction, as of reaping and threshing; sometimes in that of restitution and salvation, in the sense of gathering in. An example of the former is to be met with in Jeremiah, ch. li. 33, where he thus speaks of the destruction of Babylon. "The daughter of Babylon is as a threshing-floor, the time of her threshing is come; yet a little while, and the time of her harvest will come." Also Isaiah, ch. xvii. 5, &c. of the fall of Damascus, and the slaughter of Israel by Tiglathpileser. "And it shall be, as when the harvestman gathereth the corn, and his arm reapeth the ears." But an example of the latter is scarcely any where else to be found than in the New Testament. "The harvest," says our Saviour, "is great, but the labourers are few." There are not wanting some, however, who interpret in this sense that complaint of Israel in Jeremiah, ch. viii. 20, "The harvest is past, the summer is ended, and we are not saved." The time is past in which we thought ourselves safe, and we are not saved. Let us search out, if possible, which of the figures the harvest sustains in the present passage from the order of those transactions, which the Holy Spirit has elsewhere represented to us concerning the same times of the Church. That the treading of the winepress, by which the vintage succeeding the harvest is accomplished, is the same with that bloody slaughter executed by him who sits on the white horse, ch. xix. 15, is manifest from what is inserted in the description of the rider. "He it is who treadeth the winepress of the fierceness of the wrath of God Almighty." Now this being an acknowledged datum, it follows of course, that the prophetical parables, which equally and immediately precede each, and without any other vision intervening, must either denote the same thing, or if they are different events, yet by some means connected and interwoven with each other. Since, therefore, here. the harvest immediately precedes the vintage, and there the preparation of the nuptials of the Lamb, together with the fall of Babylon precede that fierce slaughter, it follows indisputably, that either that preparation or destruction is the harvest of which we are in search, and that they relate to the same circumstance as the harvest does, or the harvest to the same as they do. If we were to say that the devastation of Babylon was the harvest, it would sufficiently agree both with the character of the type, which implies reaping and threshing, and particularly it would favour a little the example of Jeremiah, predicting the fall of the ancient Babylon, under the same figure. The passage is the same which I just now quoted. To this likewise must be added, that since both the harvest and the vintage, as they finish the year, denote the end and consummation of all things; but the harvest would precede the vintage in time; therefore, if it were certainly known that either were applied to signify the consummation of the Roman tyranny, the harvest would very appositely designate the destruction of the city, as the first-fruits of this full destruction; the vintage succeeding that harvest would point out the extinction of the whole kingdom of the beast, to follow the former at no long interval of time. Nor is there any thing to oppose this accommodation but that one circumstance, that the laying waste of Babylon, as we have hitherto presupposed, is not found to take place immediately before that dreadful slaughter, expressed likewise by the image of the vintage, ch. xix., but another event, subsequent, as it appears, to the laying waste of Babylon, namely, the preparation for the nuptials of the Lamb, or the embellishment of his bride. Will not then the harvest be a signification of that preparation? or (it that be unsuitable) of some other event to be transacted at the same time

But what, you will ask, is that preparation of the bride? What is it which is to be transacted at the same time with this? In truth, I do not see how that preparation of the bride can be any thing else than the conversion and collection of Israel, expected for so many ages; of her, who formerly, (according to our Saviour's parable,) when invited to the nuptials of the king's son, refused to come, but now hastens to meet him, promptly and prepared. For the Gentiles, as it appears, cannot possibly be called that bride, because they have been long ago, and for many ages, espoused to Christ. The Jews, therefore, are those who are yet expected to become the spouse of the Lamb.

But with this conversion and restoration of Israel, (by which she will be adopted into the virgin company of the Lamb, and will become a part of it,) will be joined the reaping or destruction of the Turkish empire, according to what we read at the sixth phial, but under another figure, that "the water of the great river Euphrates should be dried up, that the way of the kings of the east might be prepared." For the time of this phial manifestly agrees with the time of the preparation of the bride, since, as that was introduced between the destruction of Babylon and the last slaughter of the enemies of the Church, so this phial intervenes between that which is poured out on the throne of the beast, and the last phial. That is, the Church of Christ, as it was about to become double by the conversion of Israel; so each part appears to have, at that time, its own peculiar enemy; the former the Roman beast, with its uncircumcised origin; the latter, the Mohammedan empire, over a circumcised people, and of an Ismaelitish origin, ominous to the descendants of Isaac. Of the extermination of both of which, to be accomplished at the coming of Christ, why should not the harvest represent the one, and the vintage the other?

Moreover, to this interpretation of the harvest, the prophecy of Joel will afford, if not absolutely confirmation, yet at least some appearance of probability; from which both the image of the harvest and the vintage was taken. For it is manifest, that he is there treating of the time of the conversion of Israel, even from the first words of the Oracle, (Joel, ch. iii. v. 2.) "In those days, and in that time, when I shall bring back again the captivity of Judah and Jerusalem; I will gather all nations in the valley of Jehosaphat, and will plead with them there for my people, and for my heritage Israel, whom they have scattered among the nations, and divided my land." Then follows, in the suggested type of a warlike array, "Put ye in the sickles, for the harvest is ripe. Come, get ye down, for the winepress is full, the fats overflow, for their wickedness is great."

Since, then, we may observe in this accommodation of the figure of the harvest, that the event transacted may be so compared, that either notion of the harvest, that of reaping and threshing as well as that of gathering in, may be adapted to it, the latter with reference to Israel gathered together into the garner of the Church; the former to the slaughter of enemies in conjunction with that event; yet as the matter here treated of is the last effort of the Church against its foes, I think that the notion of reaping and threshing is altogether to be preferred.

But whatever the harvest may be, the description proves that Christ himself as king will assuredly be the Lord of it, and the director of the work of reaping the corn. For to what other king than him is that title of the Son of man coming in the chariot of a cloud, attributed through the whole course of Scripture? So that, in my opinion, it is by no means safe to wrest it to any other meaning. It is rather to be collected, that the power of the Divinity in discharging the duties of that harvest, as well as in the vintage next to come, will be more conspicuous and illustrious than in any of those works, which were performed only in the names of angels.

Hitherto we have formed conjectures respecting the harvest. Let us now proceed to the vintage; which, as it usually does in the order of events, it is agreeable to reason that it should succeed the harvest.

"And another angel came out of the temple which is in heaven, he also having a sharp sickle. And another angel came out from the altar, having power over fire, and he cried with a great cry to him that had the sharp sickle, saying, Thrust in thy sharp sickle, and gather the clusters of the vine of the earth, for her grapes are fully ripe. And the angel put in his sickle upon the earth, and gathered the produce of the vine of the earth, and cast it into the great winepress of the wrath of God. And the winepress was trodden without the city, and blood came out of the winepress up to the bridles of the horses, for the space of a thousand six hundred furlongs."

This is the description of the vintage; to the interpretation of which we shall with more certainty direct our aim, because the signification of the parable is less ambiguous, and the meaning of treading the clusters is more express, since the treading of the vintage in parabolical Scripture constantly denotes a fierce, deadly, and cruel slaughter. This is our first observation. And then those words about treading the winepress of the wrath of God, inserted in that description, show that this is the same with that great slaughter in ch. xix. as I have just now observed. Therefore also, it will be the same with "the battle of the great day of the Lord God Almighty," at the last phial; for that the deadly slaughter in ch. xix. is the same as that, we cannot doubt, since both are the last destruction of the same enemy; for both ultimately impend over the beast, the false prophet, and their confederates. But it is impossible there should be more than one last slaughter of the same persons. Now, if our vintage signifies the same destruction with those, it must also impend over the same enemies, and therefore over the beast, and the false prophet. The vine, therefore, or vineyard of the earth, of which mention is here made, is the dominion of the beast. The grapes ripe for gathering are the followers of the beast, swelling with the guilt of blood, ripe for judgment. The lake, in the last place, or winepress, is the place of slaughter, the same in truth as in the seventh phial, interpreted according to the Hebrew, is called Armageddon; perhaps because there the troops or forces of the beast will be extirpated by a deadly destruction. For arma means אובדה, destruction; gedon, or geddon, וּדג, troop, army, or their army. "He gathered them together," says he, "in a place called in the Hebrew language Armageddon. (the books published by Plautinus have only the single Δ, Armagedon.) And the seventh angel poured out his phial in the air, and a great voice came out of the temple of heaven, from the throne, saying, It is done." But where the winepress, or place for treading the grapes will be, is yet hid among the secret things of God; nor is it on that account to be too curiously investigated by us, nor to be pointed out, until either the event shall disclose it, or a state of things more nearly advanced to it, shall perhaps afford some indication of it. It will be allowable however to observe, without any charge of temerity, that from so accurate a measurement of the space, for which the slaughter should extend, it may seem that the Holy Spirit directs our attention to some region, which stretches one thousand six hundred furlongs in length, for he shows us that the carnage shall take place without the city, for so many furlongs; that is, if I am not mistaken, in the region or dominion of the city. Hence it follows, that some have thought the Holy Land was marked out by that circuit, as what accurately contains so many furlongs in its length, that is, 200 Italian miles, though not more than 160 Greek, which Jerome reports in his epistle to Dardanus was the length of the Holy Land. For the Greeks, they say, measured their mile by ten furlongs, each of which were a hundred paces; but the pace (which they call orgya) was six Roman feet; so that in the whole a Greek mile contained 6000 Roman feet. The Romans, on the contrary, define the pace by five feet, the furlong by 125 paces, the mile by eight furlongs, that is, only 5000 feet. Whence it comes to pass, that the Greek mile, though it agrees with the Roman in the number of 1000 paces, is yet greater than the Roman by a fifth part. So that 200 Roman miles make no more than 160 Greek.

This is the sum of the argument. Besides, it is not altogether unimportant, in addition to this conjecture, that the name of the place is called in the Hebrew language Armageddon, as if it were to be in the land of the Hebrews. But after all, by what means could this possibly take place? Indeed, to those who imagine Antichrist is to come from the East, this opinion is very natural and easy; but not so to us, unless some one perhaps should think it probable, that the false prophet, after the overthrow of Rome, should migrate into the East, and there fix his seat; which there are not wanting

A Key to the Apocalypse

some among the followers of the beast who maintain, that is, that before the last day of judgment, the Roman pontiff shall have his habitation at Jerusalem. For certainly, that the beast with his affairs at home, placed in such a state, and in such jeopardy in the West, as is supposed, should again (as formerly in the expedition to Jerusalem) lead an army into Palestine, leaving many enemies behind him, and there at length be entirely put an end to, cannot be affirmed with any show of probability. But farther, that we who assert a Western Antichrist may not be inferior on this side to those who suppose an Eastern one, there is also a place in the neighbourhood, with which the assigned number of furlongs agrees; for instance, the Stato della Chiesa, or the possessions of the Roman Church, which, from the city of Rome to the mouth of the Po, and the marshes of Verona, extend to the space of 200 Italian miles, that is, 1600 furlongs.

But whither am I digressing? Let us at length impose a restraint on curiosity, in which perhaps we have hitherto too much indulged. Let us come to other matters which will be more worth our consideration. And therefore, in the first place, that the gatherer of the grapes, and the treader of the winepress, are not the same person; but, as the offices of the vintager and the winepresser are different, so likewise they have different agents; the vintage or gathering in, an angel furnished with a vine-hook the treading, Christ himself, as King, accompanied with heavenly horsemen, which may clearly appear from the vision of the xixth chapter (for I have often quoted it). For there St. John saw "heaven opened, and behold, a white horse, and he that sat upon it was called faithful, and true, and in righteousness does he judge, and make war,"" and he was clothed with a garment dipped in blood, and he was called by name, The Word of God."--"And the armies that were in heaven followed him on white horses, clothed in fine linen, white and clean."--"And out of his mouth proceeded a sharp sword, that with it he should smite the nations, and he shall rule them with a rod of iron, and he treadeth the winepress of the indignation and wrath of God Almighty." Can any thing be said more clearly? And therefore, in the context on which we are throwing light to the utmost of our ability, it is by no means said that the angel who gathered or cut off the clusters, was the same as trod the winepress, but only, that he cast the gathered clusters into the winepress, which being done, "the winepress was trodden without the city;" by whom, unless by Christ the King, proceeding from heaven, with his celestial troop? That doubtless is what the Holy Spirit would signify by the mention of horses immediately subjoined; "And the blood came out of the winepress, even to the horses' bridles." For why is that allusion to horses inserted, unless to admonish us by this token, that the winepress was trodden by him to whom that equestrian force belonged? To circumscribe the matter then in few words, this is the sum of the vision respecting the vintage. An angel vintager, with the assistance of the saints, the presidency over whom was committed to him for this purpose, will prune and cut off the clusters of the beast, and, during his pruning, will cause them to be gathered together at Armageddon, and those who are gathered, the Lord Jesus Christ will at length tread under at his coming; according to what St. Paul says of the "man of sin," (who is this very beast,) that he shall be destroyed by the Lord "with the brightness of his coming."

Now the harvest, as well as the vintage, is supplicated by prayers; the former, as it appears, by those of the Church universal; whence the angel who there sustains the person of the suppliants, is said generally to come out of the temple. But the latter is rather enforced by martyrs and confessors, against whom the wicked had raged with butcheries and torments, and had made them victims to Christ. On which account, the angel who proclaims to this effect, goes out of the thysiasterium, or enclosure of the altar, and is said to have power over fire, even the fire of martyrdom. It is very commonly observed, that the blood of the martyrs cries to God for vengeance. For, indeed, the Scripture every where testifies, that the Divine Power will bestow on the Church neither a state of prosperity, nor vengeance on their enemies, without the prayers of its members. So the Babylonian captivity was put an end to at the prayers of Daniel; and in the parable of the widow fatiguing the unjust judge by her clamorous entreaties, the application is, that God would be aroused in like manner by the prayers of his elect, to come at length at some fit time to avenge them. You may add, that when the trumpets were sounded for the demolition of the Roman empire, the prayers of the martyrs by incense offered up, are first recalled to the memory of God.

Hear then, Ω Christ our King! and recall to the memory of thy Father, so many suppliant prayers of thy people, for thy kingdom, so many groans of the afflicted, and of those who were slain for thy name; and when the time shall come which will appear seasonable to thee, arise, reap, and gather in the vintage!

Footnotes:

50. Isidore says he is called Πανθῆρ, omnis fera, because he is friendly to all animals except the dragon.

51. Query?--R. B. C.

52. This argument seems convincing, and how strong a proof it is, that we can look only in a certain quarter for the power here described.--R. B. C.

53. Surely this is a perversion of the text.--R. B. C.
54. Or when he offers worship to them.--R. B. C.
55. From a Letter of the French Prelates who followed the camp of those who were signed with the cross, at the end of the continuation of the sacred war.--Ed. Basil, ann. 1560, p. 240.
56. Or, "that he should give them," or, "that they should give." Greek.
57. Romiith in Hebrew signifying the same, is composed of letters forming the same number.--But see Potter's Interpretation of the Number 666, republished at Worcester by the Rev. J. עם. Butt, 1808, of which Treatise Mede speaks in the highest terms.--R. B. C.
58. Rather inflammation, excitation.
59. Because it is the rage of the serpent which causes him to discharge poison.

NOTE

Thus far, O Reader, I have been able to proceed in a detailed species of interpretation. But I can carry it no farther. In the prophecies which remain I only give instances; a part of those, in truth, which three or four years ago, I had privately communicated to my friends, on most of the apocalyptical visions. Those, whatever they are, I commend, Ω Reader, to thy candour, and beseech thee to interpret favourably; until Almighty God bestow upon me strength and leisure, and the power (unless the judgment of learned and pious men should deter me) of unfolding these prophecies, by a clew similar to that by which I expounded the former. Besides, you may see, that in these I cannot preserve the order of the chapter so exactly, since I placed the mystery of Babylon before the vision of the phials, which, however, St. John postponed; whether it was because one of the angels of the phials showed it to him, or whether he wished to subjoin a key, as it were, for unlocking all the preceding visions. Both seem to have been in view. But the same order is not always convenient to the interpreter and the historian.

Of the Metropolis of Christian Apostasy, the mystic Babylon

The metropolis of the apostasy, Babylon the mystery, or the mystic Babylon, is the city Rome, or, as we now say, the Roman see; from the spouse of Christ in former times, become not only the harlot, but also the mother of harlots. The metropolis of prostitutes, that is, the head of cities, nominally Christian, committing fornication with her.--Where, Reader, I would wish you, even in the commencement, to observe, (because we are now in the very citadel of the Apocalypse), that the great and catholic apostasy of the visible Christian Church, is defined and marked by the Holy Spirit, not for any other heresies or errors than that spiritual adultery, so earnestly reprobated also in ancient Israel. This then alone ought to be regarded as a Cynosure by him who would wish to investigate the beginning, progress, state, and decline of the apostasy of Christianity, from the records of ecclesiastical affairs. If he attend to it in this view, he may even feel what is sought for; but if otherwise, he will be disappointed or uncertain. For though Babylon herself be guilty of other errors, nay, of heresies, (for it is not a novel case for harlots and adulteresses to be infamous for other vices and crimes), yet, since the Holy Spirit has pointed out that great apostasy of the visible Church by none of those, therefore, they are to be accounted either as symptoms only of that apostasy, or as adventitious errors, equally common to other times and sects; or if the heresy were possibly of great importance, yet it was of such a kind (as that of justification and salvation being to be hoped for from the merit of works), as was late, and when the harlot was far advanced in age, admitted into the Church by the just judgment of God; lest they, who had so long and so obstinately despised the long-suffering of God, and the preaching of the witnesses, should afterwards (as we read to have been prohibited to our first parents) "stretch out their hands, and take the fruit of the tree of life, and eat, and live for ever."

Moreover, Reader, it is singular in this place, and not to be passed over with a slight remark, (of which, therefore, I have reminded thee in the Apocalyptical Key,) that this vision of the great harlot, and of the beast which carried her, is disclosed in an unusual manner to St. John, and to us, by the clearest interpretation; and undoubtedly for this end, that by the help of this interpretation, as of the chief of all the visions, the other Apocalyptical mysteries likewise,--hitherto closed, but depending upon that, by an admirable contrivance,--might be laid open. Let this reflection, then, be present to your minds, and that the angel, as far as relates to you, may not have undertaken his labours in vain, duly and rightly remember, that the interpretation of an allegory or parable (of which kind is this of the angel) is not a new parable or allegory. For what an inconsistency would this be, or more truly, insanity, on the part of an interpreter! Do not therefore listen here to I know not what ages of the world, or similar suppositions, but understand the intention of the prophesying angel as no longer allegorizing, but interpreting according to the expression, knowing that to you remains the duty, not of unfolding the meaning of an allegory, but of applying the interpretation of

A Key to the Apocalypse
it now given, to the events themselves.

To which application, as far as God has revealed it to me, I will thus lead the way.

First. The woman whom John saw sitting on the beast, "is that great city which reigneth over the kings of the earth."

Application.--What city is this but Rome [60] ?

Second. The beast which bore her who was now become a harlot, is the same beast which, even before the vision exhibited to John, existed in another form of its own, but not yet in that in which it carried the harlot. But it was afterwards to rise again from the abyss, in such a form, and in that, at length, utterly to perish. That is, the form in which it carried the harlot would be the last form of the beast, beyond which it would not prolong its existence. It follows in the same verse, (in order that you might recognise this to be the very same beast which was shown in ch. xiii.) "And the inhabitants of the earth wondered, whose names were not written in the book of life from the foundation of the world, when they beheld the beast which was, and is not, and yet is to be [61] ."--for so I read with the Complutensian edition, according to the interpretation of Primasius and Syrus, that it may agree in sense with the preceding description. "The beast which was, and is not, and shall ascend out of the abyss." In what form he was first a beast, in what he was hereafter to ascend from the abyss, we may discover from those words which the angel afterwards subjoins.

Application.--But if the woman be Rome, what can this many-formed beast be on which she rides, (that is, over which she rules,) but the Roman kingdom or empire [62] ?"

Third. The seven heads of the beast are a double type. First, there are seven mountains or hills on which the city, which was the metropolis of the beast, was situated; and besides also, seven orders of kings, or successive dynasties, and that on the same hills, (which the unity of the type denotes.)

"Hoc teneas vultus mutantem Protea node."

By this knot you may detain Proteus when he changes his appearance. Five of them, indeed, kings, consuls, tribunes, decemvirs, dictators, were even then passed away in the age of John. One (that of the Cæsars) yet remained; but that likewise was so to be changed under the Christian Cæsars, that it would appear as another dynasty, but for a very short time, yet, in truth, not be another. The last, indeed, and the eighth, as I have just said, with respect to the changed Ciesareate, but in reality only the seventh,--for there are only seven heads on the beast,--is that under which the beast was ropi4opoc, the carrier of a harlot; that is, the bearer of the mystical harlot; and in that state and appearance it was seen by John in the present vision; in whose time, indeed, it might be said it was formerly, and still was not yet come. For formerly it was a beast under the rule of the five former heads, and partly of the sixth, but it was not come in that of the last head, to wit, that of the pontificate, in which, in fine, it carried the harlot.

Application.--Now, then, Reader, attend! If the sixth head of the Roman beast, which was reigning in the age of John over the seven-hilled city, has now ceased to reign on the same for almost twelve centuries, it necessarily follows that he who now possesses the authority (since it can by no means be called a kind of seventh, and a head of a very short date) must be that last, long-lived, and real seventh dynasty of the seven hills; and, therefore, that state or republic of the nations, over which Rome now watches, and has long watched,--that dynasty which John foresaw, as to carry the harlot.

Fourth. The ten horns of the beast, the insignia of the last head, are ten kingdoms, which were not yet arisen in the age of John, but into which the body of the Roman beast was to be dilacerated in its last form, by the wound of its Cæsarean head; and which would unanimously confer all their power on the beast, renewed and re-established under the government of its last head.

Application.--Now, unless from the time in which the Cæsars ceased to reign in Rome, the Roman empire was divided and dilacerated into ten or more kingdoms, (even of nations which were foreigners and barbarians to the empire in the age of John,) when, I beseech you, or in what manner, shall we ever expect it to be divided??

Fifth. But these ten kingdoms which so coalesced under the auspices of their head, the false prophet, shall fight with the Lamb. The victory, however, will finally belong to the Lamb our Lord.

Application.--The former has been long since done, and even takes place, at the present day. The latter is now done, in some respects, but we hope will be completed at some future time, by a much more glorious victory; since, out of those ten horns, or kings, there will be some, who at length will hate the harlot, whom they have so long servilely assisted in supporting, (which, we perceive, partly fulfilled,) "will render her desolate and naked, will eat her flesh, and burn her with fire." For God, by whose providence it came to pass, that they agreed with so marvellous a consent in supporting this beast of the last head, even to the time appointed, will, at some future time, put it into their hearts to execute his will on their metropolis, the harlot. Thus far the angel.

As to what remains in the description of the allegory, that this harlot "had a golden cup in her hand, full of abominations, and filthiness of her fornication;" and also, that "she bore in her forehead her name written;" did not require the interpretation of the angel, since there is an allusion in both to the ancient custom of harlots and of the stews, where they used to drink philtres out of a golden cup to their lovers. In those places the cells were inscribed with the name of the harlots, as Tertullian shows in his book on Modesty, &c. &c. Besides, if the harlot were famous, it appears that, not only on the cell, but on her forehead, she bore her name and eulogy written, &c. &c.

Footnotes:

60. It can be no other.--R. Δ. C.
61. Loco καίπερ ἐστίν. MS. Alexand. legit πάρεσται.
62. Nothing.--C.

THE FALL OF ANTICHRIST,

Or the meaning of the Seven Phials, as far as we are yet permitted to understand it.

And first, Of the Phials generally.

The Holy Spirit propounds the history of the phials, and of the angels who pour them out, in a two-fold manner. First, generally, from the beginning of chapter xv. to the end of the fifth verse, where the vision of the seven angels holding the seven phials being related to the conclusion, before he comes to the particular description either of the angels or the phials, the narration of another vision exhibited together with them, is introduced, by which the state of the Church is described while the effusion is going on, cleansed from defilements, and the filthiness of idolatry, in that sacred laver of the temple or sea, not made as Solomon's, of brazen materials, but of crystal, and singing, during the whole time of the effusion, the ἐπινίκιον, or song of victory over the vanquished beast [63], and that while she was but just coming forth from the bath in which she was purified, and while she yet remained on the margin of the laver. He then goes on to the clothing and apparatus of the angels, and to the phials specially, from those words of the 5th verse.

"And the seven angels, having the seven last plagues, came out of the temple, clothed in linen, pure and splendid, and girt round the breast with golden girdles;" that is, adorned with the sacerdotal habit and girdle. Ezekiel c. xliv. v. 17, 18.

Take care not to join the words which we have quoted with those of the preceding verse; for what is there said of the temple of the tabernacle of testimony in heaven being opened, relates mot to the beginning, but to the end of the phials; for the temple, which, while the phials were pouring out, "was filled with smoke from the glory of God, and from his power, so that no man could enter therein," (and here there is an allusion both to the dedication of the tabernacle, Exod. c. xl. v. 34, 35, and also to the twice seven days' dedication of the temple, 1 Kings, c. viii. v. 10. 2 Chron. c. v. 13,) will be rendered so dear when the phials are completely exhausted, that the Ark of the testimony (Christ) will become conspicuous, as is the case at the sound of the seventh trumpet, ch. xi. with which it has been shown in the third Synchronism, Part 2d, the last of the phials is contemporary.

Footnote:

63. It is called the Song of Moses and of the Lamb, because the Lord alone is to be worshipped and glorified as God. Which signification of this song, as equally proceeding from Moses and the Lamb, was now promulgated to men.

HYPOTHESIS

Concerning the Phials, one by one

First, The effusion of the phials signifies the ruin of the antichristian beast.

This is apparent from the text, concerning which see Synchronism vii. part 1st. For as the former, and more ancient polity of the Roman empire was subverted by the plagues of the trumpets, so the last is to be subverted by the plagues of the phials. This is the cause of so great a similarity between them, since the last bears the image of the former Roman polity.

Secondly, The seven phials -are so many gradations of its ruin; for as the beast rose by degrees, so likewise will he be abolished by degrees.

Thirdly, Whatever that may be on which each of the phials is poured out, it suffers loss and injury by the phials; since the effusion of the phials is the effusion of the wrath of God. No interpretation, therefore, can possibly stand, by which the effusion of a phial would contribute to the good of that on which it is poured out.

Fourthly, The earth, the sea, the rivers, the sun, are something relative to the antichristian beast, which resemble the earth, the sea, the rivers, and the sun. For all the phials are poured upon the beast, and therefore each relates to something connected with the beast, or at least affecting his interest.

Fifthly, The whole body of the beast, or the antichristian universe, is tacitly compared by the

Holy Spirit, in the same manner as in the trumpets, to the mundane system, of which the different parts are the earth, the sea, the rivers, heaven, and the luminaries, so that the earth in the pontificate universe would be so called from its resemblance to the earth, the sea from the same likeness to the sea, the rivers to the rivers, and the sun to the sun in the natural world.

Sixthly, Lastly (as we have observed more than once), because God employs angels as ministers of his providence, in exciting and directing the movements and revolutions of human affairs; therefore, those things which are performed by the hands of many, are yet attributed to an angel, as the president and director of the event to be transacted, according to a common mode of speaking.

AN EXPOSITION
Of the Phials, according to the Rule of these Hypotheses

Phial the First. On the Earth, the Universe connected with the Beast

The earth, in the antichristian universe, signifies the people at large, or the Christian vulgar; the footstool (to its shame be it spoken,) of Antichrist, constructed on which, as on a base, the hierarchal papal edifice, like the tower of Babylon, lifts its head to the ethereal regions,--"Vertice ad auras ætherias tendit." On this earth of the beast, the first phial being poured out, it contracted an ailment from the effusion, so as to fill the followers of the beast with fury and violence as with ulcers, and those so fierce and malignant, that they could not be cured, nay, even a tendency to healing could not be brought on without being broken again, and thereby renewed.

This was fulfilled, when the lower orders of Christians, whether known by the names of the Waldensians, Albigensians, Wicliffites, Hussites, or by any other names, began every where to renounce the authority of the beast, crying out, that Rome was the apocalyptical Babylon, and that the pope was Antichrist. By which vapour on the earth, now glowing with the wrath of God, the followers of the beast being affected, grew all very hot with the sores of grief and indignation, by which, excited to rage, they dealt most cruelly with fire and flame against their opponents, in a wonderful manner for many years; but in vain, for they were disquieted by a bad and incurable ulcer, which the more they agitated themselves, became so much the worse from day to day. So formerly the land of Egypt, sprinkled by the Divine command with ashes of the furnace, rendered all the servants of Pharaoh, and their cattle, full of ulcers.

Now the world of the beast is in ch. xi. spiritually called Egypt, and therefore this plague of the ulcers is to be spiritually interpreted, that is, mystically, and by analogy, and this likewise in the figurative representation of the two following plagues, is to be diligently observed.

Phial the Second, On the Sea of the Bestial World

The sea, in the antichristian world, is the compass of the pontifical communion; by which not only individual Christians, but whole nations, peoples, kingdoms, provinces, dioceses, otherwise disjoined and separated from each other, are collected into one. Or, the antichristian sea is the circumference of the pontifical jurisdiction or dominion, enclosing and enfolding Christian nations, as the sea does the earth.

The second phial being poured out on this sea, it becomes thereupon "as the blood of a corpse," or cold and coagulated blood, as that of dead and slain persons, or of a member cut off, when the connexion with the fountain of life being dissolved, it is deprived of the influx of spirit and warmth. The sense is, the pontifical sea was made a sacrifice of by death, dismemberment, and butchery.

Now this was fulfilled, when by the labour of Luther, and other illustrious reformers of that acre while God in a wonderful manner favoured their undertakings, no longer some individuals only of the Christian community, but whole provinces, dioceses, kingdoms, nations, and cities, renounced communion with the beast; and having made a great mutilation of his ancient most extensive empire, forcibly wrested from the body of the beast, withdrew from it. By which event, the sea of the pontifical dominion became in great measure dead, and like the blood of a dead man, in which the pontifical animals could no longer breathe and live.

Phial the Third, On the Rivers and Fountains of Waters of the Bestial World

The rivers and fountains of waters in the world of the beast, are the ministers and defenders of the antichristian jurisdiction; whether ecclesiastical, as the jesuits, and other emissary priests, or even seculars and laymen, as the Spanish champions; to each of whom an office is committed by that jurisdiction, of managing and promoting the cause, which they call Catholic. Since, as rivers derive their origin from the sea, so likewise they apply their service and assistance to increase and maintain the same, in like manner as the rivers return into the sea.

A Key to the Apocalypse

Now these rivers, while they rashly pursue their courses, where it was no longer safe fur them to go on, become tinged with blood by the effusion of the third phial, as they likewise had formerly imbrued with blood the saints of God, and his prophets. In fact, from this phial, the affairs of the beast were to fall into such a state, that his ministers and defenders, having changed places with those whom they persecuted, were compelled to undergo the same death, by which they had been accustomed to sacrifice the saints and prophets of God, while their dominion flourished; as is clearly explained in v. 5 and 6, being the key for unlocking the parable. And this I am inclined to think was then completed with regard to ecclesiastical emissaries, and their attendants, when in our kingdom of England, during the reign of Elizabeth, of glorious memory, and even afterwards, those sanguinary managers of the authority of the beast, even by laws published for that purpose, expiated their administration by their blood, (a circumstance which had never befallen them before.) And not they only, but those who were much more formidable than them, the Spanish champions of the cause of the beast, in the endeavour to recover his dominion for the Roman Church by arms, while they thirsted for blood, drank blood in large draughts, especially in that memorable slaughter of the year 1588, and the following years, the English and Belgians, by sea and land, pouring out copiously the cup from the powerful hand of God. So that there was a wonderful cry of applause to the just and true judgments of God, not only from those islanders who were now revenging the blood of their own people formerly shed, but also from the neighbouring French, who were still groaning under the cross, and the altar; nay, in the recent butchery of the year 1572.

And thus far the phials seem to have proceeded; the rest yet remain to be poured out.

Phial the Fourth, On the Sun of the Bestial Heaven

That we may discover what the sun is in the world of the beast, we must first see what the heaven is in that world, lest otherwise, destitute of the clew of analogy, we wander too much from the mark. For the sun is not to be placed, or conceived to exist, but in a heaven suitable to it. The heaven, then, of the antichristian world is the supreme and universal pontifical power itself, or, in short, whatever exists of more sublime and regal authority in any part of the bestial world; that is, in the whole community of provinces acknowledging the Roman pontiff as their head. For so, in the natural world, all that is on high, and above the earth and waters, is called heaven, in the acceptation of the Hebrews, and of the Holy Spirit.

Now in this antichristian heaven (according to the type of the natural heaven) there are many stars, and of different magnitudes,--princes, governors, presidents, rulers, kings. There are likewise great luminaries like the sun and moon, which all appear to move round with the motion of heaven itself, and undergo their vicissitudes, from the law which governs it. Of this, indeed, the most splendid, and by far the greatest luminary which shines in the Papal firmament, is the German empire, which has been the possession of the house of Austria for about two hundred years. Is not this the sun of that heaven [64]? Now on this sun is the fourth phial forthwith to be poured out; so that he, driven out of his usual course in the heaven of the beast, and shining in a different manner, may scorch and torment with heat and fervour, even to blasphemy, the inhabitants of the antichristian world, whom he was formerly accustomed greatly to cheer with his warmth and radiance. And lo! while I am publishing these remarks, on which I had long ago written a Commentary, a report has filled the whole Christian world, while the pious are offering up their gratulations, that an avenger from God has come from. the North, to succour afflicted and depressed Germany--a king pious and fortunate, and a conqueror wherever he has come, whose successes surpass the flight of the eagle. Is not this he whom the Lord of Hosts has destined, to execute the work of this phial? So I hope and pray from my soul,--"Gird thee then with thy sword, Ω great King I proceed prosperously and reign, for the sake of truth, of meekness, and of righteousness; for thy right hand shall teach thee terrible things [65]."

Phial the Fifth, On the Throne of the Beast

The fifth phial is to be poured out on the throne or seat of the beast; that is, on Rome itself: And now the Holy Spirit no longer conceals the subject under the veil of figures or allegories, perhaps on account of the great light then to arise on those prophecies; when this sort of Mercurial sign being seen, it will no longer be ambiguous how much progress the phials have made, and how much yet remains to be completed by them.

By this destruction of the Roman city, (which I think to be the very same as is said ch. xi. 13, to follow the resurrection and ascension of the witnesses,) the name of the pontificate will not utterly perish, but will then be despoiled of its glory and splendour, so that "they shall gnaw their tongues for pain." In the meanwhile, however, still persevering in their impenitence, with obstinate minds, they will abuse their sufferings by additional blasphemy.

Phial the Sixth, On Euphrates

The sixth phial will be poured out on the great river Euphrates; so that, being dried up, a passage may be prepared for the new enemies of the beast to come from the East, that is, for the Israelites, wonderfully converted to the pure faith and worship of Christ, and now become candidates for the kingdom promised for so many ages. Whom the followers of the beast, perhaps, may be inclined to consider as the army of their fictitious antichrist, to arise from the Jews, of whom they do not hesitate to assert, that even we of this day are the forerunners. God thus avenging their obstinacy in error.

Now two things induce me to understand "the kings, to come (as it is said) from the rising of the sun," as spoken of the Jews. First, that it is the last phial but one, during which, therefore, if the Jews are not converted, it must necessarily come to pass, that they would be destroyed with the other enemies of Christ, in the number of whom they would still be included, in that great day of universal vengeance and judgment, which the next and last phial introduces. Besides the passage in Isaiah referring to the same event, brings me to this conclusion, from which, in all probability, this part of the Apocalypse is borrowed. "And the Lord," says he, ch. xi. 15, 16, "shall destroy (I should prefer, As the Lord has destroyed) the tongue of the Egyptian sea, and (I should prefer So) he shall lift up his hand upon the river, (Targum, the river Euphrates) with his mighty wind, (or Spirit) and shall smite it in the seven streams, so that men shall go over it dryshod." "And there shall be a highway for the remnant of my people which shall be from Assyria, (therefore the Euphrates is meant) as it was in the day when he came up from the laud of Egypt." Let the reader see Zach. x. 10, 11, and the Chaldee paraphrast thereon.

But what then, shall we say, is this Euphrates, whose waters shall be dried up? Whether it is to be taken according to the letter, especially in that passage of Isaiah, I somewhat doubt. In the mean time, I rather think that something of parable and allegory is sprinkled through this part of the Apocalypse, but not much; so that the analogy of the other phials may remain here likewise, well adapted to the object of the effusion. For it seems we are to understand in the same manner as the old Euphrates had, the mystical one has its Babylon also. I think the Ottoman empire will be the only obstacle to those new enemies from the East, and a defence on the part of the beast. Nor will there be wanting an example from Isaiah himself, of Euphrates thus to be understood, who, ch. viii. v. 7, has described the Assyrian army, then a borderer on that river, under the similar allegory of the Euphrates. "The Lord will cause to come up against them (that is, the Syrians and the Israelites) the waters of the river, (so the Euphrates is accustomed to be called, κατ' ἐξοχήν,) strong and many, the king of Assyria, and all his glory," (Targum, his army.) Why should not the Euphrates of the phials be taken, by a parity of reason, for the Turks, not less than the Assyrians, borderers on the Euphrates, before its desication, nay, inhabitants of the same tract?

. It contributes not a little to the establishment of this interpretation, that we explained the letting loose of that vast equestrian army, long bound on the great river Euphrates, at the sounding of the sixth trumpet, ch. ix. 15, as intended for the Turks, thence to be poured forth on the Roman world, while we were following the series of the trumpets, and the probable truth of the subject-matter. By the sixth phial, then, will this Euphratean flood be dried up. Evidently, according to what is said ch. xi. next after that destruction of the city to take place in the great earthquake, (which we have applied to the former phial,) the second woe, that is, the plague of the sixth phial, is to pass away. But we shall labour in vain in our conjectures concerning a thing which is wholly future, as to the means by which, or the authors by whom, it is to be effected; whether by the Jews themselves, (as Ezekiel, perhaps, intimates, ch. xxxviii. and xxxix.) taking possession of the Holy Land by restoration to their former state, or by some intestine dissension, opportunely preceding their return; or by both, perhaps, in successive order, or by some other cause.

Whatever it may be, their obstruction being removed, the way of approach is by some means said to be prepared for these new Christians from the East, and that, as it appears, for the purpose of undertaking an expedition against the beast, to whose destruction all the phials are subservient. For whence otherwise, and for what reason, should such a trepidation and panic seize upon the followers of the beast, and even the demons themselves, from the time of the drying up of the. river, as to occasion such a horrible and unheard-of preparation for war as is here described; unless they, with the whole diabolical cohort, feared every extremity from the accession of the new kings of the East?

Phial the Seventh, in the Air

The seventh and last phial is poured out in the air; that is, on the power of the air, or Satan, comprehending and animating in its bosom, not only the dominions of the beast, but of all the enemies of Christ our Lord, in every part of the world.

Now, as the beast drew from him spirit and life, even from his beginning, so the last fortunes of the bestial party will rely chiefly on their power and auspices, which may consist both in the array of so many confederates and auxiliaries, in the war of this last phial, collected together, as is related, by diabolical arts; and also from this circumstance, that the dragon, now Satan, not only intermeddles in their affairs by his vicars, the beast and false prophet, in levying this army of the habitable world, but that he by himself, in the last struggle of his reign, may appear to exercise his own proper and peculiar part; especially in calling forth those to a share in this war, upon whom otherwise the beast and false prophet could by no means have prevailed, either by authority or influence, or even perhaps by a representation of common danger.

Against so many enemies, thus gathered together under the auspices of the power of the air, and enclosed as in a cage at Armageddon, the seventh phial will be discharged, no longer by a human hand, but with a celestial and fulminating vengeance; (for "it is the battle of the great day, and of God Almighty.") By this the ruin of the beast will be fully consummated; not of the seat only, or the city of Babylon, as before, under the fifth trumpet, but of the state itself; that is, of the Babylonian senate and people, wherever they shall be surviving after the destruction of the city, until the extermination of all the kings and states, who had hitherto committed fornication with idols and false deities, and of the rest of the tyrants, who opposed together the holy Church of Christ, shall be completely effected.

Footnote:

64. With all due deference to the foresight of the venerable author, but with greater facilities of judging from the lapse of time since this conjecture was formed, may we not suppose France to be the country more peculiarly designated? Of this kingdom, which assumed the emblem of the sun as the mark of its dignity, Clovis or Louis was the first Christian king. In the reign of the XVIth Louis did this kingdom undergo the most stupendous revolution which has taken place for many centuries; overturning the throne and the altar, setting on fire, as we may say, the Papal world, destroying vast, armies by the valour of its troops and the force of its artillery, devastating other countries, and at length exciting the most violent opposition to its progress in surrounding nations. It was this kingdom which in Charlemagne gave the first emperor to the Papal Roman empire, though the seat of his dominion was afterwards transferred to Germany. It was in a soi-disant emperor, who copied his example, that the Pope was enthralled, and compelled to adopt the suggestions of this temporary ruler. The author of this note cannot help adding, as a remarkable circumstance, that on the 19th of January, 1793, picture of the sun the day on which the king of France was condemned, he saw, without the help of a glass, through a thin fog, large spots on the sun's surface, one of which appeared as a fissure of many digits in extent; such as he understood from Mr. Vince, Plumian Professor of Astronomy at Cambridge, were never recorded to have been seen before by the naked eye.--Vide Ann. Reg. 1793.--R. B. C.

65. This relates, I suppose, to the king of Sweden, and is surely a proof how careful we should be in the interpretation of prophetical scripture, when we see so enlightened and cautious a commentator as Mede led to apply an important part of the great scheme of prophecy to passing events.-- R. B. C.

Joseph Mede

OF THE THOUSAND YEARS

Of the Seventh Trumpet, and of the other Prophecies of wonderful Events contemporary with it

    Here, Reader, I shall in a few words explain what my opinions are, nor will I much extend my observations on a subject, which was for a long time deemed incredible, on account of inveterate prejudices, and because it is one of the most abstruse and most remarkable of all the parts of prophetic Scripture. In so great a mystery, it will be sufficient to maintain the thing in a general manner, and not to inquire too curiously into the reasons of each particular part; lest while expatiating more freely than perhaps we ought, the saying of Solomon should ring in our ears,--"In the multitude of words there wanteth not sin."

    But with relation to this subject, it relies on the irrefragable chain of apocalyptical order, which I have demonstrated above; and the agreement of the other Scriptures, especially of the prophetical ones, wonderfully confirms the same. It was so looked forward to by Christians of the age next after the apostles, that Justin Martyr attests, not only that he himself believed it, but that it was believed with the fullest assent by those, who were at that time Christians of the orthodox persuasion, in all things. Which opinion of the first Christians, whether deformed by certain additions afterwards, or improperly or erroneously understood, (as I am inclined to believe,) their posterity after one or two ages rejected. To such a degree, however, was this carried by a progressive ardour of contention, (which you will justly be surprised at, and lament,) before the matter could be proved, that those who could not otherwise get rid of the force of the opposite opinion, built on the foundation of the Apocalypse, chose rather to call in question that most divine prophecy, signed and sealed by all the disciples of the apostles, and their immediate successors, nay, openly and audaciously to undervalue its authority on that subject by their invented presumptions, than to submit and yield themselves up to the force of conviction. Until at length, having contrived a commodious interpretation of that Millennium, (as they then imagined,) leaving the authority of the Apocalypse untouched, they desisted from an undertaking, not easily to be exempted from the crime of impiety, and to be dreaded by their posterity.

    But I, Reader, (no longer to detain you in the vestibule,) so explain the whole matter, as to show that I depart as little as possible from the received opinion of the day of Christ's advent, immediately to follow the ruin of Antichrist: Do thou, then, laying aside all prejudice, weigh the matter in the fear of God, and pardon me, if I fall into any error, with a charitable judgment. Thus, then, understand it.

    The seventh trumpet, with the whole thousand days, and the other oracles referring to the same, designate that great day of judgment, אבר אניד סוי, of the ancient Jewish Church, celebrated by Christ, and his apostles; not some short space of a few hours, (as is commonly believed,) but according to the custom of the Hebrews, using a day for time indefinitely, a continued space of many years, and circumscribed by two resurrections, as termini. A day, I say, beginning from that first partial, and as it may be termed, morning judgment of Antichrist, and of the other living enemies of the Church, by the glorious appearance of our Lord in a flame of fire, and finishing at length after the reign of a thousand years, granted to the new Jerusalem, his most holy spouse on this earth, and the total destruction of new enemies hereafter to arise, _when the great day is declining, and Satan again loosed, by the universal resurrect. tion and judgment of all the dead.. Which things being finished, the impious will be transferred to Gehenna, to be for ever tormented, but the saints to live eternally with Christ in heaven.

    This, in truth, is that time of the wrath of God against the nations, and of judging the cause of those who died for Christ's sake; at which, on the sound .of the seventh trumpet, the elders rejoice with triumph, because by that God would surely "give reward unto his servants the prophets, and to the saints, and to them that fear his name, both small and great, and would destroy them that destroy the earth."

    This is "that day of judgment, and perdition of ungodly men," of which St. Peter having spoken in his 2d Epistle, c. iii. v. 7. immediately subjoins, "But beloved, be not ignorant of this one thing, that one day is with the Lord as a thou sand years, and a thousand years as one day." in which same day, indeed, the apostle with his brethren and fellow-countrymen, looks for that new appearance of things to come, of which he afterwards says, "But we, according to his promise, look for new heavens, and a new earth, wherein dwelleth righteousness." Mark! "according to his promise." But when and where was this promise to be found of new heavens and a new earth, (before John had yet seen the Apocalypse) unless in Isaiah, ch. lxv. 17, and lxvi. 22? Which promise, I should certainly be surprised, if he who had read, could imagine was to be fulfilled any where else than in the present world.

This is that kingdom also, conjoined with the appearance of Christ to judge the world, to which St. Paul alludes in his second Epistle to Timothy, ch. iv. v. 1, "I adjure thee before God, and our Lord Jesus Christ, who shall judge the quick and the dead at his appearing and kingdom." For after the last, and universal resurrection, from the same authority, 1 Corinthians, c. xv. Christ, after death, the last enemy, has been destroyed, will deliver up the kingdom to the Father, that he may be subject to him who put all things under him. But it is not said that any new kingdom is to commence at that time. The kingdom, then, which is to come, which is neither before the appearance of our Lord nor after the last resurrection, must necessarily be included between both. This is that kingdom which Daniel saw, of the Son of man, when the times of the antichristian horn being completed, or "the times of the Gentiles being fulfilled," (Luke, ch. xxi. 24,) he should appear in the clouds of heaven, when there shall be given to him power, and glory, and a kingdom, that all people, nations, and tongues, should serve him, or when (as the angel soon after explains it,) "The kingdom, power, and greatness of the kingdom, under the whole heaven, shall be given to the people of the saints of the Most High." Dan. ch. vii. 13, 14, also 18, 22, 26, 27. For, as I have just now observed, this kingdom is not to be after the last resurrection, since at that time the kingdom is not to be entered upon by the Son of Man, but, as St. Paul testifies, to be laid down, and delivered up to the Father. Now as that, the same kingdom, is treated of in both places, as well by John as by Daniel, may be proved from these two arguments. That both begin from the same terminus, namely, from the extermination of the fourth, or Roman beast. That of Daniel, when the beast who acts under the last government of "the horn with eyes," was given to be slain, and "his body delivered to the burning flame," Dan. ch. vii. v. 11, 12. 26. That of the Apocalypse, when the beast and false prophet, (that wicked horn of Daniel, having a mouth and eyes like a man) "were taken, and both cast alive into a lake of fire burning with brimstone." Secondly, it may be proved from the same session of judgment preceding both. For that the one is borrowed from the other, and that both, altogether, refer to the same event, will appear from the collation of the words in the description of each.

DANIEL, CH. VII. APOCALYPSE, CH. XX. 4. Ver. 9. I beheld till thrones were set [66], And I saw thrones, Ver. 10. And the judgment was set [67], And they sat on them,

Ver. 22. And judgment was given to the saints of the Most High [68];
And judgment was given to them.
And the saints possessed the kingdom [69].
And the saints lived and reigned with Christ a thousand years.

Moreover, I wish to give the reader this admonition: Whatever sound doctrine, generally speaking, is delivered by the Jews, whatever by our Lord in the Gospel, or in any part of the New Testament by the apostles, relative to the day of the great judgment, is drawn from this vision of Daniel, namely, the judgment to be perfected by fire--Christ's coming in the clouds of heaven,--coming in the glory of the Father, with a multitude of angels,--the saints, who are to judge the world, with him,--Antichrist to be destroyed at the brightness of his appearance, &c. So that they who endeavour to throw down the column of evangelical faith, concerning the glorious advent of Christ, neglecting the ancient tradition of the Church, must labour to transfer that prophecy to some other event.

Lastly, that I may come to a conclusion:--This is that most ample kingdom, which, according to Daniel's interpretation, was foreshown to Nebuchadnezzar in the statue, predictive of four kingdoms. Not that of the stone cut out of the mountain, while the series of the monarchies was still subsisting; (for that is the present state of Christ's kingdom;) but of the stone when the same monarchies were utterly broken in pieces and destroyed, which became a great mountain, and filled the whole world.

On these subjects, Reader, I have treated, but not asserted any thing rashly. I humbly refer the whole matter to be judged of by the Church, from the word of God,--to whose judgment, as it is fit, I willingly submit my opinion concerning this mystery.

Τῷ Θεῷ δόξη.

Footnotes:

66. So it is rendered by the Septuagint in common with the Vulgate.
67. That is, judges, as in the great sanhedrim of the Jews,--to the pattern of which the whole description is conformed.
68. That is, the power of judging. Hence that saying of St. Paul, "the saints shall judge the

world."

69. That is, with the Son of man, who came in the clouds of heaven.

A REMARKABLE PASSAGE

From a Dialogue between Justin Martyr, and Trypho, a Jew, respecting the Millennium, or the Thousand Years of the kingdom of Christ, corrected and illustrated by Notes.

TRYPHO

Now tell me the truth. Do you expect and confess, that this place, Jerusalem, is at length to be re-established, and your people to be collected together, and brought out with joy, together with Christ, and the patriarchs, and the prophets, and with these who are of our race, or even some of those who were proselytes before the coming of Christ? Or do you go to such a length, as to confess these things, that you may appear to exceed us in doubtful questions?

JUSTIN

I am not reduced to such straits, Ω Trypho, as to speak differently from what I think. I have already confessed to you, and before also, that I, and indeed many others with me, believe that it will come to pass, as you fully know. But on the contrary, I have signified to thee, that many who are [not [70]] of the pure and pious sentiment of Christians do not acknowledge this; for I pointed out to thee those who are called Christians, but are atheists, and impious heretics, because they teach all manner of blasphemous, impious, and foolish doctrines. But that you may know that I say this not only among you, I shall compose a work, as soon as I can, of these our disputations; wherein I shall insert, that I profess this very doctrine, which I acknowledge in your presence. For I am determined to follow, not men and human doctrines, but God, and the instruction delivered by him. For although you have had a verbal communication with some who are called Christians, and do not confess this, but dare to speak evil of the God of Abraham, and the God of Isaac, and the God of Jacob, and who say that there is no resurrection of the dead, but that as soon as they die, their souls are received into heaven, do not suppose that these are Christians; since, if any one think rightly, he would not say that the Sadducees were Jews, nor similar heretics of the Genistæ, and Meristæ, and Galileans, and Hellenists, and baptised Pharisees (not to tire you with hearing all I think); but those who were indeed called Jews, and sons of Abraham, and who confessed God with their lips, but their hearts (as God himself exclaims,) were far from him.

"Ἐγώ δὲ καὶ εἴ τινές εἰσιν ὀρθεγήμονες κατὰ πάντα Χριστιανοί."

"But I and all Christians, who are of the orthodox opinion," both acknowledge that there will be a resurrection of the flesh, and a thousand years' (reign) in Jerusalem, renewed, and adorned, and enlarged, as the prophets Ezekiel and Isaiah and others declare [71] .

For thus .Esaias speaks of the time of those thousand years, (Isa. c. lxv. v. 17, &c.) "For there shall be a new heaven, and a new earth, and the former shall not be remembered, nor come into mind. They shall find joy and exultation in .that which I create. For, behold, I make [for] Jerusalem an exultation, and [for] my people a joy," &c. to the end of the chapter.

But, as to that expression, "For according to the days of the tree of life [72] , are the days of my people," he subjoins, "In these words we understand the thousand years to be mysteriously signified." For as it was said to Adam, in the day in which he should eat of the tree, he should die, we know that he did not complete a thousand years. We know likewise (he proceeds,) that saying, that "the day of the Lord is as a thousand years," relates to this subject.

And a certain man among us, whose name is John, one of the twelve apostles of Christ, in that Revelation which was exhibited to him, prophesied that those of us who were faithful followers of Christ, should pass a thousand years in Jerusalem, and afterwards should be the universal, and (to say it at once) the eternal resurrection of all together, and the judgment, in which our Lord also said, that "they should neither marry nor be given in marriage, but be equal to the angels,--being the children of God, as of the resurrection." For we have prophetic gifts still existing among us up to the present time, &c.

Another Passage referring to the same subject.

After a Discourse on the great Day of Judgment, (which he calls τὴν μεγάλην ἡμέραν τῆς κρίσεως,) when the Jews should have mourned for Christ, whom they pierced, and when Christ himself, inaugurated after the order of Melchisedech, should have become the judge of quick and, dead, he immediately subjoins, "At whose second coming, do not imagine that Esaias, or the other prophets inform us, that sacrifices of blood or of libations were to be offered upon the altar, but true and spiritual praises and, thanksgivings.

A Key to the Apocalypse

Footnotes:

70. Mede has a note to allow that the negative ought here to be introduced.

71. Note by Mede.] If you except the principal articles of faith, I know not whether a similar testimony can be found to any Christian dogma. It is a great previous argument in its favour, that all the orthodox thought the same in the age next to the apostles. Justin became a Christian about thirty years after the death of St. John, in which time it is very probable many were alive who had heard the apostles teach.

72. In the Hebrew it is simply עץ, but the Septuagint has τοῦ ξύλου τῆς ζωῆς, to which the Chaldee paraphrase assents. Justin seems to have thought that the life resulting from the tree of life, or of man in the state of Paradise, would have been a thousand years, then to have been translated into a happier state and condition. But in consequence of Adam's sin, neither he nor any of his posterity attained that number of years, but died within that great day.--Mede.

Joseph Mede

THE OPINIONS
Of the Hebrew Doctors on the great Day of Judgment, and of the Reign of the Messiah then to come

Carpentarius, in his Commentary on the Alcinous of Plato, p. 322, asserts, that "the seventh millenary was called, by the whole school of the Cabalists, the great day of judgment, because then they think that God will judge the souls of all."

He means, by the name of Cabalists, (if I am not mistaken,) the Talmudic doctors, according to whom, in more than one author, that tradition is found to be recorded. For thus it is read in the Gemara Sanhedrim, Perek Chelek--R. Ketina has said, "The world subsists for six thousand years, and will be destroyed in one, of which it is said, And the Lord alone will be exalted in that day.' "But he understands the destruction which is to come, will be by fire, by which the world being refined, will be purified like gold, and will be delivered from subjection to the curse under which it now groans on account of man, into the glorious liberty of the sons of God, Rom. ch. viii. It follows a little after, in conformity with the tradition of R. Ketina, "As out of seven years, every seventh year is the year of remission, so out of the seven thousand years of the world, the seventh millenary will be the millenary of remission, as it is said, And the Lord alone shall be exalted, in that day.' It is said also in the 92d Psalm, a Psalm or Song for the Sabbath-day, that is, of the day of perfect rest. It is also said, Psalm xc. For a thousand years in thy sight are but as yesterday.'"

Here the Reader may remark two things:--First, that the ancient Jews understood that prophecy of Isaiah, ch. ii. where these words, "And the Lord alone shall be exalted in that day," occur twice,--of the day of the great judgment, and of the reign of Christ, from whose footsteps the succeeding Rabbins do not depart. "In that day,' that is, the day of judgment," says R. Schelomo. Also, "When he shall have risen to consume the earth, that is," says he, "in the day of judgment, in which the Lord shall consume the wicked of the earth," R. David Kimschi says, "In that day, that is, in the days of the Messiah, when God shall execute judgment on the wicked." And again, "And the Lord alone shall be exalted in that day, is the same as if he had said, The Lord shall be King over all the earth." Another thing to be remarked is, that the title of the 92d Psalm was thought by those Hebrew masters to have respect to the subject of the Psalm, and that it ought to be understood of the Sabbatism of a thousand years.

Now, from these premises I am decidedly of opinion, that the ancient Jews explained the day which they denominated the day of judgment as the MILLENNIUM; which is more fully confirmed from Misdrachtchillim, upon that passage of the 90th Psalm, "Comfort us now, for the days for which thou hast afflicted us," viz. says he, "in Babylon, in Greece, and under the Romans, and that in the days of the Messiah." And how many are the days of the Messiah? Jehosuah said that they are two thousand years, as it is written according to the days; that is, according to, or during, two days; for one day of the holy and blessed God is a thousand years, according to that saying, For a thousand years are in thy sight but as yesterday.'" The masters also say, that the age to come (ἐν οἰκουμένῃ τῇ μελλούσῃ Heb. ch. ii. 5.) will be one day of the Messiah. For the holy and blessed God, in the age to come, will make for himself one day, of which it is said in Zechariah, ch. xiv. "And there shall be one day which shall be known to the Lord, not day nor night [73]. And it shall come to pass that at even time it shall be light." This day is the age to come, and the revival of the dead: But in what millenary that was to come, they did not agree among themselves, and neither did that opinion of the seventh satisfy all. There were some, and not of inferior authority, who understood it of the sixth, as the house of Elias, whose tradition respecting the millennium of the great judgment is extant in these words: "The just, whom God will raise again, (namely, at the first resurrection [74],) will not again be reduced to dust. But if you inquire of those thousand years in which the blessed God will renew the world, of which it is said, And the Lord alone will be exalted in that day,' what will become of the just? Be it known, that the holy and blessed God will give them wings like eagles, that they may fly upon the face of the waters whence it is said, Psalm xlvi. 3, Therefore will we not fear when the earth shall be changed.' Perhaps you will say, it must be an affliction to them. But then occurs that passage in Isaiah, ch. xl. 31, They that wait on the Lord shall renew their strength. They shall mount up with wings as eagles.'" The same tradition, however, asserts, that the world shall not last more than six thousand years. For thus runs the tradition: "The world endures six thousand years; two thousand emptiness, two thousand years the Law; and lastly, two thousand years the day of Christ." One of which millenaries, therefore, according to this opinion, would be that great day of which it is said, "And the Lord alone shall be exalted in that day." The same was the opinion of Rabbi Asche, the son of R. Abbas, as it is there expressly said, namely, from the opinion of Chanan, son of Thahaliphas, that the holy and blessed God would not renew his world till the seventh millenary. But R. Asche had said, that it would be after the fifth millenary.

What, moreover, in addition, the Jewish masters thought concerning the reign of the Messiah in that great day to come, may be known in some measure from what I now subjoin. In the summaries of the great Rabbi Eleazar, (who lived a little after the second temple,) it is said, "As I live, saith the Lord, I will raise you up in time to come, in the resurrection of the dead, and I will gather you together with all Israel in the land of Israel." Petrus Galat. lib. xii. c. 1.

So likewise the paraphrast Jonathan, (who lived before Christ,) on the xivth of Hosea, 4 to 9, "They shall be gathered out of the midst of their captivity; they shall dwell under the shadow of their Christ; and the dead shall live, and good things shall grow up out of the earth, and there shall be a memorial of their goodness bearing fruit, and never failing, just as the remembrance of the sound of trumpets over the old wine, which used to be poured out in libation on the sanctuary."

Targum on Ps. 1. v. 3. The just shall say in the day of the great judgment, "Our God shall come and shall not keep silence, to execute vengeance for his people."

R. Saadas (one of those doctors whom they call eminent,) on that passage of Daniel, c. vii. v. 10, "And the judgment was set, and the books were opened," says, "That is the day of judgment, as it is written, Mal. c. iv. 1, Behold, the day cometh burning as a furnace.'--And the Lord of hosts shall be exalted in judgment,' Isa. c. v. ver. 16.--and also, Wherefore wait ye for me, saith the Lord.' That is the great day when the Lord shall arise to judgment." And a little after he says, "Know that with relation to what I quoted, The judgment sat, and the books were opened,' I expounded it above of the day of judgment, and the day of visitation; (Wisdom c. vii. v. 7 and 13.) that is, the day to come, when inquiry shall be made into every work of the sons of men, as well the living as the dead." The same observes on v. 18, "And the saints of the most high God shall take the kingdom." Because the Israelites rebelled against the Lord, their kingdom shall be taken from them, and shall be given to those four monarchies, which shall possess the kingdom in that age, and shall lead them captive, and shall subdue Israel to themselves, until the age to come, when the Messiah shall reign.

Compare Luke c. xxi. v. 24, &c. The Jews shall be led captive into all nations, and Jerusalem shall be trodden down by the Gentiles, until the time of the Gentiles be fulfilled. "Then shall they see the Son of man coming in a cloud," &c. And that of Tertullian against Marcion, lib. v. c. 10. "Christ, the High Priest of the circumcised priesthood, when at length it shall come to pass, that the circumcision and the people of Abraham acknowledge him, shall be deemed worthy of acceptance and benediction." To this agrees what is contained in the book of Berachoth, lib. xi. c. 1. on the faith of Peter the Galatian, and is thus read: "Ben Zuma said, It will come to pass, that Israel will not mention of the coming up out of the land of Egypt in the age to come, and in the days of the Messiah. And what is the proof of this? Because it is written, Jer. c. xxiii. "Behold, the days come, when they shall no longer say, The Lord lived], who caused the children of Israel to conic up out of the land of Egypt," &c. The wise men have said, not that the name of Egypt should be extirpated from its place, but that the wonderful things which shall come to pass in the days of those kingdoms, that is, when the Messiah shall destroy the kingdoms of the world, will be the chief in their estimation, and Egypt will be but secondary. From these and similar sayings, the reader may learn "why Jerome so often reproaches Judaism for its millenaries which indeed he does so studiously, that this may appear to have been the triumphant argument by which he would prove the error of that dogma. But however it may be with the dogma, and whether these fathers judged advisedly or not, to think with the Jews is not always to be imputed as a fault. . Otherwise, why do we not likewise explode the age to come, Gehenna, Paradise? For do not we Christians hold these in common with the Jews? Why should we not then receive those expressions of the kingdom of the heavens, and the day of judgment, delivered down from the Jewish masters? For where can they find those in the canon of the Old Testament, which however are very common among the doctors of the Jews? Besides, who now, after having heard the opinion of the ancient Hebrews concerning the thousand years of the day of judgment, would not immediately find himself induced to believe that the apostle Peter in his dissertation about the day of judgment, with the same people, (for both his Epistles were addressed to the Jews,) and immediately subjoining to it, "Be not ignorant of this, that one day is with the Lord as a thousand years," meant to confirm the tradition of the rabbis upon this very point? Especially since those words seem not to be borrowed from the Psalms, (as is generally supposed,) but from the common formula of the Jews, when speaking of that day. Nay, he will moreover reflect, that unless Christ our Lord and his apostles had made such frequent use of the expression of the day of judgment, derived from the Jewish masters, in the same sense as themselves, why do they never point it out by a single word? For is it not a very dangerous thing, nay, a mode liable to deceive, to apply the words and phrases of those who are in error in the course of doctrine, without any caution or remark that they are used in a different sense?

Such being the case, I leave to those who are able to judge of mysteries of this kind in theology, to consider whether this would be the best and easiest method of acting with the Jews; not that those very clear prophecies of events in the second and glorious advent of Christ, should be wrested by application to the first, but that they should be persuaded that no other Messiah is to be expected by them, who will fulfil all those things; mutatis mutandis however, (for the Christian is not here to be precisely of .the same opinion with the Jews, but to be guided by the measure of Christian faith,) no other than Jesus of Nazareth, whom their ancestors crucified, as the Apocalypse every where so earnestly inculcates. "Behold," says its author, just after its commencement, "Jesus Christ, the first born from the dead, who loved us, and washed us from our sins in his own blood, behold, he cometh with clouds, and every eye shall see him, even they who pierced him, and all the kindreds of the earth shall wail because of him. I am A and Ω, the First and the Last, saith the Lord, which is, and which was, and which is to come." Also he attributes that august kingdom every where to the Lamb, that is, to Jesus Christ who was slain; as ch. vii. of the multitude bearing palms, "The Lamb shall feed them," &c.; c. xvii. v. 14, "The Lamb shall subdue them, because he is King of kings, and Lord of lords;" c. xix. v: 7. "The marriage of the Lamb is come;" c. xxi. v. 9. of the New Jerusalem, "I will show you the spouse of the Lamb;" and v. 23. "The Lamb is the light thereof," &c. For while we wrest those very clear prophecies of events relative to the second coming of Christ, and apply them to the first, the Jews hold us in derision, and are more confirmed in their infidelity. This method of converting the Jews, unless I am much deceived, the apostle Peter pursued, Acts c. iii. v. 19. "Repent ye," says he, "and be converted, that your sins may be blotted out, and that [75] the times of refreshing may come from the presence of the Lord; and that he may send Jesus Christ, who was before preached unto you, whom the heavens must receive till the time of the restitution of all things, which God has spoken by the mouths of all his holy prophets, since the world began."

"Prove all things. Hold fast that which is good." 1 Thess. c. v. ver. 21.

"To our Lord and Saviour Jesus Christ, be glory both now and to the day of the age. Amen [76]." 2 Peter c. iii. last verse.

Τῷ Θεῷ δόξα διὰ Ἰησοῦ Χριστοῦ εἰς τοὺς αἰῶνας.

Ἀμήν.

THE END

LONDON: GILBERT & RIVINGTON, PRINTERS, ST. JOHN'S SQUARE.

Footnotes:

73. Query? Not a common day, composed of day and night.
74. Which all the Rabbis generally acknowledge, and also the author of the Book of Wisdom, ch. iii. 7, 8.
75. ὅπως ἄν ἔλθωσι.
76. εἰς ἡμέραν αἰῶνος.

www.ingramcontent.com/pod-product-compliance
Lightning Source LLC
Chambersburg PA
CBHW031600170426
43196CB00031B/421